iSyllabus
islam · iman · ihsan

One Year Diploma in Islamic Studies

Semester One

Understanding the Quran - Seeking Purity - Towards a Tranquil Soul 1
Understanding the Sunnah - Setting the base for Worship - Living the Law 1

© 2020 Ruzwan Mohammed.

iSyllabus

Understanding the Quran (Asl 1.01.D)

2. Who arranged the sequence of verses and chapters?

3. The start of the surahs – al-muqatta'at
    3.1 What do they mean?

4. Aspects of the Arabic Language of the Quran
    4.1 The clear (muhkam) and unclear (mutashabih)
    4.2 Mantuq and Mafhum

Did you know. Foreign vocabulary in the Quran?

1. The Makkan and Madinan Revelations
    1.1 What are the criteria for this classification?
    1.2 What are the benefits of knowing whether the revelation is Makkan or Madinan?

2. The reasons for revelation *(asbab an-nuzul)*
    2.1 One revelation: multiple reasons
    2.2 One reason: multiple revelations
    2.3 Wisdom and benefits of this knowledge

3. The theory of abrogation (an-naskh)
    3.1 Example of abrogation: The case of wine
    3.2 Benefits of this science

4. Text in context: the 'Verse of the sword' – A basis for perpetual war?
    4.1 The 'verse of the sword' and the theory of abrogation

Did you know? How to know whether the revelation is Makkan or Madinan?

1. What does *tafsir* mean?
    1.1 Why the need for Tafsir
    2.2 Early examples of Tafsir

2. Types of tafsir
    2.1 Commentary through recorded narrations (al-ma'thur)
    2.2 Commentary through examined research (ar-ra'y)
    2.3 Subtle commentary (tafsir ishari)
    5.5 An example of tafsir 'Ishari

3. Reconnecting with the sprit: The inward state of one seeking to explain the Qur'an

Did you know? There are qualifications required to do *Tafsir*?

1. The translation of the Qur'an
    1.1 What is translation and is it permitted to translate the Qur'an into a foreign language?
    1.2 What are the conditions for one translating the Qur'an into another language?
    1.3 Inadequacies of translations in conveying the meanings of the Qur'an

2. Excellence of the Qur'an and the etiquettes related to it
    2.1 The etiquette when learning and memorising the Qur'an:
    2.2 The etiquette towards the person from whom one is learning the Qur'an
    2.3 The etiquettes of listening to the Qur'an:
    2.4 The etiquette when preparing to recite the Qur'an
    2.5 The etiquettes when reciting the Qur'an

3. Abandoning the Qur'an?

Did you know? Is it better to look at a copy of Quran when reciting or from memory?

Seeking Purity (Fqh 1.01.D)

Lesson 4   Ritual Impurity *(Hukmi) 2*

Lesson 5   *Ritual Impurity (hukmi) 3*

Towards a Tranquil Soul 1 (Tzk 1.01.D)

Understanding the Sunnah (Asl 2.02.D)

---

[1] This condition of accuracy *(dabt)* is of central importance in classifying a hadith as *sahih*, as any laxity in this condition will lead to the hadith being classified in the lower category known as *hasan*.

Setting the base for Worship (Fqh 2.02.D)

Living the Law (Slw 1.02.D)

Understanding the Quran

Investigating the history, form and importance of the Quranic revelation

Module Asl 1.01.D

 iSyllabus
islam · iman · ihsan

Lesson One - What is the *Qur'an*?

Aim: By the end of this lesson the student should have gained a clear understanding of the nature and definition of the Qur'an provided by Muslim scholars.

Objectives: By the end of this lesson the student should be able to display the ability to:
1. Define what the Qur'an is both lexically as well as in the usage of scholars.
2. Summarise what has been said by scholars concerning the *'inimitable nature of the Qur'an ('ijaz)'*.
3. Detail the various types of descent through which the Qur'an reached mankind.
4. Explain why the Qur'an was revealed over an extended period of 23 years.
5. Differentiate between the Qur'an, Hadith and Hadith Qudsi.
6. Summarise the discussion regarding the first and the final portion of the Qur'anic revelation given to the Prophet *(may God bless and grant him peace)*, mentioning the various opinions in this regard.

> *"Indeed it is we that have revealed The Message, and it is We that will ensure its preservation (from corruption)."* [15:9]

2. What does the word *'Qur'an'* mean?

Many of the words used in the Sacred Law have their origins in the Arabic language used before the advent of Islam. Words such as *salah*, *du'a* and *hajj*, which conveyed a particular meaning in the past, were used in the Islamic tradition to convey new meanings which nevertheless maintained a deep association with the original usage. Scholars and linguists strove to explain the original meaning whilst at the same time attempting to define these terms in their new religious context. One important task was to point out the similarities with the original meaning, as well as venturing to furnish *reasons* as to why that word was chosen to convey its new religious meaning. This is demonstrated in their observations on the word *'Qur'an'*.

1.1 The lexical meaning

1.1.1 The word can be translated literally as *'a recitation'* from the root *'to recite'*.

1.1.2 It is said to be derived from the root word: *'qaraa'in'*, which means *'to be similar to something else'*. The explanation of this being that the Qur'an is made up of individual verses and chapters which resemble each other in beauty and content. Individual verses and chapters also complement each other for the comprehension of the Qur'anic message as a whole. This view is held by the famous linguist al-Fara'a.

1.1.3 It is also said to be a proper name with no associated meaning[2]. This opinion has been related to Imam al-Shafi'i. *[al-Zarkashi, al-Burhan]*

1.2 The technical meaning

There are a number of technical definitions given for the Qur'an, each of which relates to the particular science that seeks to explain what the Qur'an is from the vantage point of its own particular interest. **Legal jurists** seek a definition that relates to how the revelation differs from other sources of law (particularly the Prophetic Sunnah) and how this is related to linguistic import and authenticity. **Specialists in language and rhetoric** focus on the distinct literary qualities and inimitable style of the Qur'an; while **theologians** focus on the essential qualities of the Qur'an in the context of how they relate to the attributes of God. [3]

The following two definitions are in general widely used:

1.2.1 *'The inimitable speech of God, revealed to the Prophet* ﷺ *, recorded within the copies of the Qur'an (masahif), having reached us through mutawatir (large and continuous) transmission, the recitation of which is held to be an act of worship'.*

1.2.2 *'The inimitable speech of God.' [al-Zurqani, Manahil, V1, pg 16-17]*

---

[2] Pronounced without a *hamzah*: *Quran* as apposed to *Qur'an*.

[3] In the order of the sciences mentioned: *'The speech of God recorded within the copies of the Qur'an (masahif) through mutawatir transmission free of doubt' [al-Jassas]); 'The inimitable speech of God' [al-Jurjani]; 'The uncreated speech of God' [al-Nasafi].*

2. Al-Razi on *The inimitable speech of God and the preservation of the Qur'an.*

"...[Scholars] differ over how God preserves the Qur'an.

[2.1] Some say: 'He preserved the Qur'an by making it inimitable (mu'jiz), standing apart from the speech of mankind.' Therefore people were unable to expand or summarise it in any way, since if they were to attempt to do so, the literary form of the Qur'an would be altered so much that all intelligent people would realise that what was now before them was not the Qur'an. Therefore it being inimitable is similar to the way a city is fortified by an outer wall and is protected by it.'

[2.2] Others say: 'God protects and preserves it from anyone in creation being able to stand in adversarial confrontation of it.'

[2.3] It is also said: 'Mankind is unable of refute or corrupt it, as God has set apart a group of people that memorise, study and promulgate it amongst the rest of mankind until moral duty (taklif) itself remains [i.e the End of Time].'

[2.4] There are some that say: 'What is meant by preservation here is that if anyone attempted to change a letter - nay, even a dot – the people of the world would say to him: 'This is a blatant falsehood and alteration of the words of God.' Even if an esteemed Shaykh were to inadvertently mispronounce or misarticulate a word from the Qur'an, even young children would say to him, 'You are mistaken Shaykh! As it should be such and such...' [Al-Razi, Mafatih al Ghayb, al-Hijr, v9]

3. The descent and revelation of the Qur'an

The descent and revelation of the Qur'an was not a sudden event that occurred at once. Rather, it is held by scholars that there were a number of stages to the Qur'an being received from God.

3.1 Stages of Revelation

3.1.1 The revelation of the **whole Qur'an** to the Well-Preserved Tablet *(Lawh al-Mahfudh)*.

'Nay, it is an auspicious Qur'an within a Well-Preserved Tablet.' [85:21-22]

The first revelation was to what is called the *'Well-Preserved Tablet'*, a creation of light which contains all that God, from His vast knowledge, has decreed to happen. As such, it represents the knowledge and wisdom of God: That nothing occurs except by the decree and permission of the One in whose control is the dominion of the heavens and earth. Everything therefore moves according to a plan and wisdom, and the Qur'an is part of the manifestation of this divine wisdom and knowledge.

3.1.2 The descent of the **whole Qur'an** from the Well-Preserved Tablet to the *'House of Honour (Bayt al-Izzah)'* in the lowest heaven in the month of Ramadan.

'The month of Ramadan is that in which the Qur'an was revealed.' [2:185]

The second descent to the lowest heaven was *'to inform the whole of the celestial beings in the seven heavens of the onset of the final revelation to the Seal of the Prophets ﷺ of the most honoured of nations.'* [al-Zarkashi, al-Burhan, 1/323]

3.1.3 The piecemeal revelation over 23 years through Gabriel (A.S.) to the Prophet ﷺ.

'This is indeed a revelation (tanzil) from the Lord of the worlds, brought by the Trusted Spirit (Gabriel) upon your heart in order that you may become amongst those that warn.' [26:192-4]

The final descent of the Qur'an was to the Prophet ﷺ from Gabriel. *[al-Zurqani, Manahil, 1/36-9]*

4. The Qur'an and Sunnah - between revelation and inspiration

Religious guidance that has been received by the Muslim community is made up of two main sources: the Qur'anic revelation and the Prophetic example (*Sunnah*).

These are the two wellsprings of direct religious guidance. The Prophet ﷺ is reported to have said: *'I have left behind amongst you two things. As long as you hold true to them, you will never err: The Book of God and my Sunnah.'* [Malik, al-Muwatta]

Scholars have outlined the main differences between these two religious sources, and particularly what are referred to as Divine Hadith *(Hadith Qudsi)*: the Prophet ﷺ narrating the words of God through a non-Qur'anic medium.

4.1 The Qur'an

This is *'the inimitable speech of God, revealed to the Prophet ﷺ , recorded within the masahif, having reached us through mutawatir transmission, the recitation of which is held to be an act of worship.'*

> **Example: *'Say: 'If the oceans where the ink for the words of my Lord, they would run out long before the words of my Lord, even if We were to bring forth the same amount once more.' [18:109]***

4.2 The Hadith

These are reports recording the words, actions and approvals of the Prophet ﷺ . One of the most pertinent issues relating to hadith literature is that, unlike the Qur'an, the wording is rarely transmitted by a *mutawatir* chain of authority.

4.3 The Hadith Qudsi

A tradition where the Prophet ﷺ relates what God says, but it differs from the Qur'an in a number of key issues that become clear upon reflecting on the definition of the Qur'an given previously.

> **Example:** *Abu Hurayrah relates: 'I heard the Prophet ﷺ say: 'God, the Exalted, said: 'I have divided the prayer (al-Fatihah) into two halves between Myself and My servant, and My servant shall have what he asks for.' When he says:* **'All praise be to God, Lord of the worlds***' God says: 'My servant has praised Me.' When the servant says:* **'Most Gracious, Most Merciful***' God says: 'My servant has extolled Me.' When he says:* **'The Owner of the Day of Judgement***' God says: 'My servant has glorified me.' When he says:* **'You alone we worship and Your aid alone do we seek***' God says: 'This is between me and my servant and my servant shall have what he requested.' When he says:* **'Guide us to the Straight Path. The Path of those whom You have favoured, not of those who have earned Your anger or those who have gone astray***' God says: 'This is for my servant and my servant shall have what he asked for.' [Muslim]*

How does the *Qur'an* differ from the *Hadith Qudsi* ?

> **4.3.1** The wording of the Qur'an is directly from God.
> **4.3.2** The Qur'an is revealed through the medium of the Angel Gabriel.
> **4.3.3** The Qur'an is inimitable in nature.
> **4.3.4** The Qur'an has to be transmitted through *mutawatir* chains.
> **4.3.5** The recitation of the Qur'an is an act of worship.

Commenting on the wisdom of Hadith Qudsi and how they differ from the Qur'an, al-Zurqani writes:

> *'These are also the words of God, except that they do not contain the specific qualities of inimitability (i'jaz) through which the Qur'an is distinguished from all other speech. God has reserved a deep wisdom behind some of His revealed words being inimitable with others not being so [...] that of establishing a sure and definitive proof for His Prophet ﷺ as to the truthfulness of the religious message through God's inimitable speech [on the one hand] and providing an easing dispensation (takhfif) for his community through speech [which is] not so, since it is permitted to [1] narrate the latter by meaning alone and [2] for one in a state of major ritual impurity to carry and touch it.*
>
> *This issue may be aptly summarised by stating that the words of the Qur'an are held unanimously to be revealed from God; the words of 'Divine Hadith' (Hadith Qudsi) are also held to be revealed from God, according to the most well-known position, while the prophetic narrations, in areas where he did not engage in independent reasoning (ijtihad), are divinely-inspired meanings that are then articulated [into speech] by the Prophet.' [al-Zurqani, Manahil, v1, pg42]*

5. The First Revelation

> '...suddenly the Truth descended upon him ﷺ while he was in the cave of Hira. The Angel came to him and asked him to read. The Prophet ﷺ replied: **'I will not read.'**
>
> The Prophet ﷺ added: 'The Angel caught me (forcefully) and pressed me so hard that I could not bear it any more. He then released me and again asked me to read and I replied: **'I do not know how to read.'** Thereupon he caught me again and pressed me a second time till I could not bear it any more. He then released me and again asked me to read but I replied: **'What shall I read?'** Thereupon he caught me for the third time and pressed me, and then released me and said: **'Read in the name of your Lord, who has created (all that exists), created man from a clot. Read! for your Lord is the Most Generous.'** [al-Bukhari, 3; See al-Halabi, Sirah al-Halabi, v1 [3], pg 389-90]

The vast majority of scholars hold that the first revelation to the Prophet ﷺ was the beginning of Sura al-'Alaq: **'Recite in the name of your Lord' [96:1-5]** which happened while he was meditating in the cave of Hira. The Prophet ﷺ returned to his wife Khadijah shaken and she comforted and supported him. [see al-Bukhari, Kitab bad'i al-wahi].

However the companion Jabir ibn Abdillah relates that the first revelation of the Qur'an was that of Sura al-Muddaththir [Muslim]. According to al-Zarkashi, both revelations were significant in that they marked the inception of two different stages of prophethood:

> 'It is said that the first revelation revealed relating to 'Messenger-hood' (risalah) was 'O you enveloped in thy cloak [Sura al-Muddaththir]' while the first revelation relating to 'Prophethood (nabuwwah)' was 'Read in the name of your Lord', since scholars said that the latter indicates the prophethood of Muhammad ﷺ since prophethood is nothing more than revelation to an individual through the medium of an Angel with a personal religious message. As for his words 'O you enveloped in thy cloak' it is a proof and testimony of his messenger-hood, since messenger-hood is the granting of revelation to an individual through the medium of an angel with a more general religious message [meant for others]. [al-Zarkashi al-Burhan v1 pg. 293-296]

The Angel that conveyed the revelation was sometimes in its original angelic form – or else in the form of a near perfect human, such as is related in the famous 'Hadith Gabriel'. [4][al-Shami, Subal al-Huda, 2[12], pg 263-265]

6. The Last Revelation

> **'And fear the Day in which you will be returned to God. Then every soul shall be paid in full for what it earned, and none shall be wronged.' [2:281]**

[6.1] 'Scholars have offered various positions regarding what the final revelation to the Prophet ﷺ was. Some say it is the verse: **"And fear the Day in which you will be returned to God.' [2:281]**

[6.2] Al-Suddi relates that the last revelation was the verse in Sura Taubah: **'And if they turn away, then say God is enough for me, there is no God but Him and it is upon Him I rely, The Possessor and Sustainer of the vast throne.' [9:129].**

[6.3] Ubayy ibn Ka'b relates that the last revelation sent down during the time of the Prophet ﷺ was: **'There has come to you a Prophet from amongst yourselves' [9:128-129]** and he recited until the end of the sura.' [Hakim, Ahmed].

[6.4 & 6.5] Al-Bukhari relates that the final revelation was that which is **'The verse of Usury' [2:278]** [Bukhari Kitab-al Tafsir, 4544], while Imam Muslim relates that the last sura that was revealed was: **'When the victory of God arrives."** [110:1-3]

[Summary]:

'None of these opinions can be traced back explicitly to the Prophet ﷺ himself. It is therefore probable that those who held these positions did so through their own reasoning and strong

---

[4] It is also related that the angel would sometimes take on a form resembling that of the companion *Dihyah ibn Khalifah al-Kalbi* .

conjecture. Knowledge of this is not essential to the religion for people to criticise [the basic authenticity] of the revelation on account of there being no definitive answer for this.

It may be that each Companion merely reported the last thing that they individually heard from the Prophet ﷺ *on the day that he* ⊠ *passed away or just before his* ﷺ *final illness.' [al-Zarkashi al-Burhan, v1 pg. 297-300]*

Did you know?

Why the Qur'an was revealed over 23 years?

" ...thus (we revealed it in parts) that We may strengthen your heart thereby. And We have revealed it in stages." [25:32]

'If one was to enquire as to the secret of it having been revealed to earth in separate portions and why it was not revealed all at once like other revealed books [what might be said]?

Know that God Himself has taken to answering this. God says: **'Those that disbelieve say: 'Why has the Qur'an not been revealed in one instance?'** *meaning as it was for those before him from among the Prophets? God replied to this:* **'..thus (we revealed it in parts) that We may strengthen your heart thereby"** *[25:32], meaning in order that your heart be fortified, since, if revelation descends on account of each new occurrence, it helps to strengthen the heart and conditions it to be better disposed to the needs of the one to whom the message is sent. This also requires the constant descent of the Angel to him, reaffirming the covenant with him and the message that came from such an auspicious source. This would [then] be the source of such happiness that it defies expression. It is because of this that he was so overwhelmingly generous in Ramadan, on account of the frequency of the descent of Gabriel.' [Abu Shama', al-Murshid al-Wajiz, p29]*

Lesson 2 - The Preservation of the Qur'an

Aim: By the end of this lesson the student should appreciate the different phases through which the Qur'anic revelation was preserved until it was finally codified during the caliphate of 'Uthman. Students should also understand the underlying reasons for each phase of preservation of the Qur'an.

Objectives: By the end of this lesson the student should be able to:
1. Outline the two main methods through which the Qur'an has been preserved, namely the oral and written preservation.
2. Summarise the process through which the Qur'an was and continues to be preserved through the medium of oral transmission.
3. Distinguish between the three phases of the written preservation of the Qur'anic revelation.
4. Discuss whether the Qur'anic revelation was written at the time of the Prophet Muhammed (may God bless and grant him peace), providing necessary supporting evidence for this.
5. Explain why a single physical copy of the Qur'an was not left behind by the Prophet (may God bless and grant him peace)for his community.
6. Identify the reasons behind Abu Bakr collecting the various parchments of the Qur'an during his leadership, and the criteria used in this process.
7. Discuss the importance of Zayd bin Thabit in the overall written preservation of the Qur'an.
8. Explain the process of written preservation during the time of 'Uthman, pinpointing the way in which this differed from the phase of collection undertaken during the time of Abu Bakr .

"Indeed, it is We that revealed the Message, and it is We that will ensure its preservation (from corruption)." [15:9]

The preservation of the oral and literary form of the Qur'an has been the most enduring proof of its truthfulness and veracity. That this preservation has existed throughout the ages, from the time of its revelation to the present day, is not seriously contested by any credible researcher. The way that God ensured that the final revelation be protected has been detailed by Muslim scholars as presented below.

1. Oral and written preservation - Evidence attesting to a Divine origin

1.1 Oral preservation

The oral transmission of the Qur'an, as well as the associated rules of proficient recitation (*tajwid*), has been meticulously preserved from the time of the original Qur'anic revelation until the present age. This is the first and still the most stringent channel through which the revelation was and is safeguarded and to this day remains the surest method by which the integrity and authenticity of the final word of God is secured. The instruction to take care in reciting the revelation was one that was given to the Prophet ﷺ himself, and was passed on as one of the most constant religious instructions to the adherents of the faith. Therefore the Companions made it a habit to excel in the learning, study and teaching of all that was related to the Qur'an.

1.1.1 The Prophet ﷺ

"Do not overburden your tongue (concerning the Qur'an) to make haste therewith. It is for Us to collect it and promulgate it. When We have promulgated it, follow its recital. Then it is for Us to articulate it." [75: 16-19]

Commenting on this verse, Ibn Attiyyah writes: *'Al-Sha'bi said: 'The Prophet ﷺ , on account of his overwhelming concern to convey the message, and his intense striving in seeking God, may have intended to recite part of what had been revealed before the whole revelation had been complete, therefore God ordered him not to make haste in reciting until the revelation had been completed. This is the meaning of this verse. Al-Dahhak said: 'The reason for the verse (being revealed was that) the Prophet ﷺ used to fear forgetting the Qur'an and so used to studiously apply himself to the point that this became difficult and exhausting for him.'* [Ibn Attiyyah, al-Muharrir al-Wajiz on 75: 16-19]

1.1.2 The Companions

Abdullah (b. Maṣ'ud) relates: 'God's Apostle ﷺ said to me: 'Recite (of the Qur'an) for me.' I said: 'Shall I recite it to you even though it had been revealed to you?' He said: 'I like to hear [the Qur'an] from others.' So I recited Sura al-Nisa' until I reached 'How (will it be) then when We bring from each nation a witness and We bring you (O Muhammad) as a witness against these people?" [4:41]. Then he said: 'Stop!' and his eyes were shedding tears.' [Bukhari, 4582]

"This may be in order for him to reflect and fully comprehend it, since the one listening is better placed to ponder and the soul is unoccupied and more active for this than the one reciting as the latter is preoccupied with the reciting and its associated rulings. This is different from him ﷺ reciting to 'Ubayy ibn Ka'b as has preceded in the Book of [the] Merits [of the Companions], where he ﷺ intended to teach the correct manner of recitation as well as the origins of the Arabic letters (makharij al-huruf).' [Ibn Battal, Sharh al-Bukhari]

1.1.3 Preserving the word of God through studying

The narration above, and the many others, show the environment of constant teaching that took place in the early community centred on the divine revelation, a fact that can also be gathered circumstantially from the reports of the time, which mention that the Companions would be engaged in study and recitation circles. Such reports point to a community engrossed in what was for them the word of God.

Anas ibn Malik said: 'The Prophet ﷺ came to us while we were in the mosque teaching each other the Qur'an, Arabs and non-Arabs, coloured and whites, and he said: 'You are in a blessing - reciting the Book of God whilst you have the Prophet of God amongst you. There will come a time when people will aim to rectify it, even as they straighten a spear, seeking to hasten their rewards, whereas they will not be able to do so.' [Ahmed, 3/146, §12, 484]

1.2 Written preservation

The written preservation of the Qur'anic revelation, which aimed to aid the oral preservation, was completed over three stages, all of which occurred during the lifetime of the first community of Muslims and at the hands of the earliest adherents of the faith. [Abu Shah'bah, al-Madkhal, pg 260- 282]:

1.2.1 The Era of the Prophet ﷺ
1.2.2 The Era of Abu Bakr
1.2.3 The Era of Uthman

2. The Era of the Prophet ﷺ & *The revelation of the Qur'an*

'The Prophet ﷺ was taken from this life while the Qur'an had not yet been gathered in a book.' [al-Bukhari, 4986]

'This statement merely refers to a particular book having a specific description [existing]. However, the Qur'an had been written down in its entirety during the lifetime of the Prophet ﷺ . It is another matter that it had not been bound together or its chapters put in [a] sequence.' [al-Khattabi]

We can also infer from the words of Zayd ibn Thabit that even though it was not 'gathered', it had already been written down, as only that which has a physical form is gathered together. [Abu Sulayman al-Khattabi quoted by Ibn Hajr, Fath-al Bari, Hadith 4986]

2.1 Was the revelation recorded in written form during the Prophetic period?

That there was a systematic process of writing down the revelation can be established with certainty from the numerous reports related to this. The revelation was written down and reports show that parchments containing the Qur'an, despite the scarcity of writing materials, were common and in the possession of the Companions. Amongst these reports are the following:

2.1.1 The conversion of 'Umar
'My brother, you are unclean in your polytheism and only the clean may touch it.' So 'Umar rose and washed himself and his sister gave him the parchment containing a section of Sura Ta-Ha. When he had read the beginning he said: 'How fine and noble is this speech..." [Ibn Hisham, pg156-57]

2.1.2 The Prophet ﷺ calling for writing material to be brought.
'Call Zaid for me and let him bring the board, ink pot and scapula bone.' Then he said: 'Write...'
2.1.3 Material being kept for the scribes
'The material upon which the revelation had been written down was kept in the house of the Prophet ﷺ .' [Suyuti, Ulum al Qur'an 38-41, I'tiqan 1:58]

It is known that the writing of hadith was initially not allowed, as people had yet to learn to differentiate between the Qur'anic text and the words of the Prophet ﷺ . The general scarcity of writing materials at the time of the Qur'anic revelation also meant that priority was given to channelling the majority of available writing materials to ensure that the Qur'an was not only preserved through memorisation but also through writing. Once such methods of preservation were established, the permission to record anything other than the Qur'anic revelation was given.

> *'It has been said that the only reason that people were forbidden from writing hadith together with the Qur'an in one document was so that they would not become intermingled to such a degree that it would become confusing upon the reader.' [al-Khattabi, Ma'alim, 5/246]*

2.2 Why was no single copy of a Book left by the Prophet ﷺ ?

A fully compiled and sequenced copy of the Qur'an was not left by the Prophet ﷺ due to the way the Qur'an was uniquely revealed:

2.2.1 The revelation did not descend at once.
2.2.2 Some verses were abrogated in the course of the 23 years of revelation.
2.2.3 The *verses (ayat)* and chapters *(suras)* were not revealed in the order that we recite them today.
2.2.4 The Prophet ﷺ lived only a few days following the final revelation.
2.2.5 There was no chance of dispute about the Qur'an arising during the time of the Prophet ﷺ .

3. The Era of Abu Bakr - *Collecting the Suhuf (11 AH)*

During the era of Abu Bakr the Qur'an was collected in what were referred to as the *Suhuf (sing. sahifah)*: loose pieces of parchments used to write on. This was the first time that the Qur'an was collected together between two covers, thus making the entire revelation accessible to the community in one place in a written form. Needless to say the Qur'an was already memorized in its entirety by countless individuals.

3.1 Why were the *Suhuf* collected?

The impetus for this initiative during the era of Abu Bakr was simple. There was a fear of losing the oral preservation after the Battle of Yamamah, in which a large number of people who had memorised the Qur'an (*huffadh)* were killed. Since such an initiative had not been attempted during the life of the Prophet ﷺ , some Companions had reservations, but these were quickly laid to rest due to the grave nature of the situation. It was 'Umar who first highlighted the pressing need for such an initiative, but Abu Bakr's response, upon hearing 'Umar's suggestion, was: *'How can we embark upon something that the Prophet ﷺ never did?"* However, as he later elaborates: *'He continued in responding to my reservations until God reconciled me to the undertaking and I came to the same conclusion as he did.' [Al-Bukhari, 4986]*

3.2 Who was put in charge of overseeing the collection of the *suhuf* and why?

The person chosen to oversee the process was one of the brightest and most intelligent of the Companions, one who had excelled in both memorising and transcribing the Revelation for the Prophet ﷺ : Zaid ibn Thabit. *'Abu Bakr said (to him): You are a wise young man and we do not suspect you [of telling lies or of forgetfulness]; and you used to write the revelation for God's Apostle ﷺ .' [Al-Bukhari, 4986]*

3.2.1 The credentials of Zayd bin Thabit.
Zayd was blessed with several qualities that made him the clear choice for this monumental role: 1. Youth; 2. Irreproachable morals; 3. Intelligence; 4. Extensive prior experience of recording Revelation; 5. Attending the final revision of the Qur'an by Angel Gabriel with the Prophet ﷺ in the month of Ramadan. *[M.M.al-Azimi, pg 78-79; al-Jazairi, al-Tibyan].*

3.2.2 Conditions for accepting what was to be included in *suhuf* of Abu Bakr.
3.2.2.1 Testimony, along with two witnesses, that the material presented for recording had been written in the presence of the Prophet ﷺ , together with the agreement of the Companions upon this.
3.2.2.2 Testimony from memory alone – without written proof – was not accepted. Due to this, the last two verses of *Sura al-Taubah* were not recorded until they reached the Companions in a written form, even though they could recall them from memory. *[Ibn Hajr, Fath-al Bari, Hadith 4986]*

3.2.3 Zayd and his use of oral sources:
Zayd said: 'I gathered the Qur'an from the various parchments and sections of bones, as well as from the chests of men.' Al-Zarqashi says: 'This statement has caused a number of people to imagine that no one had memorised the Qur'an in its entirety during the Prophet's ﷺ lifetime and that therefore the claim of Zayd and Ubayy ibn K'ab of having memorised it are

unfounded. However, this is not so. The truth of Zayd's statement is that he searched for verses of the Qur'an from a number of different sources in order to compare them with the memorisation of those that had memorised the Qur'an. Therefore, the community participated in the compilation of the Qur'an; hence, nobody who had a section of the Qur'an was left out. In this way, nobody bore a grudge or had reason to express concern regarding the verses collected.' [Al-Zarqashi, al-Burhan]

3.3 The Result: The compilation of the Suhuf into the 'State Archives'

The order of the *ayat* within each *sura,* as well as the sequence of the *suras* themselves, was fixed. However, the sheets were still in a loose arrangement. The manuscript on which the Qur'an was collected remained with Abu Bakr until he passed away, then with 'Umar until he passed away, and finally with Hafsah, 'Umar's daughter. *[I'tiqan 1:62]*

4. The Qur'anic text during the time of 'Umar.

Although Umar is not associated with having furthered the process of codifying the Qur'anic Revelation, he did institute a systematic policy of teaching and spreading the Word of God throughout the Muslim lands. He sent eminent Companions known for their proficiency in the Qur'an, to the various cities. He sent at least ten to Basrah, as well as Ibn Mas'ud to Kufah. Mu'adh, 'Ubadah and Abu Darda were sent to Syria upon the request of the Governor Yazid ibn Abi Sufyan. Abu Darda settled in Damascus and is reported to have had over 1600 students learning from him, who he broke down into groups of ten in order to facilitate proficient learning. *[al-Dhahab, Siyar al-A'lam, V1, pg 344-46]*

5. The Era of 'Uthman - *Composing the Mushaf (25 AH)*

> *'Leader of the Believers! Save this nation before they differ about the Book, as the Jews and Christians did before them.' [al Bukhari, 4987]*

The person most associated with the collection of the Qur'an is 'Uthman, who earned the honorific title *'The Collector of the Qur'an' (Jami al-Qur'an).*

5.1 What was the reason for the Composing the Mushaf?

This can be put down to one simple point. The Prophet ﷺ had, out of necessity, taught different Arab tribes how to recite the Qur'an in their own tribal dialects, due to the difficulty faced in requiring them to abandon their native dialects. The Muslims were now arguing over the pronunciation and manner of recitation of the Qur'an. The variations were now to lead to conflicts amongst new adherents to the religion.

> *'Umar sent Ibn Mas'ud to Iraq to teach, and upon finding out that he was teaching according to the dialect of Hudhayl he said to Ibn Mas'ud: 'The Qur'an was revealed in the language of the Quraysh, so teach according to the dialect of the Quraysh and not that of Hudhayl.' [Ibn Hajr, Fath al Bari, Hadith 4986]*

5.2 The stages of the 'Uthmanic compilation

5.2.1 The *suhuf* in the possession of Hafsa was obtained.
5.2.2 'Uthman ordered Zaid ibn Thabit, (from Madinah) and three others: Abdullah ibn Zubayr, Sa'id ibn A'as and Abd al-Rahman ibn Harith (of the Quraysh), to make duplicates.
5.2.3 Any difference regarding the Qur'an was ordered to be written in the dialect of the Quraysh.
5.2.4 The final copy was recited in the assembly of the Companions *[Ibn Abi Daud al-Masahif, pp19]*
5.2.5 Final copies of the agreed upon script were sent to various parts of the Muslim lands. These were between five to eight in number.
5.2.6 All other copies were destroyed. 'Ali said *'He did that only in the presence of all of us.'*
5.2.7 All copies of the *Mushaf* were sent together with trained reciters, to ensure that all recitation was in accordance with the agreed upon script.
5.2.8 The *Mushaf* was largely free of vowels, diacritical dots and verse separators. *[al-Azmi, pg 93-107]*

> *Al-Tabrisi says: 'As for any additions to the Qur'an, this is unanimously agreed to be false. As for it being short or deficient, then this is even more impossible [...]. The knowledge of the correct transmission of the Qur'an is similar to the knowledge we have of countries; major events and occurrences; famous books and recorded poems, for the concern for preservation was intense and the conditions were well suited for it to be transmitted and safeguarded to the point that it reached a state such as to far surpass all that we have mentioned.*

Indeed, the Qur'an is the most auspicious event of Prophecy and the source of all Islamic sciences and religious rulings. Muslim scholars have reached the very summit in memorising it and protecting it to the point that they well know the grammatical points upon which they have differed as well as those related to its recitation, letters and verses. So how can it be possible that it has been changed or rendered incomplete with all that what we know of the protection and stringent accuracy [with which it has been kept]?' [al-Zarkani v1, pg 232]

If one were to ask...

"Indeed, it is We that revealed The Message, and it is We that will ensure its preservation (from corruption)." [15:9]

Despite God having assured mankind that the Qur'an would be preserved through a divine promise, it is interesting that the Companions did not wait or expect that this would happen through a divine miracle or some mysterious process from the heavens. They saw that they had a role to play in the divine plan and so they set out to become the vehicle by which the divine promise was fullfilled. In doing so they showed themselves to be to recipients of God's special favor and grace and truly represented the words of God **'You are the best community brought forth for Mankind..'**

"If one were to ask: 'Why did the Companions strive to preserve the Qur'an when God had already promised to protect it?' One could reply: 'The Companions' compilation of the Qur'an was one of the means that God used to preserve it, so that when He decreed to preserve it, He also chose the Companions to do specifically that.' [Al-Razi, Mafatih al-Ghayb, al-Hijr, V9]

Lesson 3 - The form of the Qur'an

Aim: By the end of this lesson, the student should be able to appreciate the language, form and structure of the Qur'an, as well as understand the basic issues related to how the Arabic language influences the meanings in the Qur'an.

Objectives: By the end of this lesson the student should be able to:
1. Define, both lexically as well as in technical usage, the meaning of chapter (*sura*) and verse (*ayah*).
2. Discuss who arranged both the individual verses within the chapters of the Qur'an, as well as the sequence of chapters in the Qur'anic *mushaf*.
3. Explain the use of the *'Muqatta'at'* at the start of various chapters of the Qur'an, explaining what these are and how scholars have sought to explain their functions.
4. Discuss what is meant by 'clear' and 'unclear' verses through the use of examples as well as how this affects the rulings derived from the Qur'anic revelation.
5. Mention what has been said about our ability to understand the meanings of verses that are classified as being unclear (*al-Mutashabihat*).
6. Distinguish between what are termed as *mantuq* and *mafhum* with regards to Arabic language, providing an example for each from the Qur'an.

'And if you are in any doubt concerning what we have revealed to Our Servant, then bring forth a chapter like it and call upon your witnesses other than God if you are indeed truthful. If you are unable to, and you will not be then ...' [2:23-4]

1. Chapters and Verses

1.1 Chapters: The Arabic word *sura (pl. suwar)* literally means *'an elevated plain'* or *'a fenced enclosure'*. Technically, this refers to the chapters of the Qur'an, for the following reasons:

1.1.1 The chapters of the Qur'an *elevate* the state of one that recites them.
1.1.2 The chapter *encloses* a number of verses *[Tafsir Ibn Kathir]*.
1.1.3 The chapters serve to mark out the changing portions of the Qur'an, just as the crescent moon indicates and sheds light on the different phases of the month *[Raghib al Asfahani, al-Mufradat, 434]*.

1.2 Verses: The Arabic word *ayah (pl. ayat)* is defined literally as *'a sign, a wonderful occurrence, a lesson, or a collection of different things.'*

In technical language, it is the smallest part of speech, be it a phrase or sentence, which when brought together, make up a chapter of the Qur'an. It is used in the context of a verse of the Qur'an for the following reasons:

1.2.1 The verse, on account of its miraculous nature, points to the veracity and truthfulness of the one that brought the message.
1.2.2 It inspires, by its very nature, a sense of amazement and wonder in people due to the meanings it contains. *[al-Jazairi, at-Tibyan, 195]*

2. Who arranged the sequence of verses and chapters?

2.1 The Verses: All scholars, as related by al-Zarqashi, agree that the sequence of the verses within each sura was determined by the Prophet ﷺ . *'Uthman ibn 'Affan relates that, when verses were revealed to the Prophet ﷺ , he would call the scribes and say: 'Place this verse in such and such a chapter.' [Ahmed].* He ﷺ *also said: 'Whoever recites the two verses at the end of Sura al-Baqarah at night, they will suffice them.' [al-Bukhari].*

2.2 The Chapters: The arrangement of the chapters is not a matter of consensus. Some have said that the sequence was determined by the Prophet ﷺ , while others say that it was wholly left to his Companions. A third view, which is that of many scholars, is that most of the chapters were arranged by the Prophet ﷺ , while some were left to the Companions to arrange. However, the stronger opinion appears to be that the sequence of the chapters in their present form was, like the verses, arranged by the Prophet ﷺ .

Al-Kirmani in his book *Al-Burhan*, said: *'The arrangement of the suras is from God and the Qur'an is written in the Guarded Tablet in this sequence. It was compared by Gabriel with the Prophet ﷺ in accordance with this order every year. In the final year, it was compared twice, and the last verse that was* revealed was, '**And fear a day when you will be returned back to God. Then every soul shall be paid in full for what it was earned, and none shall be wronged' [2:281]** and Gabriel ordered him ﷺ to place it between the Verse of Usury and the Verse of Debt.' [al-Zarkashi 1 [4]:353-358; al-Suyuti, al-Itiqan, 1[4], 62]

3. Al-Muqatta'at - The ambiguous opening of suras

> "**Nun! And by the Pen and that which it records! You are not by the overwhelming grace of your Lord afflicted by madness." [68:1-2]**

One of the mysterious aspects of the Qur'anic Revelation is the elusive letters at the start of a number of chapters. Much has been written on the meanings and function that they serve.

The literal meaning of *al-Muqatta'at* is *'to be cut or abbreviated'*. Twenty-nine chapters of the Qur'an start with *al-Muqatta'at* and in total, half of the Arabic alphabet is used.

> 'Those that have differed over the meanings of the broken letters can be understood to fall into two distinct groups. The first say that this is a hidden knowledge, a secret that God has kept reserved to Himself. On account of this, Abu Bakr As-Siddiq said: 'Every book has a secret, and the secret of the Qur'an lies in the openings to its chapters.'
> Al-Sha'bi said 'Knowledge of this is from those things that are mutashabih, we believe in its outward form and leave knowledge of it to God, may He be Exalted'. This has been the predominant view of scholars, in recognition of the danger of interpreting the Qur'an without firm knowledge.
> However, some have questioned this approach: 'Theologians have found fault with this first position and said: 'It is not permitted that there be something within the Qur'an that the creation cannot comprehend, since God has ordered us to ponder over it and to extract rulings from it – something which is not possible except after comprehending what is meant." [Al-Razi Tafsir al-Kabir v2 pg 3]

> [This] second group of scholars have held that the intent behind these is known, and have mentioned over twenty different opinions, some of which are close while others are not.' [al-Zarkashi al-Burhan v1 pg 261-2].

3.1 What do the *al-Muqatta'at* letters mean?

> **3.1.1** They indicate some of the names of God or the Prophet ﷺ (Ibn Abbas).
> **3.1.2** They were revealed to bewilder the disbelievers *(al-Razi)*.
> **3.1.3** They point to man's limited knowledge. '*Whoever thinks that the Qur'an is not a miracle, let them take the other half of the alphabet and create a speech that will compete with it*" (al-Baqillani).
> **3.1.4** They are a literary device to attract the attention of the listener, in keeping with the tradition of the pre-Islamic poets. [see al-Zarkashi, 1 (4), pg 261-266]

> 'This [...] has led scholars and thinkers like Al-Mubarrad, Ibn Hazm, Zamakhshari, Razi, Baydawi, Ibn Taymiyyah, Ibn Kathir – to mention only a few of them – to the conclusion that the Muqatta'at are meant to illustrate the inimitable, wondrous nature of Qur'anic revelation, which, though originating in a realm beyond the reach of human perception (al-ghayb), can be and is conveyed to man by means of the very sounds (represented by letters) of ordinary human speech.' [Asad. M, The Message of The Qur'an, Appendix II]

4. Aspects of the Arabic Language of the Qur'an

Words and phrases that are used in religious sources are classified by scholars in a number of ways, and these classifications help us understand the meaning these texts seek to convey. The different classifications mentioned may interrelate and overlap, but they all relate to the clarity (or not) of the meanings contained within a particular section of a religious text and are covered in detail in the science of *Usul al-Fiqh*.

4.1 The clear (muhkam) and unclear (mutashabih)

> "**It is He who has sent down to you the Book containing verses that are clear – they are the foundation of the Book – and others that are unclear" [3:7]**

Muhkam refers to any wording the meaning of which is understood and the explanation clear, whereas the *mutashabih* is that which is obscure as to the intended meaning. *[al-Suyuti 3:8, quoting al-Ti'bi']*

4.1.1 An example of a clear (*muhkam*) verse

"Believers! When you deal with each other in transactions involving future obligations for a fixed period of time, put them down in writing and let a scribe write down faithfully the terms between the parties." [2:282]

4.1.2 An example of an unclear (*mutashabih*) verse

'The Most Gracious is firmly established upon the Throne (of authority).' [20:5]

As the meaning and subject matter of the first verse is straightforward and easily understood, we can be sure that the intended meaning has been grasped without the need for recourse to any method of explanation. Such a religious text is also referred to as being sure and definitive in its meaning **(qati'i ad-dalalah).**

The second verse is an example of a religious text that is referred to as being unclear and conjectural in its meaning **(dhanni ad-dalalah)**[5] based on the fact that the individual words can mean a number of things. The words translated above as *'firmly established'*, *'upon'*, as well as *'Throne'* all have a number of acceptable meanings in the classical Arabic language that then require one to engage in a degree of investigation into the most appropriate meaning for each word, and then the verse as a whole. This is the main reason for the debate over this verse and others like it. *[Qadi Abu Bakr ibn al-Arabi, 'Awasim min al-Qawasim]*

The clear (*muhkam*) and unclear (*mutashabih*) is the most basic and important division when looking at the degree to which religious texts are open to interpretation. The clearer the language, the less scope there is to provide varying and novel explanations of a religious text. The more unclear the original language is, the more difference that will exist as to what is intended.

4.1.3 Can one reach an understanding of the meaning of unclear verses?

4.1.3.1 According to the opinion of Ibn Mas'ud, none except God can know the meaning of such verses. This is also related as a narration from Ibn Abbas.

4.1.3.2 According to another narration going back to Ibn Abbas, one can arrive at an understanding of unclear verses. He said: *'I am of those that that are well grounded in knowledge.'*

Al-Nawawi concludes: *'This is the preferred position since it is inconceivable that God address mankind through speech that they have no chance of understanding.' [al-Suyuti. al-Itqan, 3:5]*

4.2 *Mantuq* and *Mafhum*

4.2.1 The *Mantuq* (lit. *that which is expressed clearly and audibly*) is used for an understanding derived directly from the wording itself. An example of this is the verse providing a dispensation for the one unable to sacrifice an animal during the Hajj to fast instead. All the rulings for this are stated in the wording itself, without any need for seeking out the meaning by any logical extension.

"But if he cannot afford it, he should fast three days during the Hajj and seven days on his return, making ten days in all." [2:196]

4.2.2 *Mafhum* (lit. *that which is understood*) refers to an understanding derived from the implied meaning as opposed to the direct wording itself.

"...and do not say to them 'Uff!'" [17:23]

It is understood, but not expressly stated in the wording of the verse, that other forms of harm, be they emotional or physical, are similarly prohibited. Hence, this aspect of the Arabic language provides a meaning outside the constraints of the outward wording.

---

[5] The division of the clarity of meaning (*ad-dalalah*) is mirrored by another division based on the level of historical authenticity, or otherwise, of a religious text. If a text is so well transmitted that we cannot question its authenticity in any way, it is referred to as being of definite authenticity, *qati'i ath-thabut*. An example of this is the Qur'an.

If, on the other hand, the text has reached us in such a way that a person could make a strong case as to the text not being true and authentic as a historical document, then it is referred to as *dhanni ath-thabut*. An example of this is the vast majority of hadith literature.

Taken together, these two divisions of the religious sources provide the most important tools for achieving a balanced understanding of the Islamic faith. More practically, this allows trained scholars to reach a conclusion in issues where two or more religious texts are in apparent contradiction. *[See also notes to Searching for Purity Lesson 5; Articulating Creed Module 1 lesson 4; Hadith Lesson 3]*

Did you know?

"And if We had made this a foreign Qur'an, they would have said, 'Why are its verses not clear? What! A foreign [Book] and an Arab [Messenger]!'" [41:44]

Even though the Qur'an states that it is revealed in pure Arabic, scholars still researched the etymological origins of the words used in the Qur'an.

Classical authors differed as to whether the language of the Qur'an includes words which are not of Arabic origin. Some held that the Qur'an is wholly Arabic in origin, others that the Qur'an does contain words not previously used in the Arabic language, such as: *al-Qistas* [17:35], derived from Greek, and *al-Tur* [2:63], derived from Syriac. Others still stated that words of non-Arabic origin found in the Qur'an had nevertheless become naturalised and so became part of the Arabic language, a phenomenon that is observed in all languages.

The issue is aptly addressed and clarified by *Ibn Faris*, the fourth century grammarian. He clarifies that these words came to be used by Arabs through their interaction with other cultures before the advent of Islam and so these words were *Arabicised,* thereby clarifying the meaning of *'The Book'* being an *'Arabic' Qur'an.*

He quotes the early Qur'anic scholar and linguist, Abu 'Ubaydah, as saying:

> '*The authorities in Arabic language have claimed that there is nothing in the Qur'an which is not Arabic and that it is wholly Arabic in nature [...] The truth according to me – and God knows best – is a position that verifies both counter-positions. These words are in their origins foreign, as is stated by the scholars, except that when they arrived into the Arabic tongue, they were Arabicised through their speech and usage. They thereby took these words from their foreign state and assimilated them into the Arabic language.*
> *The Qur'an was then revealed at a time when these had become naturalised into Arabic speech. Therefore, whoever says that they are Arabic is correct and whoever holds that they are foreign is likewise correct." [Ibn Faris, al-Sahibi fi Fiqh al-Lughah, pg 33].*

It is also interesting that there are some scholars who have noted that such words that allegedly derive from other languages had their own origin in the Arabic language. *[Tafsīr Al-Tabari, Jami al-Quran]*

Lesson 4 - The Text in Context

> **Aim:** To provide a detailed understanding of the context within which the Qur'anic revelation was revealed, examining the reasons why passages of the Qur'an were sent down and investigating the theory of abrogation in providing a backdrop to the Quranic message.
>
> **Objectives:**
> By the end of this lesson, the student should be able to display the capacity to:
> 1. Differentiate between what is meant by Makkan and Madinan chapters, as well as state the three different criteria upon which this classification is based, mentioning the preferred opinion.
> 2. List the benefits of this classification.
> 3. Discuss what is meant by *'The reasons for revelation'* (*asbab an-nuzul*) together with an example.
> 4. Identify the wisdom and benefits of knowing the context in which portions of the Qur'an were revealed.
> 5. Clarify what is meant by the theory of abrogation, providing the original meaning of the word as well as an example of abrogation.
> 6. Outline the benefits this area of Qur'anic studies has in the application of Islamic law.
> 7. Relate the use of the theory of abrogation to the *'Verse of the Sword'*, examining the view that the verse replaced previous Qur'anic passages exhorting to patience and good conduct.
> 8. Mention what scholars have stated regarding the meaning of the verse, and the context within which it was revealed.

1. The Makkan and Madinan Revelation

> *"I swear by this City – while you are a resident of this City – and by the father and what he fathered. Surely we have created man troubled by affliction."* *[90:1-4]*

1.1 What are the criteria used in this classification?

One of the most important ways by which one can start to understand the Qur'an is to look at the circumstances in which different sections were revealed. That which was sent during the Makkan period – a time of persecution – will obviously thematically relate to the necessity to remain steadfast and patient in the face of oppression. The Madinan period, on the other hand, is marked by the call to believers to observe and establish justice, as well as to resist injustice in all its forms. The study of what was revealed and when, is therefore one of the best ways by which to place religious rulings in their correct context.

A large degree of one's understanding of the Qur'an stems from an appreciation of where, when and the context in which the revelation was revealed. Therefore, the entire revelation has been classified with respect to the two great cities of Islam, Makkah and Madinah, and what was revealed in each.

Scholars have three criteria by which they classify the chapters and verses into Makkan and Madinan:

1.1.1 The geographical location of revelation: That which was actually revealed in one of the two cities takes the city's name. This logically means that there would need to be a third category relating to that which was revealed in neither. *[al-Jazairi, al-Tibyan, 33]*

1.1.2 In terms of the audience addressed: That which contains *'O Mankind'* would be Makkan and that which contains *'O Believers'* is invariably Madinan (though exceptions do exist).

1.1.3 Classification relative to the Hijra from Makkah to Madinah: That which was revealed before the migration is considered Makkan, while everything revealed after this is considered to be Madinan. This is the most well known criteria to classify the two types of revelation. *[al-Zarkashi, v1[4]- pg274]*

> *"Indeed God orders you to return trusts to their rightful owners."* *[4:58]*

There are many exceptions to these general rules. The chapter entitled *Women (al-Nisa)* is considered to have been revealed after the *hijrah* in Madinah, but it contains a verse that is established with certainty to have been revealed in the city of Makkah, relating to the guardianship of the keys to the Ka'ba, in which the Prophet ﷺ ordered that they remain in the custody of 'Uthman ibn Talhah. *[al-Zarkashi,v 1[4]- 274]*

1.2 What are the benefits of knowing whether the revelation is Makkan or Madinan?

1.2.1 It aids in undertaking commentary (*tafsir*) of the Qur'an by providing a context to Islamic faith and practice as well as providing a time line which aids in identifying abrogation of rulings (*naskh*).

1.2.2 It outlines the gradual method of calling mankind to truth through wisdom and kind counsel.

1.2.3 It provides a clear insight into the Prophetic *Sirah* and its close relationship with the Qur'anic revelation. *[al-Qattan, al-Mabahith, pg59-60]*

2. The Reasons for Revelation (*asbab al-nuzul*)

Sabab (pl. asbab) literally means the underlying reason or cause, and *nuzul* means revelation or descent. Thus, this area of Qur'anic studies examines the original circumstances that led to the revelation of a section of the Qur'an. Understanding why a particular section of Qur'an was revealed, and how it addressed a need of the time, is invaluable in appreciating the wisdom of the message as a whole.

> *"To God belongs the East and the West and so wherever you turn to, here is the countenance of God. God is All-Knowing, All-Encompassing." [2:115]*

It is not clear from the verse above in *Sura al-Baqarah* what the exact meaning intended is. The reasons for revelation (*asbab an-nuzul*) provide an insight into the context of the verse. One of the narrated reports states that it was revealed in relation to a group of Companions who prayed in different directions on a pitch-black night, as they were unable to determine the direction of the Qiblah. When they mentioned this to the Prophet ﷺ , the above verse was revealed. It was sent excusing the mistake made in identifying the qiblah, as this occurred after they had attempted to ascertain the correct direction of prayer *[al-Tirmidhi]*.

Another report recorded in the hadith collection of Imam Muslim states the *asbab al-nuzul* to be about praying non-obligatory prayers on a camel while not facing the Qibla. In both cases, the context clarifies that the verse deals with the general issue of facing the Qibla while in prayer when there is an excuse present[6].

2.1 One revelation: Multiple reasons

> *"They ask you concerning the Ruh (spirit). Say, 'The Ruh is but by the command of my Lord...'" [17:85]*

Occasionally, the same section of the Qur'an was sent through the Angel Gabriel to the Prophet ﷺ as a response to differing circumstances. A prime example of this is the verse above which was a response to two different groups of people:

It was revealed in Makkah, when the Jewish Rabbis of Madinah, at the request of the Makkan idolaters, sent a question the Prophet ﷺ regarding the nature of the human soul and it is also said to have been revealed in Madinah, when the Rabbis came to ask the Prophet ﷺ about the same issue. *[al-Zarkashi, 1-124]*

2.2 One reason: Multiple revelations

> *"Their Lord responds to them, 'I will not let the deeds of anyone that does good to go to waste, be they male or female...'" [3:195]*

> *"Men and women that are Muslim, and men and women that are believers, and men and women that are obedient, and men and women that are truthful...God has prepared for them forgiveness and an immense reward." [33:35]*

> *"Do not covet what God has given to some of you over others. Men have a portion of what they acquire and women likewise..." [4:32]*

All of these verses are related to have been revealed in response to a query by Umm Salamah to the Prophet ﷺ :*"I see that God always mentions men, but not women?' [al-Suyuti, v1 pg97]*

2.3 What are the benefits of knowing *asbab al-nuzul*?

2.3.1 *'It is a powerful means by which to understand the meanings of the Qur'an'. (Ibn Daqiq al-I'id)*

2.3.2 It provides an insight into the underlying wisdom of the revelation. *[Al-Zarkhashi 1:116-123]*

---

[6] It is important in this context to note that not all reports relating to *asbab an-nuzul* can be taken at face value. *"Sometimes when a Companion says: 'This verse was revealed concerning such and such' what they sometimes mean is that this verse is of relevance to a particular ruling, and not that this is the actual initial cause of the revelation." [al-Zarkashi, 1:126]*

3. The theory of abrogation (*Al-Naskh*)

> *"We do not abrogate an ayah or cause it to be forgotten – except that We bring forth in its place one better than it or like it. Know you not that God has ability over all things?" [2:106]*

Naskh can either mean 'to remove' (*izalah*), 'to replace' (*tabdil*) or 'to copy' (*naql*). Technically, it refers to the process by which the rulings of some sections of the Qur'an are replaced by others.

It is agreed that this only affects religious commands and prohibitions and does not include such things as historical narratives and purely ethical advice. Similarly, those issues that are shared in all religious traditions, such as generic acts of worship and normative ethics and manners, cannot be abrogated. ***"And turn not your cheek away from people in pride, and walk not haughtily on earth: for God does not love anyone who acts in a boastful manner." [31:18]*** *[az-Zarkashi, 2-159-164]*

3.1 Example of abrogation: The case of wine-consumption

> *'And from the fruits of the date-palm and vines you derive both intoxicants and wholesome provision.' [16:67]*

> *'They ask you concerning wine and gambling. Say: 'They contain great harm as well as benefits for Man yet their harm is greater than their benefit'. [2:219]*

> *'Do not approach the prayer while in a state of intoxication!' [4:43]*

> *'O Believers! Indeed wine and games of chance, stone altars and divining arrows are filth from the handiwork of the Satan, so avoid them completely, that you may attain success.' [5:90]*

The case of the prohibition of the consumption of wine is a clear example of the way in which the replacement of one ruling by another in a gradual manner helped in resolving a deep-rooted issue. The benefits of gradual prohibition were mentioned by 'Aishah, when she commented on the state of the Arabs at the time. She said: *'If the first verse which was revealed had been, 'Do not drink wine,' they would have responded, 'We will never give up wine.' [Al-Bukhari]*

The wisdom of the gradual phasing-out of alcohol consumption sheds light on the way in which God takes into account the weak and fragile nature of humans and manifests His mercy. Al-Qaffal, the famous early Shafi'i scholar said: *'There was no escape from such a gradual prohibition, and this [gradual prohibition] was in effect the epitome of mercy itself'. [Al-Razi, Tafsir al-Kabir, v6 pg35]*

3.2 What are the benefits of knowing al-*Naskh*?

Knowledge of abrogation is a pre-condition for explaining the Qur'an (*tafsir*) and application of Islamic law. It is related that 'Ali passed by a man who was relating religious stories and asked him: *'Are you conversant with that which abrogates (nasikh) and that which is abrogated (mansukh)?'* He replied that he was not. 'Ali said: *'You will perish and you will cause others to perish!' [Al-Zarkashi, v2 pg158]*

4. Text in Focus: 'The Verse of the Sword' – A basis for perpetual war?

> *"But when the sacred months have passed, fight the idolaters wherever you find them, and capture them and besiege them and lay in wait for them..." [9:5]*

> *"Fight in the Way of God those who fight you, but do not initiate hostilities. God loves not the transgressors." [2:190]*

> *"...and say kind words to mankind..." [2:83]*

Can the teaching exhorting to patience conveyed in the early revelation be completely replaced with the call for perpetual war? Is the *status quo* between nations and religions that of a state of peace or a state of war? This issue has been widely discussed by early and contemporary scholars, and the ramifications of this debate have far-reaching consequences for both Muslims and non-Muslims alike. The wider issues of *Jihad* and *'Just War'* will be covered in detail in a case study later in the course. Here we will look at two of the concepts covered in this lesson and how they impact on the understanding of a religious text. The debate around *'The Verse of the Sword'* rests upon an application of the theory of abrogation (*al-naskh*), as well as an understanding of the underlying context and reason (*asbab an-nuzul*).

What is important, is that both provide an essential context which aid in an authentic understanding of the Quran and Sunnah. Commenting on the importance of context, Shaykh Abdullah Bin Bayyah writes:

> *"Based on a number of verses from the Qur'an, and during various historical periods, some have claimed that Islam was a religion of the sword. In other words, it was propelled by a thirst for conquest and war. Two typical verses that are cited to prove this assertion are: 'Prophet! strive hard against the disbelievers and hypocrites and be firm against them' [9:73] and 'But when the sacred months have passed, fight the idolaters wherever you find them' [9:5]. However, anyone who accounts for the specific context (asbab an-nazul) in which each verse was revealed, and accounts for the evolution of Islam's wars with its opponents, will conclude that there is no contradiction between these verses and those that identify the objective of warfare in Islam as being defensive." [Bin Bayyah, The Culture of Terrorism, pg 68]*

4.1 The 'Verse of the Sword' and the theory of abrogation

The Andalusian Ibn Hazm held that 114 verses that exhorted to patience, forgiveness and fighting in self-defence, were abrogated and replaced by this one verse that calls for war. Qadi Abu Bakr ibn al-Arabi, counted 75 cases of verses abrogated by this command to fight. *[Ibn Hazm, Nasikh, 17-22; Qadi Abu Bakr, al-Nasikh wal-Mansukh, 1[2]-199]*

The majority of scholars have challenged this understanding of abrogation on the basis that this verse was revealed regarding a particular situation where the Muslims were ordered to fight to preserve their very existence, and that war was only used to aid a policy of securing lasting peace in the Arabian peninsula. They therefore contest this as an instance abrogation. *[Haykal: 1456-1457]*

4.1.1 A case of straightforward abrogation?

What is clear is that the verse is not intended to provide a blanket ruling for unrestricted warfare. This particular verse, on its own, has a limited application in a contemporary context, given the conditions classical scholars have placed on its use. The prevailing state of affairs has an effect on the way that different verses are applied. It goes without saying that what is applicable in one context will not be so in another. A ruling or teaching may be temporarily suspended to take into account a situation that was extraordinary. This is the case with the verses that exhort Muslims to peace and patience on the one hand, and military engagement on the other. Al-Zarkashi says regarding this type of abrogation:

> *"...The third type (of abrogation) is when something is ordered for a particular reason and then the underlying reason ceases to exist [...]. This is a case of suspension or overlooking (mansa') [...]. From this verification (tahqiq) one can gather the weakness of what some Qur'an commentators have held regarding verses that command leniency when they state that they have [all] been abrogated by the 'Verse of the Sword'." [al-Zarkashi, v2[4] pg173]*

4.1.2 The meaning of 'idolaters'

Although the wording in the *'Verse of the Sword'* is general, including, as it does, all those that may be deemed to be *'idolaters'*, scholars are clear that those referred to are a specific group who, on account of a particular set of circumstances, were the subject of the verse.

> *"It is well-known among scholars that the following verses: 'Kill the idolaters wherever you find them,' [9:5] has been restricted in many ways and that the verse is in reference to a historical episode, namely, relating to those among the Makkan confederates who breached the Treaty of Hudaybiyyah, which led to the victory of Makkah, and that therefore, no legal rulings [...] can be derived from this verse in isolation."*

> *Among the well-known exegeses of idolaters 'al-mushrikin' from this verse (from different schools) are:*

> ***4.1.2.1*** *Those who have breached (the Treaty): 'al-nakithina khassatan' [al-Nawawi al-Jawi al-Shafi'i, Tafsir, 1:331]*
> ***4.1.2.2*** *Those who have declared war against you: "al-ladhina yuharibunakum" [Qadi Ibn al-Arabi, al Maliki, Ahkam al-Qur'an, 2:889]*
> ***4.1.2.3*** *Specifically, the jahili Arabs, and no-one else: "khassan fi mushriki l-Arabi duna ghayrihim" [al-Jassas al-Hanafi, Ahkam al-Qur'an, 3:81]' [Adapted from al-Afifi, pg 31]*

Did you know?

Did you know that there are various signs identified by scholars that shed light on the place, context and audience to which a particular section of the *Qur'an* was revealed. There are therefore specific clues used in differentiating between the Makkan and Madinan portions of the *Qur'an*.

"There are two methods of differentiating between the Makkan and Madinan revelations. One is through **narration** *(Sama') and the other is through* **deduction** *(Qiyas).*

The **narrative** *method would be the case where we are told that this was revealed in one of the two cities.*

As for the method of **deduction***, Alqamah ibn Abdillah said, 'That which only contains "O Mankind," or, "No, indeed," (kalla) or the beginning has the (broken) letters of the alphabet (al-Muqatiat), except in the case of Sura al-Baqarah and Al-Imran, and possibly the chapter of Thunder according to some [are Makkan]. Also, where there is the story of Adam and Iblis, except for Sura al-Baqarah, the revelation* **is Makkan***. Any sura that has extended stories of the Prophets and past nations is also* **Makkan***. Any sura that has a rule or legal punishment* **is Madinan***."' [Al-Zarkashi, v1-276]*

Lesson 5 - Qur'anic commentary

> **Aim:** To provide an introduction to the theory and practice of Qur'anic commentary, examining the methods and issues of importance for those undertaking an explanation of the Qur'an.
>
> **Objectives:** By the end of this lesson, students should be able to display the capacity to:
> 1. Mention what is meant by the word '*tafsir*' in its original use, as well as the use of scholars.
> 2. Outline the need and importance of this area of Qur'anic studies through a suitable example.
> 3. Identify the two main types of *tafsir*, mentioning what is intended by commentary through recorded narrations (*ma'thur*) and the various subtypes contained within this.
> 4. Mention the saying of Imam Ahmad regarding *tafsir ma'thur*, together with the explanation of this and the reason why a degree of caution should be used when undertaking *tafsir* through this method.
> 5. Outline the type of *tafsir* done through examined research (*bi ar-ra'y*), discussing the difference of opinion on its use as well as the proofs of those that allow this type of tafsir .
> 6. Summarise the pre-requisites of the one undertaking Qur'anic commentary.
> 7. Discuss what is meant by 'subtle commentary' (*al-Ishari*), together with the conditions for such Qur'anic explanation, as well as an example of its usage.

(This is) a Book which we have sent down to you, full of blessings, that you may ponder over its verses, and that people of understanding may remember" [38:29]

"Of the sciences of the Qur'an, tafsir (Qur'anic commentary) is the one that is intended for its own sake, while the rest of the sciences are like tools aiding in this process of commentary, being either directly related (to tafsir) or being one of its offshoots..." [Tafsir Ibn Juzay, 1:15]

1. What does *Tafsir* mean?

"[It is] a science by which one understands the Book of God as revealed to the Prophet ﷺ , explain its meanings and extracts its rulings and judgments." [al-Suyuti, al-Itqan, 4, pg. 169]

Tafsir refers to the process by which one understands the Qur'anic message. As mentioned in lesson three, some sections of the Qur'an are clear and require little effort for the basic meanings to be understood. Others require diligent study for a fruitful result to be obtained. Any attempt to explain the levels of the meanings of the Qur'an must be preceded by the requisite knowledge, that will aid in a correct understanding.

'In the Arabic language, the word tafsir means to make apparent (izhar) and examine/disclose (kashf). The original root meaning of this is the word 'tafsirah', which is the name given to the sample of urine-water that a doctor examines to diagnose the patient [...] In the same way, one engaged in tafsir examines the nature of a verse, its related stories and meanings, as well as the reasons for revelation.' [al-Zarkashi, 2[4], pg283]

Another term used in the context of explaining the Qur'an is **ta'wil**, which linguistically means *'to return back to'*. In the context of Qur'anic studies, it means *'explaining the Qur'anic meanings in the light of general rules and diligent study (al-nadhr al-daqiq)'. ['Ittr, Ulum al Qur'an, 73]*

1.1 Why the need for *Tafsir?*

One may argue: *'Has God not made the message so clear that we would not have any need for recourse to anything but the most rudimentary linguistic understanding?'* This is answered directly by al-Suyuti, who states that there are three main reasons for the need for the science of *tafsir*, summarised as follows:

1.1.1 The nature of Qur'anic Arabic means that the meaning will only be clear to those well-versed in the classical Arabic language.
1.1.2 The context of the verses, as well as the other conditions that are required for their understanding, are rarely alluded to in the Qur'an.
1.1.3 The language used may have multiple meanings, and may contain figurative speech and so on, thus one needs to be conversant with these to understand the meaning of the message. *[al-Suyuti, 4[4]:170]*

1.2 Early examples of *Tafsir*

1.2.1 "And eat and drink until the white thread of dawn appears to you distinct from black thread..." [2:187]

Adi Ibn Hatim relates that he said: 'Messenger of God! What is the meaning of the white thread distinct from the black thread? Are these two threads?' He ﷺ said: 'No, it is the darkness of the night and the whiteness of the day.' [Tafsir al-Tabari, 3:251]

1.2.2 *"Those that have faith and do not taint their belief with injustice (zulm)." [6:82]*

*The Companions asked: 'Which from amongst us does not wrong themselves?' The Prophet ﷺ replied: 'Have you not read the words of Luqman: '**Indeed shirk is a great injustice [31:13]**?' [al-Bukhari, 4629]*

The need for clarification is shown by the fact that Companions themselves used to seek explanations from the Prophet ﷺ about particular issues. A few common examples above make this clear. These are both also examples of what is termed '*tafsir bil-m'athur*' or commentary by means of passed-down narrations.

The second example is also an example of what is considered one of the most trusted methods of Qur'anic commentary – that of commentating on the Qur'an through the use of that Qur'an itself.

2. Types of *tafsir*

There are a number of methods by which Qur'an commentary is undertaken. One relies on the recorded sayings of the early Muslim community, without specific reference to anything other than the authority of the one giving the explanation. Another is undertaken through the use of language analysis and logical understanding, and is done while remaining observant of the general principles of the Muslim faith. Related to this is a type of *tafsir* that is undertaken by a search for the subtle indications hidden in the Quranic text.

2.1 *Commentary through recorded narrations (al-ma'thur)*[7]

2.1.1 Definition: *'Commentating upon the Qur'an through reliance on what is related from an earlier authority and in particular the first three generations of Islam.'*

2.1.2 *Types of Commentary through recorded narrations (al-ma'thur)*

2.1.2.1 Prophetic commentary. This type of *tafsir*, if narrated through a sound channel of transmission, is the most authoritative class of commentary. Examples have been given previously.
2.1.2.2 The commentary of the Companions. Having witnessed the revelation and having had the opportunity to query the Prophet ﷺ regarding the meaning of verses, the explanations related from the Companions provide an invaluable insight into the meanings of the Qur'anic revelation. Ibn Mas'ud said: *'One of us would not learn ten verses and go past them until we had understood their meanings and acted upon them.' [Tafsir al-Tabari, 1:74]*
2.1.2.3 The Followers (*Tabi'un*). While not directly classified as an integral part of narrated commentary, the Followers – who are the generation who learned from the Companions – have had an important role in preserving the explanations of the Qur'an of the first generation.

Caution in the use of *tafsir through recorded narrations (al-ma'thur)*

Imam Ahmad stated: 'Three matters have no reliable chain of narration (isnad): Qur'anic commentary (tafsir), stories of events in the future and the signs of the last day (malahim) and the chronicles of battles (maghazi)." [Ibn Taymiyyah, Muqaddimah, 49]

Though this is theoretically the most trusted type of Qur'anic commentary, a number of issues have been identified by scholars which need to be kept in mind when using such narrations, and so require caution when relating this type of *tafsir*. This relates to three main areas of concern:

One: Breaks in the chain (*isnad*) of many narrations makes it difficult to verify their authenticity.
Two: There is a well-documented genre of fabricated reports in *tafsir*.
Three: Non-verifiable Biblical sources (*Israil'iyyat*) [I'ttr, Ulum al Qur'an, 74-77].

---

[7] There are a number of famous *tafsir* works that use this methodology. Amongst these are: *Jami al-Bayan fi Tafsir al-Qur'an by Ibn Jarir al-Tabari (d.310/922); Al-Kashf wa-l-Bayan by Ahmad bin Ibrahim al-Tha'labi al-Nisaburi (d.383/993); Tafsir al-Qur'an al-Azim, by Isma'il bin 'Amr bin Kathir al-Dimashqi (d.774/1372); al-Durr al-Manthur fi-l-Tafsir bi-l-Mathur by Jalal al-Din al-Suyuti (d.911/1505)*

Use of Biblical sources (*Israil'iyyat*)

It is generally allowed to relate traditions Biblical in origin, such as the names of the twelve brothers of Yusuf (A.S.), provided that firstly that they do not contravene established Islamic texts and secondly that one does not hold them to be incontrovertibly truthful. This is indicated in the hadith *'Neither assent to what the People of the Book relate, nor accuse them of lying, but rather say 'We believe in God'.'* [al-Bukhari, 4485]

2.2 Commentary through examined research (*al-Ra'y*)[8]

> **"He gives wisdom to whom He chooses, and the one given wisdom is indeed given an abundance of good." [2:269]**

2.2.1 Definition: *'Commentating upon the Qur'an through personal exertion (ijtihad), relying upon the skills that the person undertaking the commentary is in need of.' ['Ittr, Ulum al Qur'an, pg85]*

This type of commentary, as alluded to above, is undertaken through the use of language analysis, logical understanding and reflection, while remaining observant of the general principles of the Muslim faith[9]. Commenting on the verse above, Ibn Abbas said: *'It refers to the Qur'an, specifically its explanation (tafsir) since it is read by both the righteous as well as the impious.' [al-Suyuti, 4:171].*

2.2.2 Proofs for the permissibility of Tafsir by examined research (al-Ra'y)

There has been some discussion regarding the validity of such commentary of the Qur'an, with some claiming that this is no more than the use of personal opinion to interpret the Word of God. Those that take this opinion rely upon the saying of the Prophet ﷺ : *'Whoever speaks about the Qur'an using their own opinion, then let them take their seat in the fire of Hell. [Al-Tirmidhi, 2951]*

The majority of scholars reply that the personal opinion condemned here is that which does not rely upon any supporting evidence. It may also be said that this refers to people who interpret the Qur'an by looking only at the literal wording without seeking recourse to the other sciences which the commentator is required to possess. There are numerous proofs that *tafsir* through examined research *(al-Ra'y)* is permitted:

2.2.2.1 The verses which exhort mankind to ponder over the meanings of the Qur'an: **"Do they not ponder over the Qur'an, or do they have locks upon their hearts?" [47:24]**
2.2.2.2 It is established that the Companions differed upon the meanings of the Qur'an and that they only did so based upon each having a personal understanding of the text.
2.2.2.3 The Prophet ﷺ prayed for Ibn Abbas: *'O God! Provide him with understanding of the religion and teach him its interpretation." ['Ittr, 86-87]*

2.3 Subtle commentary (Tafsir al-Ishari)

2.3.1 Definition: *'Interpreting verses of Qur'an in a way other than what is apparent, due to subtle indications which may be apparent to people with a spiritual disposition, where there is a correlation between the interpretation given and the outward meanings.' [al-Taftazani, Sharh al-Aqa'id, pg 258]*

Tafsir al-Ishari can be seen as a subset of commentary arrived at through examined research *(ar-ra'y)*, but which differs slightly in that the basis of this is not diligent research, but rather a heightened spiritual state and purity that provides a subtle insight otherwise hidden in the outward wording of a section of Qur'an.

An example of this, commonly overlooked, is what is related from Ibn Abbas concerning the chapter of the Qur'an entitled *'The Victory' (Al-Nasr)*. 'Umar asked Ibn Abbas of the meaning of the verse, *"When the victory of God arrives and the opening"*. He said: *'It is the impending passing away of the Prophet ﷺ which God is informing him of'.*

As the meaning and indication given by Ibn Abbas was not apparent to many others, it is given as proof of his ability to understand the subtle message in a way that did not oppose the outward meaning.

---

[8] There are a number of famous tafsir works that use this methodology. Amongst these are: *Al-Kashshaf, by Abu'l-Qasim Mahmud Ibn 'Umar al-Zamakhshari (d.539/1144); Mafatih al-Ghaib, by Muhammad bin 'Amr al-Husain al-Razi (d.606/1209); Anwar al-Tanzil, by 'Abd Allah bin 'Umar al-Baidawi (d.685/1286); Ruh al Ma'ani, by Shihab al-Din Muhammad al-Alusi al-Baghdadi (d.1270/1854)*

[9] It should be borne in mind that the previous type of *tafsir*, through recorded narrations (*al-ma'thur*), in many cases is arrived at through the use of examined research (*al-Ra'y*).

2.3.2 *Conditions to Subtle commentary (Tafsir al-Ishari)*
2.3.2.1 There should be an established religious principle pointing towards the meaning given.
2.3.2.2 The commentary accord with the rules of the Arabic language.
2.3.2.3 That it not be claimed that this is the sole intending meaning.
[al-Suyuti 4,197; 'Ittr, 'Ulum al-Qur'an, 97-98]

Ibn Qayyim says regarding this type of *tafsir*: '*This type of commentary is accepted if it meets four conditions: That it does not negate the [apparent] meaning of the verse; that the meaning be true in its own right; that the wording provide some sense of the meaning given; and that there be a degree of parity and link between the interpretation given and the meaning of the verse.*' *[Al-Qattan, Mabahith, pg 357-8]*

2.3.3 Example of *tafsir al-Ishari*

An example of this type of *tafsir* is that given in the story of Bilqis, in which she expresses the view that if the army of Sulayman (A.S.) was to reach her dominion, they would wreak havoc in the land and destroy them all [27:34]. This verse is taken by Shaykh Ibn 'Ajiba in his *tafsir* work to indicate a deeper meaning. He uses the outward words of the verse as a metaphor for the power of God to subdue the spiritual ills and arrogance that inhabit the human heart.

> **"She said, "Indeed when Kings enter into a city they lay waste to it and make its highest inhabitants the most abased".** *The Kings here are divinely produced impulses which come from the presence of The All-Powerful.* **"If they enter the city or village"** *meaning the heart of somebody, they decimate its outward form through destruction and punishment,* **"and make its highest inhabitants the most abased"** *meaning change its haughtiness into lowliness and its arrogance into humbleness and its richness into poverty."* *[Ibn Ajibah al-Bahr al-Madid, v5 pg227]*

3. Reconnecting with the spirit: The inward state of one seeking to explain the Qur'an

> '*Reaching the meanings of the Qur'an is based upon deliberation and reflection, knowing that the person investigating will not attain an understanding of the reality of the meanings of revelation and neither will the secrets of knowledge appear to them from the unseen while their heart is involved in any reprehensible innovation or open wrong action or their heart contains pride, personal desire, love of the world, or they have not perfected their faith, or are weak in verifying matters, or they rely upon the sayings of a commentator who has only outward knowledge, or solely relies upon their intellect. These are all veils and obstacles [to understanding], some more pervasive than others.*" *[al-Zarkashi, 2[4], pg319-320]*

Did you know?

Scholars placed conditions on the person that attempted *tafsir* to safeguard from misinterpretation.

1. Knowledge of the Arabic language.
2. Knowledge of grammar and morphology (*nahw* and *sarf*).
3. Knowledge of rhetoric (*balaghah*).
4. Knowledge of the various Qur'anic readings (*qira'at*).
5. Knowledge of the principles of faith (*usul ad-din*).
6. Knowledge of the principles of jurisprudence (*usul al-fiqh*).
7. Knowledge of the reasons for revelation, abrogation, etc.
8. Knowledge of the history and narratives of the stories contained in the Qur'an.
9. Divinely-gifted knowledge given to a person who acts according to what they have learned
10. Knowledge of basic accepted realities of natural science. *[Ittr, Ulum al-Qur'an 93-94]*

Lesson 6 - Translation and Etiquette

> **Aim:** To provide an insight into the area of Qur'anic translation through an understanding of the difficulties and limits on the use of translations. The etiquettes of interacting with the Qur'anic text, through which a meaningful relationship with the Qur'an can be developed, will also be discussed.
>
> **Objectives:** By the end of this lesson, students should be able to display the capacity to:
> 1. Identify early examples of Qur'anic translation, discussing the different types of translation and why scholars state that a purely literal translation of the Qur'an is not permitted.
> 2. Discuss, using examples, the importance of the Arabic language in conveying the meanings of the Qur'an, and how and why this is not possible in any other language.
> 3. Appreciate the importance of having proper etiquette when reading, studying and reciting the Qur'an.
> 4. Outline the main points regarding the etiquettes of interacting with the Qur'an related to memorisation, study, recitation and listening to the sacred Book.
> 5. Discuss what scholars have said regarding the importance of reflection when studying the Qur'an, and the different forms that this takes.
> 6. Summarise the issue of the abandonment of the Qur'an and the different forms that it may take, outlining the spiritual and worldly effects of doing so.
> 7. Summarise the conditions required for the one translating the Qur'an.

1. The translation of the Qur'an

"Verily we have revealed this as an Arabic Qur'an..." [12:2]

The fact that the Qur'an was revealed in Arabic has meant that its accessibility to those that do not have a familiarity with the language is somewhat restricted. This was not, however, a barrier to the teaching and expansion of the faith.

The meaning of the message was given to those that requested it, and this took place without the need to prepare a full 'translation' of the Qur'an itself. A translation from a passage from Sura Maryam was read by the Muslims in front of the Negus of Abyssinia *[Ibn Hisham [1[4]-152]*. Similarly, the Companion Salman al-Farisi was requested by some Persian converts to translate portions of the Qur'an, which he duly did. Therefore, since the earliest time, there have been examples of the meanings of the Qur'an being translated into other languages. *[See al-Zarqani, v2 pg175]*

1.1 What is translation and is it permitted to translate the Qur'an into a foreign language?

Scholars state that there are two types of translations:

1.1.1 A literal translation. Each individual word is translated to its equivalent in another language.

Scholars agree that a purely literal translation of the Qur'an, where there is little attempt to convey the meaning of the whole text, and where it aims to take the place of the original, is not possible. This is because:

1.1.1.1 The Qur'an is inimitable in nature (*mu'jiz*), such that mankind is unable to produce the like of it, even in their own languages. A literal translation would be an attempt to do just that, and would necessarily fall short of the original.

1.1.1.2 The Arabic language of the Qur'an is used to directly arrive at rulings and judgements. This is done not only from the literal meaning, but also from the implied meanings (*dalalat al-nass*) and inferences (*isharat al-nass*) from the Arabic language itself. Thus, a translation would be lacking in the ability to reproduce these meanings that are inherent in the Arabic language.

1.1.2 Translation by meaning. Here, the overall meaning of the whole text is transferred into a different language, while attempting, as much as possible, to remain faithful to the original text. Scholars agree that producing translations by meaning is not only allowed but may become a communal obligation on the Muslim community. *[Ittr, pg 116-117]*

1.2 What conditions did scholars place upon a translator of the Quran?

To ensure the reliability of the translations of the Qur'an, scholars set out some basic conditions for one translating the Qur'an into another language.

1.2.1 The translator be a Muslim, as a person who does not believe in the Divine authorship of the text may not strive to convey its full meanings.

1.2.2 Expertise and proficiency in classical Arabic as well as the language being translated into.

1.2.3 Knowledge of the linguistic, rhetorical and grammatical peculiarities of the Arabic language.

1.2.4 Familiarity with other Islamic sciences, in as much as they help in the translation of the text.

1.2.5 Reliance on authentic Qur'anic commentaries which clarify the meaning of the text.

1.2.6 Clarification that the work produced is not a translation of the Qur'an but *'a translation of some of the meanings contained within the Qur'an'*. This will clarify the fact that what is being read conveys only part of the meanings that the Qur'an contains. *[al-Zarqani, v2, 127-128; Ittr, 119]*

1.3 Inadequacies of translations in conveying the meanings of the Qur'an

The nature of the Arabic language means that it is impossible to convey accurately the original spirit and meanings of the Qur'an in another language. The eloquence contained is barely noticeable in any other language. This is particularly important to understand when seeking to translate the original Arabic. The brevity with which the Qur'an sometimes conveys many meanings is a constant challenge for translators. Sometimes there are many words intentionally not mentioned to show the eloquence of the speaker. At other times the Qur'an uses a number of words in a verse, each of which is pregnant with subtle illusions.

1.3.1 "He said: 'Oh my Lord, My bones have grown weak and grey hair has spread on my head.'" [19:4]

In the story of the Prophet Zakariyyah (A.S.), one is told of his supplicating to God to grant him a child. His old age and weakened state is described in the translation *"and grey hair has spread on my head"*, which fails to convey the powerful description offered in the Qur'an which paints the picture in a truly graphic manner. Commenting on this verse, al-Zamakhshari explains a number of rhetorical devices that bring the passage to life in the Arabic, none of which can be conveyed through a translation in any other language.

1.3.1.1 The word *'ishta'ala'* which is translated as *'spread'* actually conveys the animated connotation of sparks emitted by a fire. The implication being that Zakariyyah (A.S.), when describing the whiteness of his hair, likens it to the sparks that are emitted from a blazing fire, thus providing a highly visual aid to animate how old age had afflicted him.

1.3.1.2 The original language used in the verse places the sparking effect to the whole head, and not to the hair itself (in fact the *'hair'* are not even mentioned in the verse), thereby providing a picture of old age invading the whole head and by implication the rest of his body.

1.3.1.3 The phrase provides the impression of sparks being emitted simultaneously from many places, thereby underlying the pervasive nature of the spread of old age. The overall picture painted in these few words is impossible to convey in none but the original Arabic and any attempt to do so will fall far short.

2. Excellence of the Qur'an and the etiquettes related to it

> Anas relates that the Prophet ﷺ said: The believer who reads the Qur'an is like a citron, its smell is sweet and its taste is good. The believer who does not read the Qur'an is like a date: no smell but its taste is sweet. The evil doer who reads the Qur'an is like basil: its smell is sweet but taste bitter. The evil doer who does not read the Qur'an is like a colocynth: it has no smell and its taste is bitter. A good companion is like a perfume seller, if you do not get anything from him, you will at least experience his pleasant scent. A bad companion is like a furnace worker, if you are not covered in soot, you will be affected by its smoke.' [Abu Dawud: 4829]

> Abdullah ibn 'Amr ibn al-A'as relates from the Prophet ﷺ that he said, "Whoever reads the Qur'an, it is as if prophecy has been placed within him, except that he has not received revelation. It is not appropriate for one possessing the Qur'an to change with every new thing or to be overcome by ignorance while the Word of God is inside him." [al-Hakim: 2028]

Many of the blessings that are gained from the teachings of the Qur'an are attained and retained through the etiquette and mannerisms through which one recites and studies the sacred text itself. These not only aid understanding, but also nurture a sense of reverence for the word of God and all that is connected to God. These etiquettes can be summarised in the following points:

2.1 The etiquette when learning and memorising the Qur'an:

2.1.1 Sincerity. "And they were not ordered except to worship God in complete sincerity" [98:5]. A person may cultivate this in themselves through supplication, prayer and by focusing the heart on reciting and studying the Qur'an. In learning it, the person should be careful not to intend the attainment of any worldly benefit, as this flies in the face of acting with sincerity.

2.1.2 Perfect and rectify one's character as a means of respecting the Qur'an.

2.1.3 Cultivate a state of serenity and self-assurance emanating from the study of the Qur'an.

2.2 The etiquette towards the person from whom one is learning the Qur'an.

2.2.1 Respect and reverence for the person from whom they are learning. 'Ali said, *"The right that a scholar has upon you is that you greet all people in general, but that you single them out in welcoming them, and that you sit in front of them and that you do not point to them...'*

2.2.2 Revising and reviewing one's memorisation since the Prophet ﷺ said: *"Revise the Qur'an."*

2.3 The etiquettes of listening to the Qur'an:

2.3.1 Being in a state of Silence. God says in the Qur'an: ***"And when the Qur'an is recited then pay heed to it and remain silent" [7:204]***

Due to the greatness of listening to the recitation of Qur'an, some scholars opined that listening to the Qur'an is better than the person reciting the Qur'an themselves, since listening to it is an obligation when it is being recited, whereas reciting the Qur'an outside the prayer is not. Ibn Mas'ud relates that the Prophet ﷺ said to him, *"Recite to me."* I said, *"Oh Prophet, should I recite to you whilst it has been revealed to you?"* He said, *"I love that I hear it from somebody else."* So I recited Sura an-Nisa until I reached the verse, ***"and so how will it be when We bring a witness from each community and We bring you forth as a witness upon these people!" [4:41].*** He said to me, *"Enough!"* I looked at him and I saw that his eyes were shedding tears.'

2.4 The etiquette when preparing to recite the Qur'an

2.4.1 Purity.

2.4.2 Choosing the best time and place. All times are permitted for one to recite the Qur'an, but some times are better than others. The best is within the prayer, after which comes reciting at night, particularly in the last portions of the night, then reciting between Maghrib and Isha or after Fajr;

2.4.3 Using the *Siwak* and general dental cleanliness.

2.5 The etiquettes when reciting the Qur'an

'Aishah relates that the Prophet ﷺ said, *"The expert reader will be among the noble scribes of the Angels, and the one who stutters and for whom it is difficult will have double the reward." [al-Bukhari: 4937]*

2.5.1 Reciting the Qur'an in a slow rhythmic manner. ***"...and recite the Qur'an in a slow and rhythmic tone." [73:4]***

2.5.2 Reflection and humility: Both of these aid one in understanding the Qur'an, and allow one to access the blessings of its message. God says: ***"This is a Book that we have revealed to you, blessed, in order that you reflect over its verses..." [38: 29].*** This reflection and humility is said to be the medicine of the heart.

[Section on Reflection]

Shaykh Ibrahim al-Khawas said: *'The remedy of the heart lies in five things: in reciting the Qur'an with reflection; not eating one's fill; standing the night in prayer; making profuse supplication before Fajr; and sitting with those of pure heart.'*

One of the aids in developing reflection and humility when reciting the Qur'an is to repeat the verses while pondering over their meaning.

It is related that the Prophet ﷺ once repeated a verse through the night until morning came. The verse was: ***"If You were to punish them then they are Your servants and if You were to forgive them then indeed it is You that is Mighty and Wise" [5:118].***

It is also related by 'Abbad ibn Hamzah: *'I went to see Asma bint Abi Bakr and she was reciting the verse* ***"and so God has blessed us and saved us from the poisonous punishment" [52:27]*** *and I stood there while she repeated it and supplicated. This went on for a period of time so I went to the market place and later on came back once I had finished my business. When I returned she was still repeating it and supplicating.' [Summarized and abridged from 'Ittr, Ulum al-Quran, 267-287]*

3. Abandoning the Qur'an?

"And the Prophet says, 'My Lord, indeed my people have taken this Qur'an as something to be abandoned.'" [25:29-30]

"Leaving belief in it and attesting to its truthfulness is to abandon it; leaving reflection and contemplation of it is to abandon it; leaving acting upon its commands and shunning its prohibitions is to abandon it; to turn from it to any other speech such as poetry, singing, idle talk – any path other than it – is to abandon it. [Ibn Kathir, Tafsir al-Adhim, p1238]

The Qur'an is a book of guidance. We have not been asked to simply read its contents, but rather to understand, and furthermore, live by its guidance. Those that abandon this call have forsaken the Qur'an and neglected the essence of its teaching. There will come a time when this neglect of the eternal message of the Qur'an will become so widespread that none will remember that they recited it in their prayers and sought guidance through it in their lives. This is warned against as being the source of spiritual darkness in this world and the next.

"And whoever turns away from My Remembrance (the Qur'an), for him is a life of hardship, and We shall raise him up, on the Day of Judgement, blind. He will say: 'O My Lord, Why have you resurrected me blind, while I used to see in this world?' God will respond, 'Likewise in this manner, Our verses came to you, but you ignored them. And so, today, you shall be ignored.'" [20:124-126]

The Prophet ﷺ said: *'Islam will disappear, even as the colours of a cloth disappear, until people will not know what fasting, prayer, the rites of Hajj and charity are. The Book of God will be lifted up one night so that not even one verse will remain. A group of old people will remain who will say: 'We found our forefathers saying these words 'La ilaha illa Allah' and so we say them as well.' [Ibn Majah]*

"We ask God, the Generous, the Provider of abundance, Who has ability over all He wills, that He free us of that which procures His anger, that He make use of us in that which pleases Him – by way of the memorisation and understanding of His Book and help us uphold its teaching by day and by night in such a way that He loves and is pleased with. Indeed He is Generous and Bountiful." [Ibn Kathir, Tafsir al-Adhim, p1238]

Did you know?

Scholars differed on whether it is better to recite the Qur'an from one's memory or when looking at the physical *Mushaf* of the Qur'an. Al-Izz Ibn Abd al-Salam held that reciting from memory is better, since the aim of recitation is to reflect, and doing so from memory is more conducive to enhancing reflection.

The majority of scholars however, say that it is better to recite from the *mushaf*. Al-Nawawi said: *'I don't know any difference of opinion regarding this"*. This is because looking at the *mushaf* is in itself an act of worship. Therefore, all things being equal, it is better to recite from a copy of the Qur'an outside the prayer even if one has memorized the section of Qur'an, unless one's concentration and ability to reflect is affected. In such a case, it is better done from one's memory. *[Ittr, Ulum al-Quran]*

28

Seeking Purity

Understanding the Law and Spirituality of Ritual Purity *(al-Taharah)*

Module Fqh 1.01.D

Lesson One - Types of Impurity

> *Aim:*
> By the end of this lesson, students should be able to appreciate the importance of purification in Islamic law. They should also understand why the area of ritual purity is split into two distinct categories: that related to the purity of physical substance (*haqiqi*) and that related to ritual states *(hukmi)*.
>
> *Objectives:*
> By the end of this lesson, students should be able to display the ability to:
> 1. Summarise the wisdom of purification in Islam, as well as the significance of purifying one's body for worship.
> 2. Summarise the history of purity in Islamic law, and the background to it being made an obligation.
> 3. Identify the two categories of purity discussed in Islamic law by providing a definition, with examples, of both.
> 4. Explain what actual impurity is, as well as the two main categories of this type of impurity.
> 5. Provide examples of strong impurity, and the ruling related to this vis-a-vis what is excusable.
> 6. Provide examples of weak impurity, and the ruling related to this vis-a-vis what is excusable.

"God loves those who repent and loves those who purify themselves" [2:222]

"O you who are enveloped in the cloak! Arise and warn! Magnify your Lord! Purify your clothes! And shun all that which is impure!" [74:1-5]

One of the central teachings of the Islamic faith is the imperative to attain purity, both physical as well as spiritual. This provides the basis for all one's actions - both in terms of worship, as well as how one deals with God's creation: just as outward purity prepares one for worship and sincere devotion, it also sets the standard for social norms of cleanliness.

1. The history of purity

Scholars of the past discussed the exact time at which the rulings relating to purification were laid down and were also well aware that previous Prophets sought to purify themselves before worshipping. It is related by Imam al-Bukhari in the narrative of the prophet Ibrahim (*'alayhi salam*) and his wife Sarah, that when the king, who had evil intentions towards Sarah, sought to get close to her, she stood, performed *wudu (ritual washing)* and went into prayer. This shows that even if the method of attaining purity differed, the practice was one shared by previous manifestations of *Islam.*

1.1 When was it first obligated?

Since the verses talking about *wudu* were all revealed in Madinah, when was the Prophet ﷺ ordered to perform *wudu*? There are two views on this:

1.1.1 Makkah. This opinion, which is that of the majority of scholars, holds that *wudu* was taught and made an obligation upon the Prophet ﷺ by Gabriel after the first revelation of the Qur'an in Ramadan, while he was still in Makkah.

What then can we say about the verse in the Quran related to *wudu [5:6]* which was revealed years later in Madinah? These scholars clarify that the verse revealed in Madinah reiterated and emphasised the previously practiced actions of *wudu*, while at the same time it introduced the new dispensation for *tayammum.*

This is given support by the fact that Aishah called the verse in Surah al-Ma'idah *[5:6]* 'the verse of tayammum' and not the verse of *wudu* (the ruling for both is contained in the verse). Therefore the verse is understood to have been revealed to provide a new ruling for tayammum relating to times of water scarcity, but at the same time also served to reiterate the obligatory nature of *wudu.*

Qadi Abu Bakr ibn al-Arabi narrates with his isnad that Zayd ibn Harithah relates that *'the first time the Prophet ﷺ received revelation, Gabriel came and taught him how to perform wudu, and once they had completed the wudu, Gabriel took some water and sprinkled it upon the area of the private parts'*[10] *[al-Suhayli, Rawd al-Unuf, Bab Fard as-Salah]*

---

[10] Thereby demonstrating by example the two classifications of actual and abstract impurity mentioned below.

The well-known commentator of the Qur'an, Imam al-Qurtubi, supports the opinion that *wudu* was made an obligation in Makkah by pointing out that the prayer, of which *wudu* is a prerequisite, was made obligatory in Makkah. *'It is well known amongst authorities of the Prophetic biography, that the Prophet ﷺ , from the moment that the prayer was made obligatory upon him in Makkah, only ever prayed having performed the wudu which we know today. This points to the fact that the verse relating to wudu was only revealed so that the act [of wudu], that had already been made obligatory, also now be recited in the (Qur'anic) revelation as well.'* [al-Qurtubi, Ahkam al-Qur'an 4:43, Point 35]

1.1.2 Madinah. Others have held that it was made *fard* in Madinah after the revelation of the verse of *tayammum*. This means that *wudu* was merely *recommended* (*mandub*) during the Makkan period.

2. Impurity - Physical (*Haqiqi*) and Ritual (*Hukmi*)

There are two categories of impurities identified by scholars.

Physical impurity (*Haqiqi*) refers to actual physical substances which are required to be cleaned and removed.

Definition: Any substance whose attributes are deemed impure by the Shari'ah (e.g. wine, urine, etc.)

Ritual impurity (*Hukmi*) relates to situations where the sacred law requires one to purify oneself through cleansing in a specific way (*wudu & ghusl*), regardless of the existence of physical impurities.

Definition: A state that occurs due to having entered into what the Shari'ah views as a state of ritual impurity (e.g. deep sleep, loss of consciousness, passing wind, etc.)

3. Types of Physical impurity (*Haqiqi*) – Strong and weak impurities[11].

All substances are considered pure unless one has proof demonstrating otherwise. As stated in the legal rule (*dabit*): *'The basic ruling with regard to all substances is that they are pure.'*

3.1 Strong impurity (*mughaladhah*).

However, once we have proof of a substance being impure, it is considered a strong impurity by default. So what is a strong impurity?

Aisha said: 'I used to scratch sperm off the clothes of the Messenger ﷺ if it was dry and wash it off if it was wet.' [al-Daraqutni v1, pg 131]

Ibn Abbas relates that the Messenger of God ﷺ happened to pass by two graves and said: 'Their inhabitants are being tormented, but they are not being tormented on account of a grievous sin. One of them spread [false] tales and the other did not keep himself safe from being defiled by urine.' He then called for a fresh twig and split it into two parts, and planted one on each of the graves and said: 'Perhaps their punishment will be lessened for as long as these twigs remain fresh.' [Muslim, 575]

The following types of substances are held to be strong impurities:

3.1.1 All substances that come from the human body that would require one to perform either *wudu* or *ghusl*.

This includes blood, sperm, urine, vomit and human faeces. Due to the numerous reports ordering the removal of these substances from clothing and furnishings, they are given the default ruling of strong impurity. One exception to this is vomit if it be a small amount[12], based upon the analogy that this amount would not cause one's *wudu* to break.

3.1.2 Blood that flows from a body.

Qadi Abu Bakr ibn al-Arabi states: *'Scholars have agreed on blood being haram (to consume and sell) as well as impure such that it may be neither consumed nor made use of.'* [Ahkam al-Quran, V1, pg53]

---

[11] The Hanafi school of law classifies impurities into the two types mentioned. Due to weak impurities being rare in day to day life, these are appendixes for students information at the end of this lesson.

[12] Of an amount easily contained in the mouth without difficulty.

3.1.3 The flesh of dead animals that have not been ritually slaughtered.

3.1.4 The excrement of all animals.

3.1.5 The urine and milk of animals whose meat is forbidden to consume.

3.1.6 The sweat and saliva of impure animals. This refers specifically to pigs and dogs.

Abu Hurairah relates that the Messenger ﷺ said: "The method of purifying one of your vessels which has been licked by a dog is that it be washed seven times, the first of which should be with soil." [Related by Muslim. He also relates it with the words 'one should discard it'. Al-Tirmidhi relates the wording 'the last of which' or 'the first of which is with soil'.]

3.1.7 Grape wine The vast majority of scholars hold wine to be impure based on the prohibition of consuming wine.

The position of wine being impure as a substance is indicated by the Qur'an [5:90] as well as numerous reports from the first generations (*al-Salaf*). Mujahid is reported to have said: *'If a drop of wine falls on your clothes, wash it, for it is more potent than blood.'*[13] *[Abd al-Razzaq, Musanaf, 1/154]*

The ruling related to Strong impurity

The basic requirement for such substances is that they are to be removed and the area affected by them cleaned. However, scholars state that small amounts may be overlooked. For solid impurities, the excusable amount is approximated to just under four grams. For liquids, the surface-area of a medium sized coin or less is excusable. Practically, this means that one's prayer will be valid if performed with an amount less than this on one's clothes or body.

It should be noted that if any amount of strong impurity falls into a small amount of water, it renders the water impure and unsuitable for use in *wudu* and *ghusl*.

5. Reconnecting with the spirit – the four levels of purity

'The key to Paradise is the prayer and the key to prayer lies in purity.' [Ahmed, no:14,703].

The metaphor of the relationship between purity and the act of worship is given as that of a key to a door. One could say that the aim of life is to enter into a state where we expend our lives in servitude, adoration and worship of the One that created and fashioned us. Created from the lowest of earthly substances, we are asked to aspire to reach for the celestial realms and gain proximity to our Creator. The process of attaining Paradise differs for different people, and even as our aspirations in life differ, so too do our understanding and capacity to achieve degrees of physical and spiritual purity. Moreover, our understanding of *the key of purity* and how to use it determines the degree to which we succeed in our worship and adoration of God.

5.1 Al-Ghazali on the four levels of purity

5.1.1 *Purity from outward filth. 'Believers! When you stand to prayer, wash your faces...' [5:6]*
5.1.2 *Purity from the wrong actions of the limbs. 'Indeed God loves those that turn to Him in repentance and loves those that excel in purifying themselves.' [2:222]*
5.1.3 *Purity of heart from spiritual diseases. 'Beware of envy, for it consumes good acts even as flames consume firewood.' [Abu Dawud, 4903]*
5.1.4 *Purity of soul from other than God. 'Say '(It is) God'! Then leave them to their engrossment in futile games.' [6:91]*

In his *magnum opus*, the *Ihya 'ulum ad-Din*, Imam al-Ghazali writes of four levels of purity, beginning with outward purity and ending with inward spiritual purity. Each level of purity, he says, is integral to achieving the next, and each level is more difficult to achieve than the one before.

*'Purity has four stages: The **first** stage is the purification of the body from excrements, impurities, bodily growths and discharges. The **second** stage is the purification of the body from crimes and wrong actions. The **third** stage is the purification of the heart from blameworthy traits and reprehensible vices. The **fourth** stage is the purification of the innermost self (sirr) from everything except God [...].'*

---

[13] Some scholars include commercially-produced alcohol as a weak impurity, see Lesson 2

'No one will attain a higher stage unless he goes first through one lower. He will not reach the purification of the innermost self from other than God, unless he accomplishes first the purification of the heart from blameworthy traits and adorns it with the praiseworthy. Similarly, he will not attain to purification of the heart from blameworthy traits or adorn it with praiseworthy ones unless he accomplishes first the purification of the bodily senses from forbidden things and adorns them with good works. The more precious and noble the desired object becomes, the more difficult is its attainment, the longer the road which leads to it, and the greater the obstacles which block its path.

Do not think, therefore, that this can be attained through merely wishing or achieved through a lack of effort. He whose insight fails to distinguish between these stages will not perceive of them except the lowest, which is equivalent to the outermost husk of the desired fruit.' [al-Ghazali al-Ihya, Kitab at-Taharah]

Did you know?
The rationale behind substances being considered impurities.

The majority of impurities are taken to be so based on *Qur'anic* verses that relate to those things that are forbidden to consume. As they are forbidden to consume, some scholars also then considered them to be ritually impure. Other things are deemed impure based on their universally repugnant nature, such that the understanding of their impurity is shared amongst all peoples and cultures. Moreover, that which is produced from impure animals, such as their milk and urine, is also impure.

"Say [O Prophet]: 'In all that has been revealed to me, I do not find anything forbidden to eat, if one wants to eat thereof, unless it be carrion, or blood poured forth, or the flesh of swine – for that is indeed loathsome...'" [6:145]

Appendix on Weak impurity

In rare cases, where there are conflicting proofs from the sources of Islamic law relating to the purity or otherwise of a substance, scholars have provided a greater degree of flexibility for a small group of impurities. These are referred to as **weak impurities.**

The following substances are held to be weak impurities:

> **3.2.1 Urine of animals whose meat is permitted for consumption.** (E.g. cows)
> **3.2.2 The droppings of birds[14] that are forbidden to consume.** (E.g. falcons)

The ruling related to Weak impurity

The basic requirement for such substances is that they should be removed and the area affected by them cleaned. However scholars state that a certain amount is excusable. The excusable amount for weak impurities is approximated as less than a quarter of the total area of a section garment.

What are the practical implications of the classification of impurities into strong and weak?

> **a.** The only *difference* between them is the amount that is *excusable* when one is praying.
> **b.** They are *similar* in the way in which one purifies them (covered in Lesson Two).
> **c.** They are *similar* in that if either strong or weak impurity falls into a small amount of water, it renders the water impure and unsuitable for use in *wudu* and *ghusl*.

---

[14] *There are three types of birds with regards impurity: 1. Those that do not fly, such as chickens and certain domesticated ducks. The droppings of such birds are considered a strong impurity. 2. Those that fly, but that are forbidden to be eaten, such as eagles, falcons, etc. Their droppings are considered to be a weak impurity. 3. Those birds that fly and may be consumed, such as pigeons and sparrows. Their droppings are considered pure.*

Lesson Two - Removing Physical Impurities

Aim: By the end of this lesson, the student should be able to identify methods to remove physical impurity from the body, clothes and place of worship. They should also have an appreciation of the difference of opinion (*khilaf*) concerning the impurity of various categories of what is called alcohol.

Objectives: By the end of this lesson, the student should be able to display the ability to:
1. Provide a summary of the general rules and principles related to the removal of impurities, especially through the use of water and other liquids.
2. Outline the issues related to the purification of the body from physical impurities, with specific reference to *istinja'* and its related etiquettes.
3. Discuss the purification of clothing and how this is achieved.
4. Identify what is meant by the purification of the place of worship and how this varies depending upon the place being cleaned.
5. Identify the main methods through which impurities are removed, providing examples of each.
6. Appreciate the difference of opinion concerning the impurity of different types of alcohol and the proofs provided by each side for their position.
7. Outline the contemporary discussion of the use of synthetic alcohol and the conclusions arrived at by scholarly bodies on this issue.

'Purify your clothing, and shun all filth!' [74:4-5]

'Attaining purity of the body, clothing and the place of prayer is an obligation upon one intending to pray.' [al-Mirghinani, al-Hidayah, Bab al-Anjas]

At the time one is about to pray, one is obliged to ensure the purity of one's body, clothes and immediate place of worship. Purification for worship looks specifically at these three things and each one will be looked at in turn. The method used to remove impurities may also differ depending on what is being cleaned and so this lesson will look at the methods by which this is done.

1. General rules for the removal of impurities

1.1 Visible impurity must be cleaned until the substance seen is removed, but residual staining after washing is overlooked and need not be removed.

1.2 Non-visible impurity requires that the affected area is washed until it is reasonable to assume that the impurity has been removed, preferably by washing it three times with water or similar liquid.

2. The Body

'Therein are those that excel in purifying themselves. Indeed, God loves those that excel in purity.' [9:108]

As related by Abu Hurayrah, *[Abu Dawud, 44]* this verse was revealed concerning the inhabitants of Quba' who would make use of water after answering the call of nature (*Istinja'*). The main issue when looking at the removal of impurities from the body is the process of cleaning oneself after urinating or defecating. This is referred to as **istinja'** and is done either through the use of water, by wiping clean the body from the impurity with a solid material such as toilet paper[15], or both.

2.1. The rulings of *Istinja'*.

2.1.1 *Istinja'* is an *emphasised sunnah* (*Sunnah Mu'akadah*) if the area of filth is less than what is *fard* to wash, meaning an amount of impurity that is less than what is excused.
2.1.2 *Istinja'* becomes *essential (fard)* if the filth exceeds impurity that is deemed excusable. In such a case water should be used and failure to clean the area will invalidate any prayer performed.

---

[15] In the past, smooth stones were used for this purpose, a process referred to as '*istijmar* (literally '*to make use of stones*')

34

2.2 Etiquettes of *Istinja'*.

Hafsah reports the Messenger of God ﷺ reserved his right hand for eating, drinking, putting on clothes, taking and giving. He used the left for other actions.' [Abu Dawud]

2.2.1 Supplication when entering the lavatory: "*In the name of God. Oh Allah, I seek refuge in You from filth and impurities*" [al-Bukhari], and "*Praise to God who has taken the harmful away from me and granted me wellbeing.*" [Ibn Majah] upon leaving.

2.2.2 Refraining from speech while in the lavatory.

2.2.3 Seeking a place with the most privacy.

2.2.4 Avoiding the direction of the Qibla when answering the call of nature.

2.2.5 Not using the right hand for the purposes of cleaning.

3. Purity of Clothing

'Asma bint Abi Bakr related that a woman came to the Prophet ﷺ and said: 'Our clothes are contaminated with menstrual blood. What should we do about this?' He said: 'Scrape it, rub it with water, pour water over it and then pray in it.' [al-Bukhari and Muslim]

The Messenger of God ﷺ said: 'It is enough for you to wash the blood off, as its stain thereafter will do you no harm.' [Abu Dawud, 365]

Both dry cleaning and a normal cycle in a washing machine are sufficient to achieve the level of purity required for ritual worship.

3.1 Urine of a child

Some scholars have made an exception to the general ruling of removing impurity in the case of the urine of a male child who has not yet been weaned off breast milk. They have held that it is sufficient to spray/pour water over the area rather than actually wash it.

Umm Qays bint Mihsan reported that she came to the Messenger of God ﷺ with her child, who was not yet weaned, and she placed him in his lap and the child urinated. He did ﷺ nothing more than spraying water over it (nadaha alayhi) and did not wash it.' [Muslim, 563; al-Bukhari, 223]

There has been much discussion surrounding this hadith, with the Shafi'i school of law holding that this is a dispensation specific to a male child who has not yet been weaned and does not include female children [16]. This is also the position of the Hanbali school. This understanding is taken directly from an apparent (*dhahir*) reading of the hadith.

Others, particularly Imam Malik and the school of Abu Hanifah, have criticised the position of differentiating between males and females with regard to impurity and have stated that there is no difference in both cases as the impurities involved are essentially the same. Therefore, both need to be washed in the same way as all other impurities. This understanding is based on a number of considerations, amongst them that the word used in the hadith (*nadaha alayhi*) 'can imply washing as well as simply sprinkling.' [al-Ayni, Umdah al-Qari, 2/615-7]

4. Purity of place

Anas ibn Malik reported: 'While we were in the mosque with God's Messenger ﷺ , a desert Arab came and stood up and began to urinate in the mosque. The Companions said: 'Stop, stop!' but the Messenger of God ﷺ said: 'Don't interrupt him, leave him alone.' They then let him be. When he finished urinating, God's Messenger ﷺ called him and said to him: 'These mosques are not places meant for urine and filth, but are for the remembrance of God, prayer and the recitation of the Qur'an', or something like that. He then gave orders to one of the people, who brought a bucket of water and poured it over the spot.' [Muslim, 559]

---

[16] This is one of three positions related in the school. Al-Nawawi of the Shafi'i school states: '*One should be aware that even if there is a difference of opinion over the way that the urine of a child is cleaned, there is no difference as to it being impure. [Sharh Muslim]*

4.1 Rulings of removing impurities from places.

The method of removing impurities depends on the surface being cleaned. If the ground is hard then impurities are removed by pouring water over the area. Impurities on soft floor furnishings are removed by ensuring the removal of visible impurity. If it is not visible, then the surface is cleaned by rubbing and washing the affected area three times.

5. General methods of removing impurities.

Washing is one of many methods by which impure things become pure, but there are over thirty methods by which impurities may be removed. [*Hashiyah Ibn Abidin 1:314*].

Those most frequently employed are:

5.1 Water: *"And We sent down from the heavens water that purifies." [25:48]*

> '*It is permissible to use water to remove impurity as well as all other liquids.' [al-Mirghinani, al-Hidayah]*

Although water is the most commonly used substance for the removal of physical impurities, it is also allowed to make use of any liquid substance to remove impurities as long as the substance fulfills the following 3 criteria, that it:

flows easily; is a substance which is itself ritually pure; has properties that facilitate the removal of impurities. [*al-'Ayni, al-Binayah, 1:809*]

5.2 Dust *(turab)*: '*If one of you steps on impurity then you may clean it using dust.' [Abu Dawud, 385]*

5.3 Scraping *(farq)*: Aishah said: '*I used to scrape the remnants of semen off the clothing of the Messenger of God* ﷺ *if it was dry, and wash it if it was wet.' (Sunan al-Daraqutni)*

5.4 Wiping *(masah)*: Used for smooth, hard surfaces such as metal surfaces and mirrors.

5.5 Drying *(jafaf)*: This method is particularly used for exposed earth. Aishah said: '*The purification of the ground is its becoming dry.' [Ibn Abi Shaibah]*

5.6 Tanning *(dabgh)*: Animal skins, regardless of whether their meat is lawful for consumption or not, are purified by a process known as tanning. The Messenger of God ﷺ said: '*Any animal skin that is tanned thereby becomes purified.' [Muslim, 812]*

5.7 Chemical or physical transformation *(istihala)*

Examples of *istihala* are the changing of wine to vinegar and impure oil into soap. It is defined as: '*An alteration in the qualities and attributes of impurities, to the point that the substance ceases to be deemed impure, since the qualities of impurity no longer remain therein.' [al-Kashani, Bada'i as-Sanai']*

6. Text in Focus – The Question of Alcohol

> *"Believers! Wine, gambling, (sacrificing to) stone altars and divining arrows are filth (rijs) from the handiwork of Satan. Shun these that you may be successful." [5:90]*

> *Abu Thalaba al-Khusani relates that he came to the Messenger* ﷺ *and said: 'We neighbour the People of the Book. They cook pork in their pots and drink wine from their jars (so what should we do?). He* ﷺ *said: 'If you find other vessels, then eat and drink from them, otherwise wash them with water and then eat and drink.' [Abu Dawud, 3839]*

Based on their widespread use in the modern world within medicine and cosmetics, the purity of synthetic alcohols is one that has been the subject of research. The debate amongst Muslim scholars has revolved around two main questions: '*Does the fact that a substance is haram to consume, mean that it is also considered ritually impure?*' Secondly, '*Are all types of alcohol impure just as grape wine (kahmr) is?*

Firstly, while agreeing upon the prohibition of consuming wine made from grapes, scholars differed as to whether grape-based wine itself was also considered as an impure substance (*najis*).

6.1 The difference on the purity of grape wine

6.1.1 The majority of scholars held it to be najis *(impure).*

This is the view of the four classical schools of law, based on the following evidences:

> **6.1.1.1** It is described in the verse as '*rijs*' (filth) which in the Arabic language usually implies that a thing is physically impure.
> **6.1.1.2** The verse of the Quran orders believers to shun wine.
> **6.1.1.3** The hadith of Abu Thalaba orders the washing of vessels containing wine.

6.1.2 A minority of early scholars held wine to be pure.

This is held by, amongst others, Rabi'ah al-Ra'i, one of the teachers of Imam Malik, Laith ibn Sa'ad, a contemporary of Malik and Imam al-Muzani, one of the main pupils of al-Shafi'i. Their reasoning was:

> **6.1.2.1** Everything on earth is pure unless proven otherwise.
> **6.1.2.2** When the verses were revealed, people spilt out the contents of the wine-jars into the streets of Madinah. They would not have done this had it been impure.
> **6.1.2.3** The reason that early Muslims *(Salaf)* strove to stay well clear of having any contact with wine was to instill a hatred for it in themselves and not because it was considered ritually impure.
> **6.1.2.4** The use of the Arabic word '*rijs*' denoting filth is figurative in the verse. The word '*rijs*' is also used in the verse to describe the three other things condemned, yet all agree that the materials used in gambling, divining arrows and stone altars are pure, therefore so too wine.

Commenting on the fact that something being *haram* does not mean that it is impure, the Yemeni jurist al-*Sanani says:*

> *'[B]eing prohibited does not necessitate that an object itself is impure. For example, hashish is prohibited but it is pure, so something prohibited is not necessarily impure. [Despite being haram for men] silk and gold are pure by consensus. [Hence] every impure thing is prohibited [to make use of], but not vice-versa. [...But] if a ruling states that something is impure, it is also prohibited (haram).' [al-Sanani, Subul al-Salam]*

Even Imam an-Nawawi, who otherwise holds wine to be impure, concedes this point. *'There is no manifest indication (to its impurity) in the verse, since 'filth', according to the linguists, means dirtiness, and this does not necessitate impurity per se. Likewise, the command to 'avoid' does not necessarily imply its impurity.' [al-Nawawi, al-Majmu'] [Ibn 'Ashur, al-Tahrir wa al-Tanwir, 6-21-26; Nur ad-Din I'ttr, 'Ilam al-Anam, 91-93]*

6.2 Modern uses of synthetic alcohol

The widespread use of synthetic alcohol in medicine and industries has meant that most contemporary scholars have reviewed the general ruling relating to the impurity of alcohol, and have ruled synthetic alcohol to be pure based on the following reasons:

> **6.2.1** Relying on the minority opinion of the purity of wine mentioned above.
> **6.2.2** Synthetic alcohol is commercially produced by the hydration of the hydrocarbon ethene, whereas traditional alcohol is produced by the fermentation of sugars with yeast etc.
> **6.2.3** Fermented alcohol contains over forty distinguishing components such as smell and taste that make it sought after as liquor. Synthetic alcohol does not have these qualities and may be poisonous.

The 8th Islamic Medical Symposium, which met in Kuwait in 1995, released a general edict stating the following: *'[T]here is no Islamic legal impediment to the use of synthetic alcohol in medicinal procedures [...] this dispensation does not extend to wine, as it is unlawful to make use of it in the first instance.' [al Mawad al-Muharamah, Dr. N. Hamad, pg 47-51]*

Others, such as the late Badr ud-Din al-Hassani of Damascus, have stated that synthetic alcohol is to be treated as a weak impurity due to it being prevalent and unavoidable in modern society.

Lesson Three - Ritual Impurity *(Hukmi)* 1

Aim: By the end of this lesson, the student will appreciate what is meant by ritual impurity *(hukmi)*. They will be able to identify what major ritual impurity is in relation firstly to what causes it and secondly the actions forbidden whilst in such a state.

Objectives: By the end of this lesson, a student should be able to display the ability to:
1. Define what is meant by both 'minor' and 'major' ritual impurity and how they differ.
2. Identify the three things that cause major ritual impurity.
3. Summarise what is meant by the word *'janabah'* in Islamic law, and detail how this is caused.
4. Detail the main issues relating to menstrual bleeding *(hayd)*, and in particular how it is defined and its minimum and maximum duration.
5. Detail the main issues relating to post-natal bleeding *(nifas)* and in particular how it is defined and its minimum and maximum duration.
6. Understand what is meant by the term *'dysfunctional uterine bleeding'* *(istihada)* and its rulings.
7. List those things that men and women in a state of major ritual impurity are forbidden from doing.

1. Ritual impurity *(hadath)*.

"They ask you concerning menstruation. Say: that is an impurity, therefore avoid (marital relations with) wives during menses and do not approach them till they have purified themselves" [2:222]

"...if you are in a state of major ritual impurity (janabah) then purify yourselves..." [5:6]

What is meant by *'ritual impurity'*? This is best explained as any situation where, even though the body of a person appears to be free of physical impurities, the sacred law obliges one to perform either *wudu* or *ghusl*. It therefore refers to abstract states rather than actual physical substances. It is defined as: *'A state that occurs due to having entered into what the Shari'ah views as abstract legal impurity (e.g. deep sleep, loss of consciousness, passing wind).*

Ritual impurity is broken down into two types and they differ mainly in the manner in which one leaves such a state.

    1.1 Major *(hadath al-akbar)* requiring one to bathe *(ghusl)* or perform tayammum.
    1.2 Minor *(hadath al-asghar)* requiring one to perform ablution *(wudu)* or tayammum.

2. Major ritual impurity (Hadath al-akbar*)*

The Prophet ﷺ *said "(The use of) Water (to wash) is only (an obligation ensuing) from (the emission of) water."* [Muslim, 775]

This can be studied by examining the following questions:

What causes it? What actions are forbidden while in such a state? How does one remove such a state?

    2.1 What causes Major ritual impurity?

        2.1.1 Janabah. This is a state which either the male and female enter into either by:

            2.1.1.1 The emission of sexual fluid after arousal, which then requires *ghusl*.

'Ali reported that the Prophet ﷺ *said: "....If you ejaculate then perform ghusl."* [Abu Dawud, 206]

Umm Sulaym said, "O Messenger of God ﷺ *! God is not ashamed of the truth. Does a woman have to do ghusl if she has a wet dream?" He said, "Yes, if she sees liquid."* [Al-Bukhari, 282]

2.1.1.2 Sexual intercourse. *Ghusl* is obligatory upon penetration[17] – regardless of ejaculation.

> *Abu Musa came to Aisha and said to her: "It upsets me that the Companions of the Prophet ﷺ have differed about a matter I myself am embarrassed to ask you about." She said "What is that? Ask me whatever you can ask your own mother." He then asked about one that has intercourse with his wife and does not ejaculate. She said, "When the private parts of each partner meet ghusl is obligatory." Upon hearing this, Abu Musa said: "I will never ask another person concerning this." [Muslim, 785]*

> *Abu Hurayrah relates that the Prophet ﷺ said: "If a man lies between the four limbs (of his wife) and exerts himself then ghusl becomes an obligation." [This hadith is agreed upon by Bukhari and Muslim. Imam Muslim narration adds "even if he does not ejaculate".]*

2.1.2 Hayd

> *Aishah related that the Messenger of God ﷺ said: "Do not pray during your period. After it has ended perform ghusl and pray." [Al-Bukhari, 331]*

Hayd is defined as: *The normal blood discharge that comes from the womb of a female from the time of puberty up until the age of 55 years, as long as the bleeding does not occur during pregnancy and is not caused by illness.*

It may be a red, yellow or muddy coloured liquid seen by a woman during the days of her cycle. The womenfolk of Madinah used to send Aishah small boxes containing stained cotton (to ascertain whether or not they had finished their periods) and she would say to them: *'Do not hasten (to assume purity) until you see pure white cotton.' [Muwatta, Bab Tuhr al Hayd]*

2.1.2.1 The Duration of menstruation

The minimum period that menstruation lasts is **three days** and it legally lasts no more than **ten days.** Sufyan ath-Thawri said: *'The minimum period for menstruation is three days and the maximum is ten.'*

There is no maximum time for purity between cycles and the **shortest** legal period of purity between two separate periods of menstruation is **fifteen days.**[18]

2.1.3 *Nifas: Post natal bleeding.*

Definition: *The blood flowing from the womb after having given birth.*

Post-childbirth bleeding is considered to last no longer than forty days and there is no minimum period for its duration. This ruling has been established by no primary religious text. Al-Hasan al-Basri said: *'Once forty days are complete, she should wash and then pray.' [Abd ar-Razzaq, al-Musanaf V1-313]*

2.1.4 *Istihadah:* Dysfunctional uterine bleeding.

Definition: *Prolonged flow of blood - either less than **three days** or longer than **ten,** in the case of menstruation, or over **forty** days in the case of nifas.*

2.1.4.1 Rulings for women suffering from *istihadah*:

A woman in this state is not prevented from performing normal acts of worship or full marital relations. After having performed *ghusl,* the women should then simply perform *wudu* at the time of each prayer, and this does not need to be renewed until the next prayer time, even if there is intermittent bleeding.

> *The Prophet ﷺ said to a woman affected by istihadah 'Do wudu for every prayer." [Abu Dawud, 126]*

> *'Umm Salamah asked the Messenger ﷺ about istihadah. He said she should wait for the days and nights of her normal period, and calculate them, and should leave praying during those days. She should then perform ghusl, wrap something around her private parts and then pray.' [Malik, Bab al-Mustahadah]*

---

[17] Defined as the full head of the male member entering into the private part of the female.

[18] Therefore if a women completes her cycle past ten days and then starts to bleed again within fifteen days, this bleeding will not be taken as a new cycle but is considered as *istihadah* (dysfunctional uterine bleeding) mentioned below.

3. Actions forbidden for those in a state of major ritual impurity

3.1 The Prayer

> *"...if you are in a state of major ritual impurity (janabah), then purify yourselves..."* [5:6]

3.2 The circumambulation of the *Ka'bah (tawaf)*

> *"The Prophet ﷺ said: 'Indeed the tawaf around the Ka'bah is like the prayer, except that you can talk, and so whoever speaks, let them speak only good.'* [al-Tirmidhi, 960]

3.3 Touch or recite the Qur'an

> *'The woman during her period and a person in the state of janabah should not read anything from the Qur'an."* [al-Tirmidhi, 131]

> *Ali said that nothing kept the Prophet ﷺ from reciting the Qur'an – except the state of janabah.'* [al-Tirmidhi, 146].

3.3.1 Related rulings on touching or reciting the Qur'an.

It is also not permissible to touch the *mushaf (copy of the Qur'an)* through one's garment which is being worn at the time, such as the sleeve or the edge of one's clothes.

Given that women have no way of removing themselves from this state while in *hayd* or *nifas*, there are various exceptions to this general prohibition. The non-direct handling of the *mushaf* is permitted, as is staggered or broken reading, reading sections of the Qur'an that are also supplications with the intention of supplication. It is permitted to touch the *mushaf* through a covering, such as a cloth covering or bag, with the condition that it is not permanently attached to the *mushaf* itself.

> *'If the woman (during hayd) recites the Fatihah, or any other verses that denote the meaning of dua, with the intention of supplication, and does not intend to recite the Qur'an as a Qur'anic recitation per se, there is no harm in that. As for sections that do not carry the meaning of supplication, such as Surah Lahab, then the associated intention is of no consequence.'* [Ibn Abidin, Radd al-Muhtar]

3.4 Entering the Masjid

> *'The Prophet ﷺ said: 'Direct those houses away from the masjid, as it is not permitted for a woman menstruating or a person in janabah to enter the masjid.'* [Abu Dawud, 232]

3.4.1 What is considered a masjid?

It is not permitted to enter a masjid in such a state. This ruling does not include places that are temporary places of worship (*musala*). This is an area that has not been made an endowment (*waqf*) or is not yet intended to become a permanent masjid. An area of land only becomes a masjid once the deeds for the area have been made an endowment barring transferral of ownership back to a private individual. The area reserved for use as a masjid also has to be clearly demarcated.

> *'It is a condition for a place to be considered a masjid that the lower and upper floors need [also] to be a masjid, so that the rights [and ownership] of people is waived from it, as God says 'And verily the mosques are for God [alone]..."* [Ibn Abidin, Radd al-Mukhtar 3:370]

There is no prohibition as to the visitation of the graveyard for those in such a state.

4. Specific rulings for women

Women in the state of *hayd* and *nifas* should observe two further points:

4.1 The obligation to fast and pray is removed.

> *Aishah was asked: 'Why must we make up the fasts missed but not the prayers?' She said: 'That is what the Messenger ﷺ told us to do. We were told to make up the fasts and not the prayers.'* [Muslim, 761]

4.2 Sexual intercourse is not permitted between the husband and wife during this period.

"...therefore avoid (marital relations with) wives during menses and do not approach them till they have purified themselves" [2:222]

In terms of sexual intimacy between spouses, there is a general dispensation during the period of *hayd and nifas* allowing a degree of intimacy as indicated by the hadith: *'You may do what you please above the loincloth.' [Abu Dawud, 212]*

The majority of scholars have mentioned that the body between the navel and the knee is prohibited to pleasure or be pleasured, except through a covering.

Did you know?

General cleanliness - The acts of fitrah

Abu Hurayrah reported that the Messenger of God (may God bless and grant him peace) said: 'Five things are part of one's fitrah: shaving the pubic hairs, circumcision, trimming the mustache, removing the hair under the arms and trimming the nails." [Muslim]

There are certain natural traits which have their origins in ancient sunnah of previous Prophets that also help maintain general cleanliness. These have been passed down through different nations as a sign of the natural state of man. A number of these are recorded in prophetic hadith.

Anas ibn Malik said: 'The period for us to trim the moustache, cut the nails, pluck out the underarm hairs and cut the pubic hairs was forty nights.' [Al-Nasa'i]

Lesson 4- Ritual Impurity *(Hukmi) 2*

> ***Aims***: This lesson will provide students with a discussion of how to remove the state of major ritual impurity through the performance of the *ghusl*, as well as looking at the causes of minor ritual impurity and what is forbidden for a person in such a state.
>
> ***Objectives:*** By the end of this lesson, a student should be able to display the ability to:
> 1. Summarise, with a brief explanation, the essential elements of the *ghusl*.
> 2. List the sunnah (recommended) acts of the *ghusl*.
> 3. Detail the four occasions when it is recommended to perform *ghusl*.
> 4. Explain what is meant by minor ritual impurity.
> 5. Discuss the causes of minor ritual impurity.
> 6. List the occasions when the performance of *wudu* is recommended.

1. How to remove the state of Major ritual impurity.

> *"...if you are in a state of major ritual impurity (janabah) then purify yourselves..." [5:6]*

Major ritual impurity (*hadath al-akbar*) requires one to bathe (*ghusl*) or perform *tayammum*.

2. The essentials of ghusl

There are *three essential (fard)* elements of *ghusl*. If any of these are not performed properly the *ghusl* will be considered invalid and will have to be rectified or repeated:

2.1 Washing the body

Ghusl literally means 'washing' and is done by *"pouring water once over what one is able to of the whole body without unnecessary difficulty." [al-Kashani, Badai'i, 1-142]*. This includes the hair.

2.1.1 The hair

> *Abu Hurairah relates that the Prophet ﷺ said: "Below every hair is a portion of major ritual impurity therefore, wash your hair and clean your skin"* *[Related by Abu Dawud and al-Tirmidhi]*

> *Aisha came to know that Abdullah ibn Amr was ordering women to undo their plaits for ghusl. She said, "It is amazing that he orders women to undo their plaits for ghusl. Why doesn't he order them to shave their heads! The Messenger ﷺ and I used to bathe from one vessel and all I did was pour three handfuls of water over my head." [Muslim, 747]*

2.1.1.1 It is essential for men that water reach the roots of their hair, regardless of whether that is the head or the beard. This is also the case for a woman who has short hair.

2.1.1.2 There is a dispensation for women with braids or plaits in that they are not required to undo their hair, provided water reaches the roots of the hair.

2.2 *Gargling water in the mouth*

2.3 *Sniffing water into the nostrils.*

3. The sunnah (recommended) acts of *ghusl*

> *Aisha relates: 'When the Prophet ﷺ used to bathe on account of major ritual impurity, he would start by washing his hands. Then he would pour water from his right hand to his left and wash his private parts. He would then perform wu'du as he would for prayer, take some water and move his fingers through to the roots of his hair until he was sure that they were completely soaked, then he would pour water over his head three times, then he would pour water over the rest of his body and would wash his feet." [al-Bukhari and Muslim]*

3.1 Mentioning the name of God (*Basmalah*)

> *"The curtain between the eyes of jinn and the 'awrah of humans when they de-robe is to say, 'In the Name of God'"* [Tabarani, al-Majmu al-Awsat, 3:130]

3.2 Intention.

3.3 Washing one's hands before commencing.

3.4 Washing one's private parts.

3.5 Performing the full *wudu*, except for the feet, which should be washed at the end of the *ghusl*.

3.6 Rubbing the body while pouring water over it.

4. The four occasions when ghusl is a sunnah

4.1 Friday prayers

4.2 The Eid prayers

4.3 The day of *Arafah* for those on Hajj.

4.4 When donning the *ihram* for Hajj.

5. Minor ritual impurity (hadath al-asghar)

Minor ritual impurity (*hadath al-asghar*) requires one to perform ablution (*wudu*) or perform tayammum.

> **"Believers! When you rise for prayer, wash your faces and hands to the elbows, wipe your heads and wash your feet to the ankles."** [5:6]

> *"God does not accept the prayer of any one of you who has nullified his wudu until he performs it again."* [al-Bukhari, 135]

As with Major ritual impurity, this can be studied by examining the following questions:

What causes it? What actions are forbidden while in such a state? How does one remove such a state?

6. What causes it?

> Aishah relates that the Messenger ﷺ said: *"Whoever vomits, suffers from a nose bleed, regurgitates food up to the mouth or emits prostratic fluid should leave [the prayer] and perform wu'du and then they should build upon their prayer. In doing all of this they should not speak."* [Imam Ahmad]

6.1 Normal secretions from the private parts

> *"...or one of you comes after answering the call of nature..."* [4:43]

6.2 Bleeding or any other impurity coming from a part of the body

> *"Wudu is required by all flowing blood."* [al-Daraqutni, 1:163]

> *Ata ibn Abi Rabah said, "If blood flows, then one should do wudu, but if it appears and does not flow, then there is no need for wudu."* [Abd al-Razzaq, Musannaf, 1:143]

6.3 Vomiting a mouthful or more.

6.4 Sleep

Any loss of consciousness also follows the same ruling as sleep. Sleeping while lying down or reclining requires the performance of *wudu*, even for a short period, if the person has fallen into a deep sleep. This type of sleep is described as one where the person drops something that they were holding, or are no longer able to make out voices or sounds around them.

> *"The Prophet ﷺ used to command us not to remove our leather socks when we were travelling unless we were in a state of janabah – in other words, not due to defecating, urinating or sleep." [al-Tirmidhi, 96]*

Sleeping while standing, or in the positions of the prayer, or while sitting in such a way as one's buttocks are firmly seated does not nullify wudu.

> *Anas ibn Malik relates: "The companions of the Prophet ﷺ used to wait for 'Isha prayer to the point that their heads would bow down, then they would stand and pray without [renewing] wu'du". [Related by Abu Dawud and Muslim]*

6.5 Laughing loudly while in the prayer

> *'While the Prophet ﷺ was praying with people, a man with a sight problem stumbled into a covered well and fell. Some people burst out laughing. The Prophet ﷺ commanded those that had done so to repeat their wudu, and their prayers.' [al-Daraqutni, 1:169]*

7. Actions forbidden while in such a state

7.1 Prayer

> **"O Believers! When you rise for the prayer, wash your faces and hands, wipe your heads and wash your feet to the ankles." [5:6]**

This is the case regardless of the type of prayer, such as the funeral prayer.

7.2 The *sajdah* of recitation

This is a prostration performed when one recites or hears a section of the Qur'an that requires a prostration to be made. Al-Zuhri said, "One should not do a sajdah unless one is pure."

7.3 Touching the Qur'an

> **"Indeed this is an honorable Qur'an in a Well-Preserved Tablet, which none but those purified may touch." [56:77-79]**

> *In a letter sent to 'Amr ibn Hazm, the Prophet ﷺ had dictated: "None is to touch the Qur'an but one that is purified." [Muwatta, 108]*

The verbal recitation of the Qur'an is however allowed in a state of minor ritual impurity.

> *'Ali said "The Messenger ﷺ used to recite the Qur'an, and nothing would keep him from this except janabah." [Abu Hanifah, Kitab al-Athar]*

7.4 Tawaf

Wudu is *wajib*[19] for the circumambulation (*tawaf*) of the Kabah during *'Umrah* and *Hajj*. While not null and void if performed without *wudu*, one is nevertheless required to either repeat the *tawaf* or sacrifice an animal as an expiation for the shortcoming.

8. When being in *wudu* is a recommended (*sunnah*) act.

It is sunnah in a general sense that one stay in a state of purity at all times.

> *The Prophet ﷺ awoke one morning and called for Bilal and said to him, "Bilal! How did you arrive in Paradise before me? I entered Paradise yesterday and heard the sound of your footsteps in front of me!" Bilal said, "I have never given the call to prayer except that I prayed two rakat after it, and I have never lost my wudu except that I have replenished it immediately." The Prophet ﷺ then said, "It is for this!" [al-Mundhiri, al-Targhib, 1:163]*

---

[19] An obligation less than that of an essential *fard* act.

There are other occasions when it is **sunnah** to be in *wudu.*

8.1 When going to sleep.

'When you (intend to) lie on your bed, do wudu, lie on your right side and say "God! I submit my face to you. I entrust my affairs to you..." [Ibn Abi Shaybah, 1:111]

8.2 In a state of *janabah*, if one intends to eat, drink or sleep.

"If the Prophet ﷺ was in a state of janabah and wanted to eat or sleep, he would make wudu." [Muslim, 699]

9. Recommended times for *wudu*:

9.1 Washing a dead body and carrying it.
9.2 Reciting the Qur'an or Prophetic traditions.
9.3 For sacred learning.
9.4 For visiting the Prophet ﷺ
9.5 When performing the Sa'i;
9.6 In order to remove oneself from a difference of opinion among the scholars. [ash-Shurnbulali, Maraqih al-Falah, pg43]

Did you know?

Conserving water.

The Prophet (may God bless and grant him peace) used small amounts of water for washing and ordered his Companions to do the same. It is recorded that he *(may God bless and grant him peace)* used around 3 litres for bathing (*ghusl*) and half a litre for *wudu.*

Abdullah ibn 'Umar narrated that the Messenger of God (may God bless and grant him peace) passed by Sa'd while he was performing ablution and said: 'What is this extravagance, Sa'd?' He said, "Is there extravagance in the use of water?" He said: "Yes, even if you are at a flowing river." [Ahmad]

Anas said, "The Prophet (may God bless and grant him peace) used to perform ghusl with a sa'a (3.25 litres according to the Hanafi school, 2 litres according to the majority of schools) of water. He also used to make wudu with one mudd (between 812.5- 510 ml) of water." [al-Bukhari and Muslim]

'Ubaidillah ibn Abu Yazid narrated that a man asked Ibn 'Abbas, "How much water is sufficient for wudu?" He answered, "One mudd." "And how much is sufficient for ghusl?" He said, "One sa'a." The man said, "That is not sufficient for me." "Ibn 'Abbas said, "No? It was sufficient for one better than you, the Messenger of God (may God bless and grant him peace)." [Ahmad, 1/289]

Lesson 5 - Ritual Impurity (hukmi) 3

> **Aims:** Students will be provided with an explanation of how minor ritual impurity is removed through *wudu*, as well as a discussion on the issue of wiping over one's footwear while performing *wudu*.
>
> **Objectives:** By the end of this lesson, a student should be able to display the ability to:
> 1. List, with explanations, the essential acts involved in performing *wudu*.
> 2. Discuss the significance of the sunnah acts of *wudu*.
> 3. Distinguish between those acts that are essential in *wudu* and those that are sunnah.
> 4. Summarise the *fiqh* of wiping over one's footwear, mentioning the essential elements for doing so.
> 5. Appreciate the underlying reasons for the disagreement over which type of footwear it is permitted to wipe over and which it is not.
> 6. Define what is meant by *khuff* and *jawrab* in the Arabic language, clarifying the description of each.
> 7. Mention the detailed reason that scholars have differed over this issue.

1. How to remove the state of minor ritual impurity – performing *wudu*

> ***"O Believers! When you rise for the prayer, wash your faces and hands up to the elbows, wipe your heads and wash your feet to the ankles..." [5:6]***

Humran relates that 'Uthman ibn 'Affan called for water to make wudu, then he washed his hands three times, rinsed out his mouth and sniffed up some water [into his nose] and blew it out. He then washed his face three times, then his right arm to the elbows three times and then repeated that for the left. Then he wiped his head and washed his right foot to the ankle three times then repeated that for the left. Then he said, "I saw the Prophet ﷺ perform wudu like this wudu of mine. [and say 'Whoever does wudu' like this after which then prays two rakah in which he does not become distracted, they will have their past wrong actions forgiven]." [Agreed upon]

1.1 The essential elements *(fard)* of *wudu*

The four essential elements of *wudu*, without the performance of which any acts of worship will be incorrect, are all mentioned in the Quranic verse mentioned above. These are:

1.1.1 Washing one's face from the top of the forehead (where one's normal hairline is) to the bottom of the chin in length, and from earlobe to earlobe in width.
1.1.2 Washing the arms up to and including the elbows
1.1.3 Wiping one's head approximated to be at least one quarter of the head area.
1.1.4 Washing the feet up to and including the ankles

For both the arms and feet, even though the elbows and ankles are not specifically mentioned, they are implied in the verse. Al-Zamakhshari said, *"The Arabic word 'up to' (ilaa) [in 'wash your faces and hands up to the elbows'] implies the meaning of extremity without indicating whether or not this is included in the ruling or not [...] the vast majority of scholars veered towards caution and judged that they be included in the command to wash." [Tafsir al-Kashaf, 1:610]*

2. The blessing of sunnah acts – forgiveness from minor wrong actions

As they are not expressly mentioned in the Qur'anic verse, all other acts habitually performed in *wudu* are non-essential and have varying degrees of recommendation associated with them. Those established by Prophetic practice are mentioned below.

These are acts that form part of the exemplary practice of the Prophet ﷺ , but are not considered obligatory, as the Prophet ﷺ did not adhere to them all the time and did not usually reprimand his Companions for not performing them. However, the reward for such actions is immense. The Prophet ﷺ said, *'When a believing (mu'min) or submitting (muslim) servant makes wudu' and washes his face, every wrong action he has committed with his eye is removed with the water, or the drops of water' [Muslim].*

He ﷺ also said: *"Shall I not inform you of what removes wrong actions and raises one's status? Perfecting wudu in difficult circumstances, taking plenty of steps to the masjid and waiting for one prayer after another as that is [a type of] ribat (guarding the frontiers)." [Muslim, 587]*

2.1 The sunnah acts of *wudu*

2.1.1 Intention to perform the act for the pleasure of God.

2.1.2 Mentioning the name of God: *Abu Hurairah relates that the Prophet* ﷺ *said: "There is no wu'du for one that does not mention of the name of God when performing it" [Ahmed]*

2.1.3 Washing one's hands before commencing. Aws ibn Abi Aws said, *"I saw the Prophet* ﷺ *perform wudu, and he washed his hands three times." [al-Nasa'i, 83]*

2.1.4 *Cleaning one's teeth:* *The Prophet* ﷺ *said: "If it wasn't for it being a hardship upon my community, I would have ordered them to make use of the siwaq with every wu'du."[Related by Malik]*

2.1.5 Gargling the mouth with water (*madmadah*) [al-Bukhari, 191]

2.1.6 Taking water into one's nose (*istinshaq*) and blowing it out *(istinthar):* *"When one of you performs wudu, they should take up water through their nostrils, then blow it out." [Bukhari, 162]*

2.1.7 Washing three times: *"A man came to the Prophet* ﷺ *and asked him, "How is wudu performed? The Prophet* ﷺ *called for some water and washed his hands up to his wrists thrice, then washed his face thrice..." [Abu Dawud, 135]*

2.1.8 Wiping the whole head: *"...then he wiped his whole head with his hands. He started with the front of the head then moved to the back, and then returned with his hands to the front..." [al-Bukhari, 174].* Abu Dawud said, *"All the sound narrations reported from 'Uthman indicate that the head is to be wiped once, as they mention the washing of all other parts three times."*

2.1.9 Wiping one's ears: *'Ali narrated that the Messenger of God* ﷺ *used the same water to wipe his ears that he used to wipe his head.' [Abu Dawud, 117]*

2.1.10 Running one's fingers through the beard (*takhlil):* *Anas ibn Malik said that when the Messenger of God* ﷺ *performed wudu, he would take a handful of water, put it under his jaw and pass it through his beard, and he would say, "This is what my Lord God ordered me to do." [Abu Dawud, 145]*

2.1.11 Running one's fingers through the fingers and toes: *The Prophet* ﷺ *said, "When you perform wudu, then run your fingers through your [other] fingers." [At-Tirmidhi, 38].* It is related also that 'Ali used to move his ring whilst doing *wudu*.

2.1.12 Rubbing one's limbs while washing them: *'Abdullah ibn Zaid related that when the Messenger* ﷺ *performed wudu, he rubbed his limbs.' (Ahmed, 16488)*

2.1.13 Following the sequence mentioned in the verse of wudu. *Jabir ibn Abdullah narrates: "Start with what God has started with" [Narrated by al-Nisa'i]*

2.1.14 Starting with the right side: This is the sunnah in *wudu* as in other actions. *'Aishah said, "The Messenger* ﷺ *loved to begin with his right side when putting on his shoes, arranging his hair, cleaning or purifying himself and in all his acts." [al-Bukhari, 168]*

2.1.15 Non-interrupted performance of all the acts of *wudu*: This means that the actions of *wudu* should not be separated by actions not related to *wudu* itself.

2.1.16 Avoiding wasting water: Abdullah Ibn Mughaful narrated that he heard the Messenger ﷺ say, *"There will be from amongst my nation those who will exaggerate in making supplication and in purifying themselves." [Abu Dawud, 96]*

2.1.17 Supplicating after performing wudu: Although there is nothing confirmed regarding supplications *during* the wudu, there are several narrations as to what to supplicate with after one completes wudu. 'Umar reported that the Prophet ﷺ said, *"If one completes and perfects wudu and says "I testify that there is no god but God, the One who has no partner, and that Muhammad is his slave and Messenger. O Allah, cause me to be amongst the repentant and make me from amongst those that excel in purity," the eight gates of Paradise will be opened for him and he may enter it through any of them he chooses." [Tirmidhi, 55]*

3. Wiping over leather socks (khuffs) and other acceptable footwear

3.1 **Rulings:**

> **3.1.1 Essential (*fard*) elements of wiping the *khuff*:** It is *fard* to wipe over the top of the *khuff* once an area that is at least three fingers in width.
> **3.1.2 Sunnah elements of wiping the *khuff*:** It is sunnah to draw all five fingers from the toes over the upper part of the foot to above the ankles.

3.2 Method of wearing khuff.

One performs the full *wudu* including the washing of the feet. After the feet are dried, one can put on the *khuff* anytime before the *wudu* has been broken and one is now able to wipe over the *khuff* as needed.

3.3 Associated rulings

> **3.3.1** The duration for which one may wipe over the *khuff* is a period of 24 hours in the case of a non-traveller and 72 hours in the case of a traveller.
> **3.3.2** The period from which the dispensation to wipe the *khuff* starts is from the time when one's *wudu* breaks after having put on the *khuff*.
> **3.3.3** Wiping over the *khuff* is not permitted if one is required to perform *ghusl*.

3.4 What nullifies the dispensation of wiping over the khuff?

> **3.4.1** The elapsing of the designated time period.
> **3.4.2** Removing the *khuff* from one's feet.
> **3.4.3** Requiring ghusl.

4. Text in focus – Wiping over footwear

> ***"...and wash your feet to the ankles" [5:6]***
> ***"And God desires ease for you, not hardship..." [2:185]***

The issue of whether it is permitted to wipe over one's footwear, particularly cloth socks, has been the subject of much ongoing debate and confusion. The original ruling of only washing one's feet is established by the Qur'anic text, allowing nothing but the washing of feet. The dispensation for one not to wash one's feet while performing *wudu* is related in the Prophetic sunnah as a means of easing hardship during travel and cold weather, etc. Therefore the debate revolves around the permission given by the Prophet ﷺ to wipe over what are called '*khuff*' and '*jawarib*' and the meaning of these two words.

4.1 The question of wiping over the *khuff*

Scholars permitted the dispensation of wiping over footwear rather than washing one's feet in *wudu* only after it was established by multiple (*mutawatir*) narrations going back to the Prophet ﷺ . Hasan al-Basri said: '*Seventy people from among the Companions narrated to me that they saw the Prophet ﷺ wipe over khuff.*' Abu Hanifah said, "*I did not hold to the permissibility of wiping [khuff] until the evidence became clearer to me than the light of day.*" *[al-Ayni, al-Binayah, 1:554]*

4.2 The evidence

Al-Mughirah Ibn Shu'bah said, "*I was with the Messenger ﷺ one night during an expedition. I poured water for him to do wudu, he washed his face and arms and wiped his head, and when I went to remove his khuff from his feet, he said, 'Leave them, as I put them on while I was in a state of purity,' and [proceeded to] wipe over them.*" *[Al-Bukhari, 206]*

There are numerous narrations relating to this, as well as a scholarly consensus (*Ijma*) as to the permissibility of wiping over *khuff*.

4.3 What are *khuff*?

> "*Khuff are leather footwear that covers up to the ankles.*" *[Shawkani, Nayl al-Awtar, 1:212]*

4.4 Conditions on what constitutes a *khuff*

Though linguistically the Arabs used the word *khuff* primarily to denote a type of leather footwear, scholars, except for the Maliki school, did not take this as an integral condition as to what constitutes a *khuff*.

A general summary of an agreed description of the other schools of law would be:

4.4.1 That they cover the area up to and including the ankles.

4.4.2 That it be possible to walk wearing the *khuff* i.e. that they are suitable to walk in, thereby taking the place of normal footwear. This is approximated by the Hanafi school to around 3 miles walking.

4.4.3 While other schools of thought do not put such an approximation on how long the footwear should last, they generally hold that they should be of a nature that withstands normal daily wear and tear.

4.5 Scholars position on wiping over the *jawrab*

What is a *jawrab*?

Jawrab: footwear made from wool worn to provide warmth. [al-Zabidi, Taj al-'Urus, 2:156]

Al-Mughirah Ibn Shu'bah said, "The Prophet ﷺ made wudu and wiped over his jawrab and sandals." [Abu Dawud, 159; al-Tirmidhi, 99]

This hadith is related by the same companion who related the previous hadith concerning wiping over the *khuff*. Over and above the initial dispensation established by multiple chains of narration (*mutawatir*)allowing wiping over *khuff*, there is only one solitary narration recorded which mentions wiping over what Arabs referred to as a *jawrab*.

4.6 Opinions on the hadith of al-Mughirah ibn Shu'bah

4.6.1 Some rejected the narration outright, with Maliki school restricting wiping over anything save leather footwear, holding the initial dispensation to be for the *khuff* alone. They point out that nature of dispensations is that they must be restricted in their usage (in this instance that of wiping over the *khuff* alone). *[Ibn al-Arabi, al-Aridah al-Awhadhi, 1:149; al-Qarafi , al-Dhakhirah, 1:333]*

4.6.2 It is well established in Islamic law that following actions (as opposed to sayings) is conditional on having an understanding of the context and environment where such an instance took place. The condition (thickness, etc) of the footwear which were wiped is unknown. *[Ittr, Dirasat, 76]*

4.6.3 Other scholars, such as Imam Ahmad, Abu Yusuf and al-Shaybani, have allowed wiping over such footwear with the condition that they fulfill the same basic conditions as *khuff*.

4.6.4 *Imam Ahmad said: "Wiping over the jawrab is not permissible unless it is thick-textured (jawrab safiq) and stands alone on one's leg without collapsing, just like the khuff, as people used to wipe on the jawrab because, in their usage, it provided the same function as the khuff and stood up on the leg like the khuff, allowing one to come and go with it." [Ibn Qudama, al-Mughni, 1:374-375]*

4.6.5 It is narrated that Imam Abu Hanifah, in his final illness, wiped over his *jawrab* and said: *"Today I did something which I never used to do: I wiped over my jawrab." [al-Kashani, Badai', 1:83]*

Did you know?

A question of Creed (*Aqidah*)?

Early scholars mentioned the issue of wiping over the *khuff* in their books of *Aqidah* (Islamic creed), as it is an example of a religious practice established through a continuous multiple chain of narration (*mutawatir*) going back to the Prophet (*may God bless and grant him peace*). To reject such well established narrations was seen as being akin to rejecting the Qur'anic text itself and hence would undermine the very core of how religious teaching is established. Hence, al-Karkhi said, *"I fear disbelief for the one that does not believe in wiping over the Khuff."* [Ayni, al-Binayyah, 1:554]

The hadith on the topic of *khuff* are an example of religious text that have been established as being definitively authentic due to the large number of people that report them. This is sometimes referred to as **'qati'i al-thabut'**, meaning '*conclusively established*' such that one cannot doubt its epistemic value. No one can doubt that the Prophet (*may God bless and grant him peace*) actually did this, though they may differ as to how it is explained.

The opposite of this is what is referred to as **'dhanni al-thabut'**, where there may be some doubt remaining as to the truthfulness of a report due to factors that are investigated in the science of hadith.

Lesson 6- *Tayammum*

> ***Aims:*** Students will be introduced to the theory and practice of *tayammum* and investigate when it is used. They will also be provided with a summary of the rulings related to ritual purity during illness.
>
> ***Objectives:*** By the end of this lesson, a student should be able to display the ability to:
> 1. Explain what is meant by *tayammum* and what type of ritual impurity it is used for.
> 2. Detail the four conditions that need to be met before one may perform *tayammum*.
> 3. List the sunnah acts of *tayammum*.
> 4. Discuss what nullifies *tayammum*.
> 5. Mention how, while ill, one decides whether to perform *wudu*, *ghusl*, or tayammum.
> 6. Summarise the relationship between *tayammum* and wiping over bandages and plaster-casts.
> 7. Discuss the rulings relating to people with illnesses that lead to a perpetual loss of *wudu* (*ma'dhur*) and the three conditions relating to the start, continuation and end of such a state.
> 8. Appreciate the significance of purity as key to other acts of worship and devotion.

Tayammum[20] is the word given to the process by which one can attain ritual purity, removing both major and minor ritual impurity by the use of dry earth. It was given as a dispensation to believers for times when it becomes difficult or impossible to make use of water for *wudu* or *ghusl*.

> ***"And if you are ill, or on a journey, or one of you comes from the privy, or if you have had marital relations with women and you do not find water, then take for yourselves clean sand and rub your faces and your hands therewith. Indeed, God is Compassionate and Forgiving." [4:43]***

> *Jabir ibn Abdullah relates that the Prophet ﷺ said: 'I have been given five things which no one before me had been given. I was given victory through awe which preceded me by a month's journey. The whole earth was made a place of prostration for me and ritually pure, so when the time to pray comes upon my Community they may pray...' [Agreed upon]*

> *Abu Juhaym relates the Messenger of God ﷺ came after answering the call of nature and I greeted him with salam, but he did not return my greeting. He struck the wall once with his hand and wiped his face, then he struck it a second time and wiped his hands up to his elbows, then he responded to my greeting. [Abu Dawud, 331]*

> *Abu Dharr al-Ghafari relates that the Prophet ﷺ said, "Indeed the earth is a purification for the Muslim, even if he does not find water for ten years, and if he finds water, then let him make use of it, since that is better." [al-Tirmidhi, 124]*

1. The four conditions for the performance of *tayammum*

1.1 Intention:

One should intend to perform a worship which is not correct without purity.

1.2 An excuse that permits *tayammum*:

There are two types of excuses:
- The lack of water for purification
- The inability to use water

1.2.1 Lack of water:
Imran ibn Hussain said, "We were with the Messenger of God ﷺ during a journey and he led the people in prayer. After he finished, he saw a man sitting alone who had not prayed with the people. He asked, 'So and so, what has prevented you from praying with us?' He replied, 'I am in the state of janabah and there is no water.' The Prophet ﷺ said, 'Perform tayammum with clean earth, for that will suffice you.'" [Al-Bukhari]

The general guidelines related to a lack of water are as follows:

---

[20] *Tayammum* was originally used by the Arabs as a word meaning *'to look out and intend to search for something'*. The reason this word is used for the action of using dry earth for purification is that a person unable to make use of water is asked to seek out and look for a material that is suitable to be used for *tayammum*. [Al-Azhari, al-Sihah]

If water is available, but is a mile or more away, it is permitted to perform *tayammum*.
In the case of someone who does not find water at the beginning of a prayer time, but who hopes to do so by its end, it is recommended to delay praying to the latest time of prayer then perform *tayammum* and pray.
If one thinks it possible that water may be found in the vicinity, then it is not permitted to do *tayammum* without having searched for it.

1.2.2 The inability to use water:

Jabir said, "We set out on a journey. One of our people was hurt by a stone, injuring his head. He then had a wet dream. He asked his companions, 'Do you find any concession for me to perform tayammum?' They said, 'We do not find any concession for you while you are able to use water." He performed ghusl and died because of it. When we went to the Prophet ﷺ , the incident was reported to him. He said, 'They killed him, may God kill them. Why did they not ask concerning that which they did not know about? The cure for ignorance is to ask. It would have been enough for him to perform tayammum.'" [Abu Dawud, 336]

This may be due to an inability to reach water; only having a basic quantity which meets one's urgent needs such as drinking and cooking; that one is ill and fears that using water will aggravate the illness; or that one is in a state of *janabah* and fears for one's health if one was to use water.

1.3 That it be performed with soil

It is only permitted to perform *tayammum* with pure earth. 'Earth' here refers to whatever naturally covers the earth's surface, being of the same genus such as the earth such as sand, stone and dust[21].

1.4 Wiping over the whole of the face and arms to the elbows.

The definition of '*face*' and '*arms*' here is the same as in the lesson on *wudu*.

2. Sunnah acts in *tayammum*

There are six sunnah acts in *tayammum*:
   2.1 Saying the '*Basmallah*'.
   2.2 Following the sequence of acts.
   2.3 Continuation between the acts without a break.
   2.4 Moving the hands to and fro in the soil or ground.
   2.5 Shaking the hands of excess dust.
   2.6 Spreading open the fingers while striking the earth.

3. Related rulings of tayammum

Abu Sa'id al-Khudri said, "Two men went out on a journey. The time of prayer came and they had no water so they performed tayammum with pure earth, and prayed. Later, one of them repeated his prayer with wudu and the other did not. When they rejoined the Prophet ⌧, they mentioned this to him. He said to the one who did not repeat his prayer, 'You have acted according to the sunnah and your prayer is sufficient for you.' He said to the other, 'You will get a double reward.'" [Abu Dawud, 338]

3.1 What type of illness permits the use of *tayammum*?

It is sufficient that one has a good degree of certainty *(ghalab al-dhann)* that one's illness will increase or that the healing process will be delayed by the use of water, be that through past experience or through the information provided by a competent medical authority.

3.2 What are the restrictions to the use of *tayammum* for worship?

There is no limit as to the type or quantity of worship one is allowed to perform with *tayammum*, as it takes the place of other types of purification until it is nullified.

3.3 What nullifies *tayammum*?

3.3.1 All that which nullifies *wudu*.

---

[21] Anyone in a situation where there is neither water nor dry dust for *tayammum*, should imitate the actions for the prayer and later make up the prayer performed in such a way.

51

3.3.2 Accessibility of water, or the ability to use it, regardless of whether this happens before or while praying. In such a case one must perform *wudu* and then resume the prayer, but any prayer(s) completed before one gains accessibility to water do not have to be repeated.

4. Injuries and *wudu* - washing or *tayammum*?

4.1 In a state of minor ritual impurity, to ascertain whether to perform *wudu* or *tayammum*, one counts each member of the four limbs that are cleaned in *wudu* (face, arms, head and feet).

4.2 If the majority of the members are affected by wounds, then one performs *tayammum*, otherwise one washes the limbs that are sound and wipes over the wound or bandage as detailed below.

5. Injuries and *ghusl*- washing or *tayammum*?

5.1 In a state of major ritual impurity, to ascertain whether to perform *ghusl* or *tayammum*, one compares the whole body area with the area of the wound – if the majority of the body area is wounded, then one performs *tayammum*, otherwise one washes the body and wipes over the bandage.

5.2 If it is not practical to wash the body without affecting the wound (such as a back-wound that would become wet if one poured water on the head), all the area from the wound and above is counted as wounded.

5.3 If one has wounds on the hands preventing one doing *wudu* or *ghusl*, then *tayammum* is performed.

6. Wiping over bandages and plaster casts

6.1 It is permitted for people who are wearing bandages and plaster casts to wipe over these in conjunction with performing *wudu* or *ghusl*. The condition for wiping over them is that one be unable to wipe over the wound itself.

6.2 It is not a condition to have been in a state of purity when the covering was initially worn or applied.

6.3 It is sufficient that one wipes over the majority of the bandage and this only need be done once.

6.4 A person requiring *wudu* and a person in a state of *janabah* are the same in this regard.

6.5 If one has put on such a covering on part of the body, it is not required to repeat wiping over a new bandage if the original one has to be changed.

7. Rulings relating to people with illnesses that lead to a perpetual loss of *wudu* (*ma'dhur*)

The Prophet ﷺ said: 'Do wudu for every prayer.'

Individuals who suffer from urine incontinence, a wound which does not cease to bleed, or any ailment which entails the secretion of a substance that nullifies one's *wudu* need only do *wudu* once for each prayer time. Thereafter, they may perform any *fard* or voluntary prayer they wish to, within the time of that prayer.

7.1 The conditions for this dispensation

7.1.1 The initial illness should be one that afflicts a person and occupies the whole timeframe of one prayer. There should be no break in the illness allowing for the performance of *wudu* and prayer free of the illness.

7.2 How long does this dispensation last?

7.2.1 A person will continue to have the benefits of this dispensation even if they are afflicted by the illness once during the time of that prayer. In other words, it is not a condition that the illness be continuous during the time of the prayer in question.

7.3 When does this dispensation end?

The person suffering from the illness ceases to benefit from this dispensation if:

7.3.1 The illness fails to appear for the timeframe of one whole prayer.

7.3.1 The wudu breaks due to any reason other than the ailment in question, in which case *wudu* needs to be performed again.

7.3.2 Once the time of that prayer elapses, the *wudu* becomes invalid and should be renewed.

8. Purifying the best part of the body to perform the best act of worship

Few individuals perform the acts of *wudu* without pondering, even for a moment, the significance of each act of purity, or of the meaning inherent in attaining purity of body, clothing and place as a preparation for standing in front of the Lord of all of creation. Much has been written on this and amongst the most soul-stirring articulations in this regard are the words of Abu Abdillah al-Bukhari, who writes the following on the wisdom of the actions of the wudu:

> *"Purity is the best state attainable by creation, something which is deemed praiseworthy by all of fair disposition and sound mind. The best action that all of creation may partake and excel in as well as the most agreeable condition to be in is that of attaining purity from all defilements that may afflict one.*

> *If we were left to our own devices and ventured to decide what to clean, we would seek to clean our whole body, since worship is done by all parts of the body. However, God, Who is worshipped, the Merciful and Loving, favoured us and ordered us to wash only part of the body and waived cleaning the rest, allowing the purity of four parts of the body to substitute for the whole of the body, which themselves represent the four elements [...]*

> *He ordered to merely wipe over the head rather that wash it, so that the clothes of the one performing wudu do not get soaked. The One who ordained purity in such a way as to save one from getting soaked is more likely to extend His mercy by forgiving wrong actions in order that the body be saved from being burned by Jehanam [...]*

> *He ordered that the face be washed, since with it, prostration is done. He ordered the hands to be washed as it is upon them that one relies. He ordered that the feet be washed since it is by them that one stands.*

> *He apportioned the head a role in purity as it contains the face, which is the epitome of all perfection. In the same way that all human perfection is in the face, similarly all perfection in worship is in the prostration (sajdah), therefore, it is through this symbol of human perfection that prostration is made. [The prostration] is closeness to the One to whom there is no temporal closeness or distance and so He said, **"Prostrate and draw near [96:19]"**. [Abu Abdillah al-Bukhari, Mahasin al-Islam, pg 9-10]*

Towards a Tranquil Soul 1

Understanding the theory and practice of Purifying the Heart

Module Tzk 1.01.D

iSyllabus
islam · iman · ihsan

Lesson One - Human Nature & Purification of the Heart

Aim: By the end of this lesson, students should understand the importance of the science of *tazkiyyah* and how it relates to the human being. They will gain an insight into human nature in as much as it relates to spiritual self-betterment and end with a study of the usage of terms such as 'heart' (*qalb*), 'intellect' (*'aql*), 'soul' (*ruh*), and 'spirit' (*nafs*).

Objectives: By the end of this lesson students should be able to display the ability to:
1. Explain why *tazkiyyah* is one of the most important disciplines to study and apply.
2. Summarise the *shari'ah* ruling regarding its study.
3. Discuss the nature of the human and how knowing this helps one understand *tazkiyyah*.
4. Explain the meaning of each of the following terms; 'heart' (*qalb*), 'intelligence' (*'aql*), 'soul' (*ruh*), and 'spirit' (*nafs*).
5. Summarise the manner in which these terms are both similar and different from each other.
6. Outline, with a brief explanation, the three stages of the *nafs*.

1. The subject matter of *tazkiyyah*

There is arguably no area of concern that is more important in the life of a human than knowing who they are and the relationship they have with their Creator. This area of knowledge is referred to as *tazkiyyah* or *purification of the heart,* and examines the nature of the human and the spiritual ailments and diseases with which they are afflicted. The ultimate aim of *tazkiyyah* is perfection in worship and adoration of God (*ihsan*).

According to Ibn 'Ajiba, the science of *tazkiyyah* relates to two things. Firstly knowing God and secondly knowing what it is to be human. However these are not mutually exclusive since knowledge of the self leads to knowledge of God.

> *'The subject matter of this science is God himself, since it looks into the ability [of an individual] to come to have knowledge [of Him] either through a decisive proof, or by witnessing and direct perception. The first is for those who are [still] seeking, while the latter relates to those who have arrived. It is also said that the subject matter of this science is the ego (nafs), heart (qalb) and soul (ruh) since it looks into purifying and refining them. This is closely related to the first, since whoever knows himself comes to know his Lord.' [Ibn 'Ajiba, Iqadh al-Himam, pg6]*

2. *Tazkiyyah* - How necessary is it?

> ***'The day in which neither wealth nor children will be of any use, except for whoever comes to God with a sound heart.'*** *[26:88-89]*

> *'Imam al-Shadhili said: 'The one that does not engage in this science of ours will die continually committing wrong actions while not knowing it.' [Ibn Ajiba, Iqadh al-Himam, 8]*

The only thing that will benefit humans on the day they are resurrected will be a sound heart. It is defined as a heart free of spiritual blemishes such as associating partners with God (*shirk*), vanity, pride, love of the world and heedlessness. Central to the Prophet's ﷺ mission was the purification of the hearts of the believers and as such, the scholars of this community have been unanimous in stating the imperative for all human beings to give due attention to this science. Ibn Taymiyyah, for example, compares the struggle against the ego with outward *Jihad* against injustice, indeed noting that the former is more pressing.

> *'If the nafs leans towards that which is forbidden, one is ordered to resist this [...] in the same way that one is ordered to undertake jihad against one that openly orders to sin against God [...] rather people are in more need of this, as this is an obligation on every individual, while the other jihad is obligatory on the community as a whole [...].*
>
> *It is related that the Prophet ﷺ said: 'The true muhajir (one who emigrates) is the one who leaves what has been prohibited by God.' [Abu Daud 2481]. The Messenger ﷺ also said, 'The true warrior is the one that struggles with their own self.' [al-Tirmidhi, 1621][Ibn Taymiyyah, Tazkiyyah an-Nafs, 51-52]*

The *shari'ah* ruling related to the study of this science is summarised by the famous Shafi'i jurist al-Nawawi as follows:

'As for knowledge of the heart, being aware of the ailments of the heart such as envy, pride and the like, al-Ghazali has stated that having knowledge of their definitions, underlying causes, cures and treatments is an individual obligation.

Others have stated that if a person who is morally responsible has been graced with being safe of these unlawful [spiritual] ailments then this will suffice him. They are not [in such a situation] obliged to seek out their cures. However if this is not the case then the person should reflect; If they can cure these ailments without a course of study then they may do so, in the same way that one is obliged to resist and spurn fornication and the like without learning the detailed reasons for doing so.

If, however, a person is not capable of this, except through the aforementioned branch of knowledge, then it becomes a personal obligation [on them]. Ultimately it is God that knows best.' [Al-Nawawi, Muqadimah al-Majmu, v1 [25], pg 65]

3. The meaning of Man

Before looking at spiritual ailments that afflict humans, it is necessary to first enquire into the nature of the human being, the subject matter of this science. The Arabic language is extremely rich - many words are used to refer to the same meaning and words also have different origins or linguistic roots that help us appreciate the reason why a word is used for a particular meaning. The word *Insan* is one such word, and it is said to derive from a number of different root words. Why is the human referred to as *al-Insan?* There are a number of theories:

> *[3.1] Due to his negligence and forgetfulness (nisyan).*

> *[3.2] He provides and requires affection (uns) from others.*

> *[3.3] He attains knowledge and understanding through perception (iynas). [al-Fayruzabadi, Al-Basai'r, v2 pg31]*

The human is not created self-sufficient and, being a social animal, requires basic amenities and resources to survive and procreate. The search for these basic amenities inevitably leads to the development of a struggle of sorts between the otherworldly, angelic nature of man and the worldly, self-centered aspects of the human being. Indeed, it was a feeling of superiority and being cherished that led to the downfall of one of the two sons of Adam (A.S.). The physical form of man is such that he is created to consume and procreate, even if merely for his own immediate survival.

It is related in the Prophetic sources that when God created Adam (A.S.), Iblis circled around him, all the while observing his physical form. When he saw Adam's (A.S.) capacity to consume, Iblis said: *'He has been created in a way that he will not be able to control himself.' [Ahmed, §12561]*

This insatiable nature of humans to consume is starkly portrayed in the following prophetic hadith: *'If the sons of Adam had two valleys of gold they would still seek out a third, yet the only thing that will satiate them is the dust (of their own graves), and God forgives those that turn to Him.' [al-Bukhari, 6436]*

It is also important that we understand what it is that makes us human. Is it the spirit, soul or intellect? What role does the heart, the centre of discussions on spiritual knowledge, play in our humanity?

4. The four elements. The Heart (*qalb*), Intellect ('*aql*), Soul (*ruh*), and Spirit (*nafs*).

There are a number of terms used in Arabic to describe the essential life-force which makes us human. Each of these terms has a particular meaning and connotation and is therefore a distinct entity in its own right. However, all four of these terms are also used to refer to the same subtle spiritual force through which the human being lives and perceives. As a result of this shared usage, the terms Soul (*ruh*), Heart (*qalb*), Intellect ('*aql*), Ego/Spirit (*nafs*) are used interchangeably when we read the works of the masters of the science of tazkiyyah.

4.1 The Heart (*qalb*)

The **heart** (*qalb*) is primarily used to refer to the piece of flesh in the chest cavity of man, an organ shared with other animals, an organ through which blood is pumped to the extremities of the body. It is also used in the science of *tazkiyyah* to indicate a subtle spiritual and cognitive force, and is referred to as such in the Qur'an and Prophetic traditions. This subtle spiritual force has a connection of sorts with the physical heart, which we are only now starting to understand. Imam al-Ghazali explains the heart as follows:

"...When the term 'heart' is used in the Qur'an and the sunnah, it refers to that quality within man which comprehends and discerns the real nature of things. This may be sometimes be alluded to by way of metaphor to the heart within one's breast due to the connection between this subtle substance [about which we are concerned] and the physical heart. Even though this subtle substance is connected to all parts of the body, the connection it has to the physical heart is still primary..." [Ihya Ulum al-Din, Kitab 'Aja'ib al-Qalb]

4.2 The Intellect ('aql)

The **intellect** ('aql) is used to refer to the force of knowledge, and the capacity through which one knows. It can sometimes be used to refer to a subtle force through which one perceives and understands, a meaning shared with the other words explained here such as heart.

4.3 The Soul (ruh)

Similarly the **soul** (ruh) is used, as al-Ghazali states, to refer to *'...a subtle entity, the source of which lies in the cavity of the physical heart, and which pervades the other parts of the body by means of the arteries.'* It can also be used to refer to the meaning given to the heart previously.

4.4 The Ego (nafs)

Lastly the **ego** (nafs) can be used to refer to the destructive side of man within which the faculties of anger, appetite and the like exist. Although this is the main usage of the term *nafs*, it may also be used synonymously with the heart in certain situations. The *nafs* is understood by some to be the *ruh* when it is established in the body. As will be seen below, the *nafs* itself does not remain the same through a persons lifetime, but goes through various stations of development during the process of disciplining the *nafs*.

> *'Al-Suhayli refers to the discussion among the scholars over whether the soul (ruh) and the ego(nafs) are one and the same thing, or different. He established that the ruh is subtle and ephemeral, similar to air, flowing through the body like water through the capillaries of a tree.*
>
> *He goes on to state that the soul (ruh), which the angel breathes into the feotus is the nafs and, provided that it connects with the body, it then acquires the quality of being either meritorious or blameworthy - it will either be a soul which is tranquil or else one oft-commanding to evil.*
>
> *He said, 'Just as water is the lifeblood of a tree and [yet] when it is mixed with another substance it acquires another name. If water mixes with grapes and the grapes are then pressed, it becomes either a sweet draught or wine. It is no longer called water, except in a metaphorical sense. Similarly the ruh is not referred to as the nafs and vice versa except by way of such an explanation.*
>
> *It may be said in conclusion: The ruh is the origin and essence of the nafs, which in turn is made up of the ruh through its connection to the body. They are the same in one sense, but not in others.' [Ibn Kathir, Tafsir Sura Isra v85]*

5. The three stations of the ego (nafs)

The spirit/ego is further broken down into three main types, depending on the degree of its spiritual development and maturity.

5.1 *Al-Nafs al-Ammarah bil Su'u. (The spirit that commands to evil)*

> *Sufyan al-Thawri said: 'Never have I dealt with anything stronger against me than my own ego; it was one time with me, and one time against me.'*
>
> *'Struggle against your lower ego with the four swords of training: eat little, sleep little, speak little, and be patient when people harm you. Only then will the ego walk the path of obedience, like a fleeing horseman in the field of battle.' [Yahya ibn Mu'adh ar-Razi]*

The lowest of these stations is referred, as stated in the Qur'an, as *'The spirit that commands to evil'*, of which the Prophet Yusuf (A.S) says **"And I do not defend myself, for indeed the spirit indeed commands to evil" [12:53].** In this state it is wholly in the control of the appetite and desires, with little importance being given to correct conduct and living an ethical life. It therefore leads to excess and tyranny. The only path of action is to subdue it through *tazkiyyah*.

Indeed, some people may lead their whole life in this base state, servants of their base desires with no intent for their own spiritual betterment. What is known is that without careful attention and nurturing, the soul languishes in this desert of neglect only to die before physical death.

5.2 *Al-Nafs al-Lawwamah. (The Self-blaming soul)*

> *The Messenger* ⬚ *said, "There are two impulses in the soul, one from an angel which calls towards good and confirms truth; whoever finds this, let him know it is from God and praise Him. Another comes from the enemy which leads to doubt and denies truth and forbids good; whoever finds this, let him seek refuge in God from the accursed devil.' Then he* ⬚ *recited:* **"The devil shows you fear of poverty and enjoins evil upon you" [2:268]** *[Tirmidhi]*

The next level of the spirit is referred to as the self-blaming soul, where the individual is attempting to rectify the conduct of the spirit through applying the dictates of the sacred law and the accepted norms of good conduct. Through acts such as fasting, charity and upholding justice, the spirit is brought back from the earlier self-destructive state to one where it starts to recognise its true value. This is referred to in the words of God: **'Should I not swear by the self blaming soul?' [75:2]**

5.3 *Al-Nafs al-Mutma'inna. (The Tranquil soul)*

> **"But as for him who feared to stand before his Lord and restrained his soul from lust. The Garden will be his home." [79:40-41]**

Having trained the soul to good conduct and habituated it to a moral life, the soul attains tranquility and peace after its initial turbidity and flux. This state is the pinnacle of the ascent the soul and the ultimate aim of sacred law (*shari'ah*) and religion (*din*).

As al-Ghazali describes it: *'Tranquil under His commandment and through denial of fleshly appetite, the previous agitation has passed behind it and it is called the tranquil soul. Of such a soul God says:* **'O soul which was attained tranquility! Return back to your Lord, pleased and pleasing [to Him]. Enter [the company of] My select servants! Enter Paradise!' (89:27-28)**. *[Ihya Ulum al-Din, Kitab 'Aja'ib al-Qalb]*

Lesson Two - Diagnosing the Spiritual Heart

> *Aim:* By the end of this lesson, students will appreciate how the word *qalb* (heart) is used differently in religious sources, as well as the factors that affect the spiritual health of the heart, leading to its death.
>
> ***Objectives:***
> By the end of this lesson, students should be able to display the ability to:
> 1. Discuss the different ways the word *qalb* is used in the Qur'an, hadith and works of scholars.
> 2. Explain, using the work of Ibn Qayyim, how trials and tribulations are the underlying cause of the ailments of the heart.
> 3. Identify the main ways by which to recognise a healthy heart.
> 4. Identify the main ways by which to recognise a dead heart.
> 5. Mention what causes a dead heart.
> 6. Discuss why remorse over past wrong actions is a key to spiritual awakening.

Central to the science of tazkiyyah is examining the function of the human heart. It is described as fulfilling a number of tasks, and is used synonymously with the intellect in many contexts. Are there any peculiarities in how the word '*qalb*' or heart is used in the Qur'an, Prophetic traditions and the works written by the masters of the heart?

1. The heart (*qalb*) in religious texts

1.1 The Qur'an

> *"And follow not that which you have no knowledge of. Verily, the hearing, sight and the heart, each of these will be questioned." [17:36]*

The use of the term *heart* in all religious texts is primarily to refer to the subtle spiritual faculty within the human that is the seat of understanding and moral responsibility. This is certainly the dominant use of the word in the Qur'an, appearing over 130 times in both the plural and singular forms, where it is seen as the centre of understanding and faith. It is through experiencing life that it attains its purpose of knowledge of the divine.

> *"Have they not travelled in the earth that they gain hearts by which they understand and ears with which to hear? It is not the eyes that are afflicted by blindness but rather the hearts that dwell in the breasts of Man." [22:46]*

1.2 The Sunnah

> *"...Indeed there is in the human body a morsel of flesh that if it is healthy, the body is healthy and if it is corrupt the body is corrupt. It is surely the heart." [al-Bukhari, 52]*

When one looks at the Prophetic traditions one observes, together with that mentioned above, another subtle usage of the word, depicting the heart as a litmus test for the vitality of the human soul itself and the origin of one's intentions. Commenting on the above hadith, Ibn Rajab al-Hanbali makes a link between the actions and the heart saying *"This indicates that the vitality (salah) of actions is only measured by the spiritual vitality (salah) of the heart." [Jami' al-Ulum wal-Hikam]*

The heart is challenged by the trials and temptations that are decreed by God for humans and depending on the manner in which one reacts and the action one takes, the human heart is either strengthened or weakened. If the heart is weakened, it falls victim to an array of spiritual illnesses. The two main categories of spiritual diseases, defective understanding and doubts *(shubuhat)* and Carnal Desires *(shahawat)*, lead on from this.

1.2.1 The two types of heart in the Sunnah

> *Hudhayfah relates that the Messenger ﷺ said: 'Trials will affect hearts, even as an interwoven reed mat [absorbs a liquid], bit by bit. Any heart that allows itself to be affected by these trials will have a black mark put on it. However, any heart that is not affected by them will have a white mark put on it. The result will be two [types] of heart: One pure white, not harmed by trials as long as the heavens and earth endure; another will be dark and like a rusty, overturned vessel, being absorbed with its desires, unable to recognize good, nor reject evil' [Muslim, 369].*

"Hearts, when tested with trials, become one of two types:

[The first is] a heart, which, when exposed to such trials, absorbs it like a sponge that soaks up water, leaving a stain. Such a heart continues to soak up the trials that are presented to it, until it becomes dark and corrupted - which is what is meant by "an over-turned vessel"[...]

[The second is] the pure heart, in which the light of faith is bright and its radiance is illuminating. When trials are presented to such a heart, it rejects and turns away from them. This further increases its light, illumination and strength.

These trials that afflict the heart are the underlying cause of the diseases of the heart. They are the carnal desires (shahawat) on the one hand and defective understanding and doubts (shubuhat) on the other [...].

The first corrupts one's intentions and motives, while the latter corrupts one's cognition and belief.' [Ibn al-Qayyim, Ighathat ul-Luhfan, v1, pg11]

1.3 The Scholars

'...The other members of the body, on the other hand, are merely followers, slaves and instruments which the heart uses and employs even as the King employs his servants, the shepherd makes use of his flock or the artisan utilises his tools.' [Al-Ghazali, Ihya 'Ulum al-Din]

When one looks at how scholars of this science, particularly Imam al-Muhasabi and later al-Ghazali, viewed the function of the heart, one comes to the conclusion that the heart is akin to the controlling centre of the human. The other parts of the body, such as the eyes and tongue, are subservient to it, but yet able to influence it for better or for worse.

Through focusing on this very specific usage of the word *qalb*, scholars can study the volitional role of the heart and from there explore the various spiritual diseases that the human may become afflicted with during their life.

Most of what remains of this module and Module Two on Tazkiyyah will be an exploration of their writing on this theme.

2. Checking the pulse - Signs of life and death

"Corruption has appeared on land and sea as a result of what the hands of Man have acquired" [30:41]

It is reported that Abu Bakr said: 'The Land refers to the tongue and the sea to the heart. If the tongue is corrupt, people cry over it and if the heart is corrupt, then it is the Angels that weep over it.' [Ibn Hajar al-Asqalani, Preparing for the Day of Judgement, pg 3]

2.1 The healthy heart - What are the signs of a healthy heart?

One of the most important requirements in purifying the heart is initially assessing its spiritual health. This leads to a simple question: How can one tell if one's heart is spiritually healthy?

There are many signs pointing to the health of the 'heart', most of which have to do with the way one deals with new situations. Whether these situations are good or not, they provide an insight into how the heart is functioning. A healthy response, in accordance with religious teachings and moral teachings, shows that the person is blessed with a sound heart. For example, overlooking injustice done to oneself for the sake of God shows that one is more eagerly expectant of the reward of God's pleasure than seeking redress in this world. Numerous examples in the Qur'an and Sunnah contain different signs that point to the existence of a healthy heart.

2.1.1 *"Believers are those whose hearts tremble when God is mentioned, whose faith increases when His signs are recited to them and who put their trust in God" [8:2]*

2.1.2. *"....and do not put any rancour in our hearts towards those that have faith. Indeed you are All-Gentle and Merciful." [59:10]*

2.1.3 *The Prophet ﷺ said: 'Whoever is pleased with their good actions and saddened with their bad actions then that is a true believer." [Ahmed, v1:18]*

2.1.4 *The Prophet ﷺ said: 'Are any of you able to be like Abi Damdam? He used to give up his own personal honour as a charity for people!' [Ibn al-Sinni, Amal al-Yawm wa al-Laylah, § 22]*

2.2 The dead heart - What are the signs of a dead heart?

"...They have hearts that they do not understand with, eyes they do not see with and ears they do not hear with. Such people are like cattle, rather more astray. It is they who are [in reality] heedless." (7:179)

The failure to use the spiritual capacity of the heart; take heed from the end of previous nations; to fail to reflect over the signs that God has placed in the Universe and a general neglectful heedlessness (*ghaflah*) are just some amongst many signs of a dead heart mentioned in primary religious sources.

Scholars have stated the main signs of a dead heart as being a lack of remorse and care over one's bad spiritual state. This is one of the best symptomatic ways of assessing the spiritual life of one's heart. As the spiritual master Imam Ibn Ata' illah states in one of his aphorisms:

'Amongst the signs of a dead heart is a lack of remorse over missing out good acts and showing no regret over committing wrong actions.' [Ibn Ata' illah al-Iskandri, al-Hikam no.48]

2.2.1 What causes the death of the heart?

There are three categories of acts that will lead to the death of the heart. The spiritual recklessness entailed in these acts means that a person will quickly develop a hardened heart after which the death of the heart will be imminent. One should take immediate heed of these causes and signs, noting how God, through His all-encompassing Mercy, has set down signs by which one can take oneself to account and rectify one's conduct to give life to the heart once more.

"The death of the heart is caused by one of three things:
Love of the world; heedlessness of the remembrance of God; and allowing the limbs to freely commit acts of disobedience.

Life is given to the heart by three things:
Making do with a little of the world (zuhd); being constantly engaged in the remembrance of God (dhikr); and keeping company with those beloved to God (awliyah).

The signs of [the heart] being dead lies in three things:
A lack of remorse over missing out good acts; showing no regret over committing wrong actions; and keeping company of those who are like the dead on account of their blatant heedlessness (al-ghafilin al-amwat)."

This is because acts of obedience coming from a servant [of God] are a harbinger of eternal felicity (sa'adah), while acts of disobedience are a sign of eternal damnation (shaqawah). The heart only survives nourished by gnosis (ma'rifah) [of God] and faith. Therefore it is pained by whatever leads it to eternal damnation and conversely, it is given joy by what leads it to eternal felicity.' [Ibn Ajibah, Iqadh al-Himam, pg 105]

3. Spiritual awakening - Feeling heartfelt remorse over wasted days

'Amongst the most elevated stations to aid one's spiritual awakening is a realisation of the days in one's life that have been allowed to go to waste. This can lead to a firm, heartfelt resolve to compensate for lost time and fill one's remaining days with piety and goodness. A soul so awakened will become miserly about wasting a moment, even a breath, engaged in that which is not helpful in its journey to God [...].

*There are three things that heighten one's remorse for wasted days, helping one focus on compensating for them in the remaining days of one's life; **[seeking] knowledge, giving one's ear to good counsel and admonition, and keeping the company of the righteous**.*

The more one knows the worth of actions and enormity of their consequences, the more one realises the enormity of one's loss. Similarly, one's responsiveness to the sincere promptings of one's own heart will determine how great any improvement will be. Keeping the company of people who have great concern for the condition of their own hearts and who have a spiritual resolve (himmah) in attaining the highest levels [of spiritual perfection] will greatly help the path of the one engaged in such a spiritual sojourn.' [Ibn Qayyim al-Jawziyyah, Madarij al-Salikin, V1, pg 245]

Lesson Three - *Taqwa* & preserving the Eyes and Ears.

Aim: By the end of this lesson, students will appreciate the starting point of the purification of the heart: the cultivation of *taqwa* and how this relates to the physical body. They will also understand that each of the seven organs of the body have an aspect of *taqwa* that need be attained. In particular this lesson will look into the *taqwa* as related to the eyes and ears.

Objectives: By the end of this lesson, students should be able to display the ability to:
1. Define what is meant by *taqwa*.
2. Summarise the ten steps outlined in the Quran that help nurture *taqwa* in an individual.
3. Explain what the five stations of *taqwa* are.
4. Discuss the relationship between the heart and the seven organs in achieving *taqwa* and what scholars have said regarding rectifying the heart and the limbs.
5. Identify the role and importance of the hearing and sight in purifying the heart.
6. Outline the practical steps through which one may rectify and protect both one's hearing and sight.

Yahya ibn Muadh: 'How sad is the state of the sons of Adam! Mining stones out of the earth has become easier for them than removing themselves from wrong actions.' [al-Dhahabi, Si'yar 'Alam al-Nubala', v13, pg 15-16]

1. *Taqwa* and the Purification of the Heart

Taqwa comes from an Arabic root word that means to seek to protect oneself, be wary and careful. It is translated variously as fear or more appropriately God-consciousness. Scholars have defined it in many ways, one of the most comprehensive of which is the following:

*'**Acting in obedience** to God through a guiding light from God with the intention of seeking His pleasure. It also entails the **leaving of acts of disobedience** through a guiding light from God out of being fearfully apprehensive of God's punishment.' [al-Suyuti, al-Durr al-Manthur, v1[14], pg61]*

2. *Taqwa* - Steps and Stations

There are a number of actions and exercises outlined by scholars of the heart that help one in becoming God-conscious. These provide the basis for further purification of the soul from both the wrong actions associated with the seven organs of the body, but also the hidden ailments and sicknesses that exist in the heart such as arrogance and vanity. The Andalusian scholars Ibn Juzay al-Kalbi states that the Qur'anic usage of the word *taqwa* is connected to specific qualities and actions and they revolve around what he refers to as the *'Ten steps to Taqwa'*.[22] One of these which he singles out is having *'Sincere Love of God' because of the words of the one who said:*

> "You disobey God while you make apparent that you love Him,
>> This, by my life, in analogy is a marvel.
> If your love were sincere you would obey Him,
>> Truly, the lover towards the one he loves is obedient."

And to God be attributed the good of the poet who recited:

> 'She said, upon being questioned about the state of her beloved:
>> 'For the sake of God, describe him to me and do not omit or exaggerate!'
> So I said: 'If he had feared death on account of intense thirst,
>> and you said: 'Stop! Don't approach the water!' he would not have approached.'

---

[22] *"The ten steps which create taqwa are having: Fearful apprehension of punishment in the next world; Fearful apprehension [of punishment] in this world; Hope of worldly reward; Hope of reward in the next; Fearful apprehension of the Reckoning (hisab); Bashfulness (al-haya'a) before God which is the station of watchfulness (al-muraqabah); Gratitude for His blessings by obeying Him; Knowledge, as indicated by His words: 'Of [all] His servants, only such as are endowed with [innate] knowledge stand [truly] in awe of God.' [35:28]; Dutiful honouring of His majesty, which is the station of awe (al-Hayba) and Sincere Love [Kitab al-Tashil fi Ulum al-Tanzil,V1 [2], pg 98]*

2.2 The 5 stations of *Taqwa*

Not all people start their journey of acquiring *taqwa* from the same starting point. Nor do they all reach the same station or level in perfecting *taqwa*. The level that Prophets, may God bless them all and grant them peace, reached in their worship and *taqwa*, cannot be attained by normal people. As the poet al-Busiri says about the Messenger of God ﷺ :

> *'And you continued in your ascent until you attained a station*
> *- a distance of two bows length- that will never be reached nor sought.'*

In line with this, there are a number of stations of *taqwa*, each one leading to the next. One cannot arrive at a station without first passing through and perfecting the one before. Each station is gained by guarding oneself from things that stand in the way of spiritual progress at that station.

> ***Taqwa* can be from:**
> **2.2.1 disbelief** *which is the station of* **Submission** *(al-Islam)*
> **2.2.2 the forbidden** *which is the station of* **Repentance** *(al-Tawba)*
> **2.2.3 doubtful matters** *which is the station of* **Scrupulousness** *(al-Wara')*
> **2.2.4 extraneous matters** *which is the station of* **Doing without** *(al-Zuhd)*
> **2.2.5 'other than God' occupying the heart** *which is the station of* **Vigilance** *(al-Muraqabah)*
> [Ibn Juzay, Tasfiyyah al-Qulub, pg 76]

3. *Taqwa* and preserving the seven organs of the body from wrong action

The human body is one of the greatest blessings that one is given by God. Through it, one is able to understand, make use of, and interact with the world around us. It is a trust from God and should be treated as such. Therefore, committing wrong actions using the bodily organs has been described as the height of ungratefulness and transgression.

> *'Know that you only manage to commit wrong actions through limbs of your body which are a blessing with which God has honoured you and which are a trust in your possession. That you use a blessing of God to disobey Him is the height of ungratefulness (kufran). Your treachery with regard to a trust left in your safekeeping is also the height of transgression (tughyan)."* [Al-Ghazzali, Bidayat al-Hidayah, pg 59]

Imam al-Ghazali goes on to single out seven limbs of the body when he speaks about cultivating *taqwa* and in doing so, he underlines the important role they play in the development of diseases of the heart. They are important as they have been observed by spiritual masters to influence the health of the spiritual heart and the manner by which they influence the heart, is through the actions they perform.

The manner of minimizing their negative influence and rectifying the limbs, is by gradually weaning oneself from wrong actions and then performing good actions, which will in turn further help in rectifying the limbs.

> *'Therefore, Oh pitiful one! Preserve the whole of your body from wrong actions, specifically your seven limbs, since Hellfire "...**has seven doors, each of which has an allotted place" [15:44]** and none is assigned to these seven doors except one that disobeys God with these seven limbs of the body. They are: the eyes, ears, tongue, stomach, private parts, hands and feet.'* [al-Ghazali, Bidayat al-Hidayah, pg 60]

3.1 The rectification of the heart and limbs.

Using the body for actions that please God is a means of pursuing *taqwa*. Both the heart and limbs are rectified by two simple processes. The first is by removing the indiscretion of both the heart and limbs. The second is that one should seek to acquire praiseworthy qualities related to the heart and limbs. The scholars of the heart also teach that leaving negative traits comes before the acquisition of praiseworthy ones.

3.1.1 The rectification of the limbs is through two acts: *Leaving wrong actions (ijtinab) and performing good actions (imtithal)*

3.1.2 The rectification of the heart is through two acts: *Divesting oneself of blameworthy qualities (takhali) and acquiring praiseworthy qualities (tahali)* [Ibn 'Ajiba, Sharh al-Hikam, pg11]

4. The ears, eyes and the heart

> *"Has man ever known a moment in time when he was something unworthy of mention? We created man from a single mingled drop to test him and We created him hearing and seeing."* *[76:1-2]*

The ears and eyes play a pivotal role in achieving *taqwa*. Developmentally, the hearing is the first faculty from which one gathers information about one's environment, after which sight engages with the surroundings. It is only after this that one's intellect seeks to make sense of what is perceived. Both hearing and sight are constantly referred to in the Qur'an as a blessing from God. As they are the first port of call with the outside world, it is only natural that these two senses are the quickest in affecting the spiritual health of the heart through the temptations of the *dunyah*, or worldly life.

> *"And God brought you out of your mother's wombs while you knew nothing, and He gave you hearing, sight and hearts, that you may give thanks."* *[16:78]*

> *"And follow not that which you have no knowledge of. Verily, the hearing, sight and heart (fu'ad) each of these will be questioned."* *[17:36]*

4.1 The ears

> *"...And so We sealed their ears in the Cave for a number of years."* *[18:11]*

In the story of the *'Seven Sleepers'* related in the Qur'an, God mentions that He sealed their ears (and not their eyes) and that they are made to fall asleep in a cave, only to be awakened after a long passage of time.

The commentator Ibn Atiyyah said that the ears are mentioned in the Qur'an specifically as they are the one faculty by which one's sleep is usually disrupted, and so God numbed their faculty of hearing so that they could remain unaware of their surroundings *[Tafsir al-Muharir al-Wajiz]*.

Hearing is multidirectional, unlike sight, therefore it goes without saying that protecting one's hearing from transgression is more difficult that preserving one's sight.

4.1.1 Plan of action to protect one's hearing

> *'and when they pass by worthless talk, they pass with dignity and when they are reminded of the signs of their Lord they do not turn their backs, deaf and blind to them'* *[25:72]*

> *It is related that Ibn Mas'ud passed by an assembly of people engaged in vain talk and walked passed and ignored them. The next day the Prophet ﷺ praised him saying 'Ibn Mas'ud has spent his whole day, morning and evening, dignified.' [Tafsir ibn Kathir, verse 25:72]*

The cure for the wrong actions of the ears is simple yet difficult to implement. It entails what has been mentioned previously, namely leaving wrong actions *(ijtinab)* associated with the ears. The importance of doing so can not be overstated, since many a time one's laxity in this regard may leads to baseless ill-thoughts or suspicions becoming intrenched in the heart. Imam Malik once said *'Do not lend your ear to someone whose heart is deviant, as you know not to which your [own] heart will become attached to'.*

Protection of one's hearing is closely related to the wrong actions of the tongue, which will be looked at in the next lesson. The protection of one's heart and its spiritual wellbeing is largely dependent on how cautious one is to not listen to the wrong action emanating from other's speech *'...and so be careful not to listen to innovation, back-biting, foul language, delving into falsehood or mentioning the bad qualities of other people...' [al-Ghazali, Bidayah al-Hidayah, pg 60]*

4.2 The eyes

> *"The capacity of sight is one of the doors to the heart, indeed the most destructive pathways to it [pg17]... Sins related to sight are amongst those that are erased by good actions since the sacred law (Shar') has not deemed it a major wrong action (kabirah) since the hadith of Abu Hurayrah states that the expiation of this happens by means of wudu': 'When a believing (mu'min) or submitting (muslim) servant makes wudu' and washes his face, every wrong action he has committed with his eye is removed with the water, or the drops of water' [Muslim]." [Abu al-Hasan ibn al-Qattan al-Fasi said: Kitab al-nazar fi ahkam al-nazar pg35]*

The eyes are one's gateway to the world outside, and are a means by which one observes the wonders of creation which leads to a re-affirmation of our natural *fitrah,* state of belief in the Divine. They are also an access point of the lower qualities of the world (*dunyah*) - described as *'sweet and luscious'* by the Prophet ﷺ on account of which he ﷺ advised us to have *taqwa* with regards to the world. [*al-Bukhari*]

As with the ears and the faculty of hearing, the Qur'an gives clear advice as to the best means of protecting the eyes from indiscretion and wrong action. It puts the emphasis on the one looking to guard their sight in case the heart is affected by what it sees and there are clear spiritual benefits related to protecting one's sight from *haram*.

In an age of rampant commercialisation of all aspects of human life, both public and private, the visual qualities of things are constantly being altered and augmented to make them even more enticing to one's sight, especially those which both divine law and normative morality would have deemed to be detrimental to one's spiritual health. In such a situation, protecting one's sight from viewing gratuitous violence and sexually explicit content becomes all the more of an imperative.

4.1.2 Plan of action to protect one's eyes

"Tell the believing men to lower their gaze and guard their modesty [...] and tell the believing women to lower their gaze and guard their modesty" [24:30-31]

The Prophet ﷺ said: A glance is the poisoned arrow of the Satan. Whoever lowers their gaze for the sake of God, He will provide in its place a type of faith the sweetness of which they will find in their heart.' [al-Tabarani, Mu'jam al-Kabir, V10 §10,362]

The practice of lowering one's gaze is not simply to look to the ground and constantly avert one's sight from those things that sully one's heart. When done in a way that is indicative of the heightened etiquette of the one that makes it their want to practice it, it becomes a powerful act with deep spiritual and social meaning.

The benefit experienced by lowering one's gaze helps to make protecting one's sight the source of strength and health for the heart. This simple yet profound practice allows one to observe the relationship that exists between good conduct and the health of the spiritual heart. The more it is done, the more benefit one gains.

Did you know?

"The perfection of taqwa lies in the existence of uprightness (al-istiqamah), which is to bring the nafs round to displaying the etiquette of the Qur'an and the Sunna. [...] this cannot be completed without a teacher who gives good counsel or else a pure intentioned companion who points out what is most suitable in rectifying an individual's situation since what is beneficial for some may be detrimental and harmful for others." [Al-Zarruq, al-Qawaid, no:64]

Lesson 4 - Preserving the Tongue & Sincerity

Aim: By the end of this lesson, students will understand the relationship between one's speech and the cultivation of sincerity in one's heart. They will also be able to pinpoint the major ailments of the tongue as well as work towards creating an effective plan of action to combat these ailments.

Objectives: By the end of this lesson students should be able to display the ability to:
1. Outline the relationship that exists between sincerity and the tongue and why an understanding of this is important in the study of *tazkiyyah*.
2. Define what sincerity means when related to belief and actions, as well as pinpoint the opposite of sincerity in both cases.
3. Discuss what the function of the tongue is and what is meant by cultivating sincerity through one's speech.
4. List the major diseases of the tongue as mentioned by Imam al-Ghazali.
5. Discuss whether backbiting and lying are ever permitted?
6. Provide a comprehensive and practical plan of action to deal with the diseases of the tongue.

'The Beneficent, who taught the Qur'an, created the Human, and taught him articulate speech.' [55:1-4]

1. Sincerity and the tongue

'Al-Shafi'i said: 'Only one endowed with sincerity will really grasp the nature of hypocrisy.'

This means that it is impossible to know the reality of hypocrisy and see its subtle shades except by one who resolutely seeks out sincerity. Such a person will strive for a long time - searching, meditating and examining at length within themselves - until eventually they come to know something of what hypocrisy is. However this does not happen for everyone. Rather it only happens for the few. Therefore it is the height of ignorance for any individual to claim that they have come to know what hypocrisy is.' [Al-Nawawi, Bustan al-'Arifin, p.53]

One of the most important tasks in purifying the heart is to cultivate true sincerity in one's belief and actions. *Ikhlas*, or sincerity, is checking and rectifying one's intention to the point that whatever we believe or do corresponds to what our intention is. It is to remain true to God and focused on why we do what we do. God says **"They were only commanded to worship God sincerely with the religion solely for Him" [98:5]**

The tongue has an important role to play in this search for *Ikhlas* as it is the limb that testifies and provides evidence of what is in the heart. If one's speech corresponds to what is in the heart, it indicates one's sincerity, and if not, then one stands accused of hypocrisy: saying other than what the heart contains.

The Prophet ﷺ said: 'The first of people judged on the Day of Resurrection will be a man who was martyred, who is then brought into the Divine presence and will be mentioned by his blessings which he will acknowledge and it will be asked of him: 'Why did you fight?' He will reply: 'I fought for your sake and was martyred'. God, the Exalted, will say: 'You lie! You fought so that it could be said about you that you are a courageous man, and thus it was said'. He will then be ordered to be taken to the Fire. Then someone who has studied the Qur'an and taught it will be brought to the Divine presence and shown his blessings and he will acknowledge them. When he is asked what he did with them he will respond: 'I studied knowledge and transmitted it and I recited the Qur'an for your sake. It is said to him 'You lie! Rather you did so that it be said about you: 'You are learned' and so it was said'. He is then ordered to be taken to the Fire and dragged along his face and thrust into it.' [Muslim, 4923]

1.1 Cultivating sincerity through the tongue

'It is related that one day the master of Luqman the wise ordered him to slaughter a sheep and to bring him the two best parts of it afterwards. Luqman brought forth the animal's heart and the tongue. The master, expecting a better cut of meat, became annoyed and sent him back saying "If this is the best then what is the worst?"
Luqman left and came back after a while, returning again with the heart and tongue. Luqman said to his master, 'This is the heart and tongue. If they are pure then they are the best parts of the body but if not, they are the worst part of the body.' [Tafsir al-Qurtubi, 14:62]

Is it possible to achieve sincerity of the heart through our limbs? If so, then which part of the body is instrumental in helping us achieve that?

We know that the way we act and behave has an effect on our faith. Listening to the Qur'an leaves the believer with a sense of tranquility and stillness. Being lazy and lax in performing one's prayers is also seen to have a detrimental effect on one's *Iman*. From looking at the religious sources one can observe that there is a clear link between the health of the heart and the actions of our tongues. Our speech gives an immediate insight into the health of our heart and so observing ourselves and how we speak is a good way of assessing how much work we need to do to tackle our spiritual diseases. Ultimately, the purpose of speech is to communicate ideas, to converse and exhort people to good and one should keep in mind this when speaking.

> *'As for the tongue, it has been created for you so you make profuse remembrance of God, recite His Book, guide people by [your speech] to His path and give expression to what is in yourself in terms of needs, both religious and worldly.' [Al-Ghazali, Bidayah al-Hidayah, p238]*

2. The Diseases of the Tongue

> *Abd al-Rahman ibn Sakhr related that the Prophet ﷺ said: 'A person utters words, the consequence of which he gives no thought to, for which he will fall through the fire of Hell for a period of seventy years.' [al-Tirmidhi, 2314]*

Imam Al-Ghazali mentions 20 diseases related to the tongue in his book *'Ihya 'Ulum ad-Din'*. In his work *'The Beginning of Guidance'*, he summarises these to 8 diseases: lying; breaking one's promise; backbiting; argumentation; talking oneself up; cursing other people; praying against mankind; jest and mockery.

> *"...If you use [the tongue] for a task other than what it was created for then you have indeed been ungrateful to God for the blessing therein. It is the most potent limb working against you and against the rest of mankind since '....nothing leads mankind to the fire on their faces except for the harvest of their own tongues' [...]*

Therefore, protect your tongue from 8 traits:

2.1 *Lying:* *Protect your tongue from this in both seriousness and jest. Don't habituate your tongue to lying in jest lest it leads you to lying in seriousness since lying is the mother of all great wrong actions. If you become known by this, your uprightness will cease to exist as will the trustworthiness of your speech and people will belittle you and judge you as nothing [...]*

2.2 *Not keeping one's promises:* *Beware of promising something and not living up to it. It is rather more befitting that your beneficence to mankind be expressed through your actions and not your words [...]. The Prophet ﷺ said: 'There are three attributes, whoever has them is a hypocrite even if he fasts and prays. When he speaks he lies; when he promises he breaks his promise and when he is given a trust he betrays it.' [Ahmed, 10938]*

2.3 *Protecting the tongue from backbiting:* *This is when you mention a person in a way that they would hate if they were to hear you. If you are not truthful in what you say then you are an unjust slanderer. The Prophet ﷺ said: 'If what you have said exists in that person then you have backbitten him and if it doesn't then you have slandered him.' [Muslim, 2789]*

2.4 *Argumentation and debating.*

2.5 *Talking up one's own self:* *'And do not talk yourselves up as He is more aware of whoever has taqwah.' [Quran 53:32]*

2.6 *Cursing.*

2.7 *Praying against people.*

2.8 *Jesting, mockery and belittling people.*

... So these are the sources of the diseases of the tongue. Nothing can help you in combatting these apart from solitude and holding to silence, except in what is necessary.' [Al-Ghazali Bidayah al-Hidayah, 238-261]

3. Exceptions to the wrong actions of the Tongue

3.1 Is it always forbidden to lie or relay fiction?

> *Humaid b. 'Abd al-Rahman b. 'Auf reported that his mother Umm Kulthum bint 'Uqba, one of the first emigrants who pledged allegiance to God's Apostle ☒ , said that she heard him ☒ say 'A liar is not one who tries to bring reconciliation amongst people, stating what is good, or conveys good'.*

> *Ibn Shihab [al-Zuhri] said that he did not hear that exemption was granted in anything of what the people speak as a 'lie' but in three cases: in battle; bringing reconciliation between people; words of the husband to his wife and the words of a wife to her husband. [Muslim, 6633]*

Scholars differ as to what this permission means. Some have taken this literally, stating that if there is an overwhelming benefit in relaying an untruth it then becomes permitted. They gathered support for this from the fact that there is no disagreement as to the permissibility of saving someone's life by such means.

Others, amongst them [Muhibb al-Din] al-Tabari, state that lying is not allowed at all, though it is permitted to be *'disingenuous with the truth'* (al-tawriyyah), which is making it appear as if one is saying one thing while in fact intending another. So for example if a person wanted to reconcile between two parties they would convey only the good from the other's speech, leaving out that which is negative and likewise when conveying the response. *[See al-Nawawi, Sharh Sahih Muslim]*

3.2 Is backbiting ever permitted?

It is permitted, and sometimes an obligation, to convey information about someone which they may not like to be known with the condition that there is a well-defined wider benefit in doing so. Otherwise it is *haram*.

> *"One should be aware that 'backbiting' is permitted if there is a legitimate shar'iah aim behind it which can only be attained by such means as in the case of seeking redress for oppression [...]; seeking others' aid in changing what is unanimously considered evil [...]; seeking a fatwa where one says: 'Such and such has harmed in such a way. Is he permitted to do so...'; and warning others to be wary of someone (al-tahdhir), which has various permutations." [al-Khalawi, al-Durrar al-Mubaha fi al-Hadhr wal-Ibaha, pg185-6]*

4. Plan of action

4.1 Solitude and holding to silence.

This should be done in balance and in proportion to the problem one is seeking to rectify. Imam al-Qushayri said *'Silence at the proper time is the attribute of men, just as speech at the proper time is one of the noblest of qualities.'*

> *It is related of Abu Bakr as-Siddiq that he used to place small pebbles in his mouth so as to prevent himself from speaking unnecessarily. He used to point to his tongue and say: 'This is the thing which has so often brought me close to destruction.' [Al-Ghazali, Bidayah al-Hidayah, 261]*

4.2 Committing oneself to a regime of leaving the diseases of the tongue.

One can do this by cultivating a habit of good speech and reflecting before speaking, and penalising oneself for falling short.

> *Hasan Al Basri said: 'The tongue of the believer lies behind his heart. When he intends to speak he reflects over it with his heart and only then does he go ahead to say it with his tongue. The tongue of the hypocrite lies in front of his heart. If he wants to say something he just says it without reflecting over it with his heart.' [al-Zabidi, Ithaf as-Sadat al-Muttaqin v9: pg140]*

4.3 Being vigilant of one's words.

Taking oneself to task at the end of the day for one's words.

> *'It is said that Rabiah ibn Khuthaym did not speak on anything regarding the world for twenty years. When he used to wake in the morning he used to put aside ink, paper and a pen and*

later write down everything he uttered to take himself for account of it in the evening before he slept'. [al-Zabidi, Ithaf as-Sadat al-Muttaqin v9: pg 145]

5. Prophetic gems regarding the tongue

The Prophet ﷺ said: *'When the son of Adam awakes in the morning, all of his limbs speak to the tongue [as if to say]: 'Fear God in regard to us for indeed if you are upright we will be upright and if you are astray we will fall astray.'* [Al-Tirmidhi, 2407]

The Prophet ﷺ said: *'Do not talk excessively without remembering God, because such excessive talk without the mention of God causes the heart to harden and the furthest person from God is a person with a hard heart.'* [Al-Tirmidhi, 2411]

The Prophet ﷺ said: *'The faith of a servant is not put right until his heart is put right, and his heart is not put right until his tongue is put right.'* [Ahmed, v3 pg197]

Did you know?

Excessive speech leads to negative results that are not restricted to this world. Once it becomes a habit, one loses sight of consequences of such an action and gives little regard to what awaits one on the other side.

Abu Talib al-Makki said:

'Excessive speech points to a lack of scrupulousness (wara'), a lack of taqwa, a lengthy calling to account (hisab), the unrolling of the scroll, a great number of claimants that connect the person wronged to the perpetrator [of injustice], a lengthy testimony from the noble scribes [and not least] a constant turning away from the Noble King. [This is because] words are a key for the major sins of the tongue: lying, slander, backbiting, and false testimony. [Ibn 'Ajiba, Sharh al-Hikam]

Lesson 5 - Breaking the Two Desires

Aim: By the end of this lesson, students will understand what are referred to as the *'Two Desires'* and what role they play in determining the health of the heart. It will look at the importance of the stomach in achieving spiritual health. The benefits of hunger as well as the practical steps that should be taken to combat gluttony will also be outlined. Finally it will relate gluttony to the wrong actions of the private parts.

Objectives: By the end of this lesson, students should be able to display the ability to:
1. Discuss what gluttony is, its importance and what organ it relates to.
2. Explain what the spiritual effects of gluttony are.
3. List and discuss the main benefits of hunger as a means of combatting gluttony.
4. Outline a plan of action that can aid in combating gluttony.
5. Discuss the importance of avoiding excess food and drink.
6. Explain how fasting can be used to create a habit for curing gluttony
7. Outline the importance of consuming halal and its relationship with gluttony.
8. Discuss the relationship between gluttony and preserving the private parts from wrong action.
9. Mention the two reasons why humans have been endowed with sexual desire.
10. Discuss the importance of protecting one's private parts in promoting spiritual health.

1. The Stomach and the *'The Two Desires'*

When God created Adam (A.S.), Iblis circled around him observing his form, and when he saw Adam's (A.S.) capacity to consume, he said: 'He has been created in a way that he will not be able to control himself.' [Ahmed, 12561]

'Fudayl ibn 'Iyad said: 'The Shaytan said: 'If I win over the son of Adam with one of four things I will not seek anything else from him: eating too much; being arrogant; considering one's actions to be substantial and forgetting one's wrong actions.' [Al-'Ujhuri, Fada'il Shahr Ramadan, p155]

The desire to eat and drink is a human need that aids one in gaining strength to perform acts of good. It is also essential in sustaining one's body, which is a trust from God. Excess in this regard leads to gluttony, which in turn affects the rest of the body, particularly the desires of the private parts. These two appetites of the stomach and the private parts are referred to by al-Ghazali as *'The Two Desires'*.

Controlling them has been seen as essential in all ethical traditions for curing the heart of its spiritual ills. Reducing the consumption of food and drink is one of the simplest, yet important, ways by which to aid in increasing the spiritual health of the heart. On the other hand, neglect of this aspect of one's life is said by scholars of this science to lead to hard-heartedness. Research has shown that is true as much of the physical heart as it is of the spiritual.

2. Al-Ghazali on the benefits of hunger

Reflecting over the spiritual and temporal benefits of controlling one's consumption of food and drink is one of the most effective ways by which to move towards rectifying any excess in this regard. Imam Al-Ghazali speaks of these as follows:

'We say, then, that hunger has ten benefits:

2.1 Purification of the heart and the awakening of intuition, as well as the focusing of one's spiritual perception since satiation causes dullness and blinds the heart [...]. Abu Sulayman al-Darani said: 'Indulge in hunger because it humbles the nafs, renders the heart tender, and allows one to inherit heavenly knowledge.'

2.2 Tenderness and purity of heart, which prepares it to attain the delight of contemplation and the impact of dhikr [...].

2.3 Submission, abasement, the elimination of ungodliness, and what is more evil, namely oppressiveness and obliviousness of God Almighty [...]. The Prophet ﷺ *said: 'No, I would rather hunger a day and be filled a day; for if I were to hunger, I would become patient and humble. Were I to be filled, I would be grateful.' [al-Tirmidhi]*

       71

2.4 Not forgetting the trials and torments from God on those that are afflicted by them. *He who is satiated is oblivious of the one who hungers, and of hunger itself. The mindful servant does not see the affliction in others without remembering the afflictions of the Hereafter. He becomes mindful through his own thirsting of the thirsting of created beings in the wide plains of The Resurrection [...].*

2.5 One of the greatest of all is in curbing the lusts of all defiances *and to thereby take charge of the nafs that commands to evil (al-nafs al-ammarah bil su'u). The source of all defiances are one's lusts which are fuelled by food in each instance: curbing them weakens every desire and urge. Happiness lies in one taking charge of one's self, and misery is in the nafs taking possession of the person. Just as a beast of burden can only be controlled when weakened by hunger, so too the nafs. Should it be fed to fill, it gains strength, becomes uncontrollable and runs away [...].*

'Aishah said: 'The first innovation after [the passing away of] the Messenger ﷺ was satiation. When the bellies were filled, their self (nafs) propelled them into the world.' [...]

2.6 Warding off sleep and maintaining continuous wakefulness.

2.7 Facilitating continuous worship.

2.8 Soundness of the body as a result of little food. *It is achieved by eating less and warding off sicknesses caused by excessive food intake. [...] A wise doctor once condemned overeating saying: 'The most beneficial thing a person can consume is the pomegranate, while the most damaging is salt [23]. I prefer that one decrease one's consumption of salt rather than increase in the consumption of pomegranate.'*

2.9 Lessening one's financial outgoings. *[...] A person habituated to eating his fill will find that his belly will become like a creditor [in pursuit of him] who it is impossible to shake off, seizing him by the throat each day, saying: 'What will you feed me today?'*

2.10 The tenth benefit is in being responsive and generous, *giving food to orphans and to the poor from any surplus that he has so that on the Day of Resurrection he dwell in the shade of his own charity as mentioned in narrations.' [Summarised from Al-Ghazali, Ihya Ulum al-Din, V5- pg 301-318]*

3. Plan of action

The path towards curing gluttony is to slowly wean and reduce one's overconsumption of food and drink. In a society where there is a massive industry created to make us consume more than we need to, this is not a simple task. The process is slow and needs to be carried out over a sustained period of time, creating a habit which the body will then become accustomed to. This process - related to disciplining the *nafs* - has been compared to the weaning of a baby from reliance on breast milk to eventually consuming solids. It may be slow but is necessary for the long-term health of the child. As al-Busiri says in his poem *al-Burdah:*

> *'And the nafs is like a child, if neglected grows being*
> *accustomed to breast-feeding yet if you wean it, it is weaned'*

3.1 Avoiding excess. One should attempt to eat enough to fulfill the right of one's body.

"...and eat and drink but not to excess, surely God loves not the excessive" [7:31]

Ibn Ma'di-Karib relates: 'I heard the Messenger of God ﷺ saying: 'No human ever filled a vessel worse than the stomach. Sufficient for a son of Adam are some morsels to keep his back straight. If it must be, then let one-third be for food, one-third for drink and one-third to aid breathing.' [Ahmad]

'Aishah, referring to the austere lifestyle lead by the Messenger of God ﷺ and his family, said: 'We, the family of Muhammed, used to live through a whole month without lighting a fire. It was just dates and water.'

---

[23] *'As it inflames the blood, weakens the eyesight and harms the brain and lungs'. [al-Zabidi, Ithaf as-Sadat al-Muttaqin v7: pg 400. Quoted by Winters, Al-Ghazali on Disciplining the Soul, pg 128]*

> *'It is related of Hasan al-Basri that he offered some food to a companion of his who then said to him: 'I have eaten until I am no longer able to eat.' To which Hasan exclaimed: 'Subhan Allah! Does a Muslim eat until he is no longer able to eat?'*

3.2 A regime of regular fasting.

Fasting is the easiest way of controlling one's consumption of food and drink and there are many times during the whole year that it is recommended to fast. There are monthly and weekly fasts that can help us create good habits in this regard.

> *Ibn Milhan al-Qaysi related from his father that he said: 'The Messenger of God ﷺ used to instruct us to fast the days of the full moon: the thirteenth, fourteenth and fifteenth. He ﷺ said: 'They are equivalent to fasting the year.' [al-Nisai, 2419]*

> *When he ﷺ was asked about fasting on Monday, God's Messenger ﷺ said: 'On this day, I was born, given prophethood, and revelation first came to me.' [Muslim]*

> *Abu Hurayrah related that God's Messenger ﷺ said: 'Deeds are presented on Mondays and Thursdays, so I like that my deeds be presented while I am fasting.' [al-Tirmidhi, 747]*

3.3 Eating what is halal and wholesome.

> **"Believers! Eat of the pure that We have provided for you" [2:172]**

This means that one should be careful that one's *rizq* and sustenance is sought from only pure and permitted means. This is not always easy to determine in the modern age, where one's job and profession entails carrying out many different roles. One should always consult a trusted and well-versed scholar who understands both the sacred law and the complexities of the modern workplace for advice on such matters.

> **"O Messengers! Eat of the pure things and do righteous deeds" [23:51]**

> *Ibn Abbas commented on this verse saying: '[God] commanded them to perform righteous actions after commanding them to consume pure food as a reminder that one does not gain any benefit from one's actions until one has rectified one's livelihood and provisions"* [24]

4. Guarding the private parts

> **"...and those that protect their private parts" [23:5]**
> **"...and do not approach fornication, for it is foul and leads to a foul path" [17:32]**

The organs most closely related to the stomach are the private parts, and sexual desire has a strong link with the overconsumption of food and drink. They are so closely related that Imam al-Ghazali discusses them in the same section of his monumental book *'al-Ihya'*. The treatment of excess regarding sexual desire is mostly related to what is *haram*. This entails freeing oneself of all vices related to the private parts which are stated to be prohibited in the sacred law and are amongst the major wrong actions (*kaba'ir*), namely adultery and fornication. Masturbation is also included in the list of *haram* acts related to the private parts as it is deemed to be unseemly to human nature. Hence protecting the private parts of *haram* is one of the paths towards subduing the *nafs*.

> *The Prophet ﷺ said: 'Whoever guards for me his tongue and private parts, I guarantee him a place in the Garden.' [al-Bukhari, 6474]*

The wholesome alternative of marriage is encouraged as a means of fulfilling one's desires. Indeed, enjoying one's spouse sexually has been described by the Prophet ﷺ as an act of charity. Though there are undoubted vices associated with sexual desire, it has been placed in the human for two vital benefits:

> *"Know that it has been placed in humanity for two benefits. One of them is to allow humans to experience its pleasures and measure thereby the pleasures of the Hereafter [...] The second benefit is perpetuating one's offspring ..." [Al-Ghazali, Ihya, v9,89]*

---

[24] See Finance Module Rzq 502, Lesson 1

4.1 Protecting one's chastity and Divine mercy

'The Prophet ﷺ said: 'Seven people will be in the Divine shade on a Day when there will be no shade save His shade [...] a person that is called by a women of standing and beauty and he says "I fear God..." [al-Bukhari, 1423]

"It is related that Sulayman ibn Yassar, accompanied by a companion, left Medina intending to perform the Pilgrimage. When they arrived at al-Abwa', his companion left for the market to buy something, taking with him the mat of leather on which they used to eat.

Sulayman remained seated in the tent. Since his face was unusually handsome, he had been noticed by a bedouin woman who was on a nearby hill who now descended and went to him. When she saw the beauty of his face she drew closer until she stood before him wearing a veil and gloves. She unveiled her face, and it was like a piece of the moon. 'Satisfy me!' she said.
He thought that she was referring to food, so he picked up some leftovers and gave them to her. 'I don't want that,' she said. 'I want what a man gives to his wife.' 'Satan has sent you to me!' he exclaimed, and then, setting his head between his knees, began to sob and weep without interruption. Beholding this sight, she drew on her veil once more and went away to her family.

His companion returned, and, upon seeing that his eyes were swollen from tears and that his voice was subdued, asked what had made him weep. 'Something good,' he told him. 'I remembered my children'. 'No, by God,' his companion said. 'You have some tale to tell. You were with your children only three days ago or thereabouts'. He persisted in questioning him until he had heard about the bedouin woman.

He thereupon put down the leather mat and started to weep bitterly. Sulayman asked him: 'Why are you weeping?' He replied, 'It is more appropriate that I weep than you. I fear that had I been in your place I may not have refused her!' And then they wept together for a long time.' [Al-Ghazali, Ihya Ulum al-Din, V5- pg 301-318]

Lesson 6 - Preserving the hands and feet

> **Aim:** By the end of this lesson, students will understand the function of the two most distant bodily limbs that effect spiritual health: the hands and feet. The effect of wrong actions by the seven limbs will be outlined so that necessary habits can be created to remedy any imbalances. Students will also come to understand the importance of bringing about a change in the way that spiritual issues are viewed and what needs to be done for spiritual progress to be achieved successfully.
>
> **Objectives:** By the end of this lesson, students should be able to display the ability to:
> 1. Outline the relationship between the spiritual heart and the various organs of the body.
> 2. Outline the function of the hands and mention the main wrong actions related to them.
> 3. Outline the function of the feet and mention the main wrong actions related to them.
> 4. Mention what Shaykh al-Zarruq says are the foundations of treating the ailments of the soul.
> 5. Explain why it is important to be balanced and realistic about bringing change to oneself.
> 6. Relate the concept of *Tawbah* (repentance) to the science of *tazkiyyah*, outlining the conditions of successful *Tawbah* with reference to *'the three R's of Tawba'*.

1. The Heart and the Limbs

In the previous lessons, we looked at what the subject matter of *tazkiyyah* is, the nature of the human heart and its connection to the limbs. It is known that from one perspective it is the heart that controls the actions of the rest of the body. As the Prophet ﷺ said:

> *'..Indeed there is in the human body a morsel of flesh that if it is healthy the body is healthy and if it is corrupt the body is corrupt. Surely it is the heart.' [al-Bukhari, 52]*

However the spiritual masters of the Islamic tradition also point out that wrong actions of the outer limbs can, and do, have an effect on the spiritual health of the heart. As wrong actions are committed, the heart is negatively affected and will fall into a spiral of spiritual decay, unless steps are taken to rectify one's actions.

In this section from his *'Epistle to the Seekers of Guidance'*, Imam al-Muhasibi, shares his reflections on the human condition, and how the excesses of the limbs impact on the human heart.

> *'I looked and saw that the basis of transgression that emanates from the heart comes from the hearing, sight, speech, appetite, clothing and place of residence.*
> *Excess with regard to hearing leads to forgetfulness and heedlessness;*
> *Excess with regard to sight leads to heedlessness and confusion;*
> *Excess with regard to the tongue leads to pretension in speech and heresy;*
> *Excess with regard to food leads to greed and desire;*
> *Excess with regard to clothing leads to boasting and haughtiness;*
> *Excess with regard to habitation lead to extravagance and pride.*
> *You should know that safeguarding the limbs is a duty, just as abstaining from excess is a virtue.' [al-Muhasibi, Risalah al-Mustarshidin, pg 254]*

2. Guarding the hands

> *'Aishah said: 'I never saw the Messenger of God ﷺ take revenge when wronged at any time as long as it was not something held sacred by the God. He ﷺ never struck anything with his hand except when fighting for the cause of God and he ﷺ never struck a servant or a woman.' [Muslim]*

One's hands can be the means by which we offer aid to others with charity and are used in the fight against injustice and tyranny. They can also be the organs used to harm others, spread insurrection, war and insecurity. Preserving the hands from injustice is described by the Messenger ﷺ as the basic sign of a Muslim.

> The Prophet ﷺ said: *'The Muslim is the one from whose tongue and hand other Muslims are safe, and the muhajir is the one that leaves that which God has forbidden.' [al-Bukhari, 10]*

2.1 Plan of action for preserving the hands from injustice.

> *'Be careful to protect [the hands] from striking anyone; handling wealth that is unlawful; harming any of God's creation; misappropriating a trust (amanah) or something you have*

that belongs to another (wadia'ah) or even writing with your hands something that it is not permitted for you to utter as the pen is considered as one of the two 'tongues'. Preserve your pen as you would your tongue. As Dhu Nun al-Misri wrote:

> *'There is none that sets pen to paper except that*
> *time will keep and preserve what his hands set down*
>
> *So be wary of allowing your hands to write anything save*
> *that which, on the Day of Rising, you would be pleased to set eyes on'* [25]

3. Guarding the feet

'Have they not travelled on the earth so as to gain hearts by which they understand and ears with which to hear? It is not the eyes that are afflicted by blindness but rather the hearts that dwell in the breasts of Man.' [22:46]

Abu Sa'id al-Khudri relates that the Prophet ﷺ said: From amongst the Tribe of Israel there was a man who had murdered ninety-nine people. He then set out asking [on the possibility of repentance]. He came upon a monk and asked him if he had any possibility of performing repentance. He replied: 'No' and so the man killed him. [Yet] he continued to enquire until a man of knowledge advised him to go to such and such village. However he died on his way there and [fell with] his chest facing towards that village.

The angels of mercy and the angels of punishment quarrelled amongst themselves [on his fate]. God ordered the village [to which he was going] to come closer, and ordered the village [from which he had left] to become distant. He then ordered them to measure the distances between his body and the two villages and he was found to be one span closer to the village [to which he was going] and so was forgiven.' [al-Bukhari, 3470]

The feet are the means by which we sojourn on the earth and are therefore a blessing from God. They are also essential in travelling and moving towards acts of good. They therefore provide evidence of our innermost motives and intentions and upon this we will be judged. On the other hand, they are also the means by which we may approach the *haram* and frequent places that are hated by God. It is because of this that our feet will be called to give testimony against us on the Day of Judgement. *'Today We will set a seal on their mouths, and so their hands speak to Us, and their feet bear witness as to what they have earned.' [Qur'an, 36:65]*

3.1 Plan of action for preserving the feet from wrong actions

'As for one's feet, prevent them from going to that which is haram or to seek out the door of a tyrannical ruler, since going to oppressive leaders without any overriding need is a major wrong action since it is a show of humility towards them as well as [a sign] of rewarding them upon their oppressive actions. God has ordered that one shun them 'And incline not towards the oppressors, such that the Fire touches you.' [11:113] It is also a means by which their numbers are shown to be great (takthir li-sawadihim).' [Bidayat ul-Hidayah, pg 271-2]

The Prophet ﷺ said to Ka'b ibn 'Urjah: 'O Ka'b may God protect you from frequenting the rulers who will come to rule after my time. Those who seek favours at their doors, believe in their lies, and support them in their tyranny are not of us, and I am not of them. I will not intercede for them on Judgement Day. However those who may pass through their doors yet do not believe in their lies or support them in their tyranny are from us, and I am from them. I will intercede for them and quench their thirst on Judgement Day, serving water to them from my fountain.' [al-Tirmidhi]

4. Spiritual awakening and change

The most important step in the path to spiritual purification is the first. A sound and proper intention is already assured, as a person who has realised the need for ridding the *nafs* of negative qualities and characteristics will only have done so after much self-reflection. Changing one's condition means realising that change is needed, and then to awaken to the task ahead. At the core of the task ahead is removing headlessness (*ghaflah*) of God from one's heart, since it is seen by many scholars as the precipitating source of all other internal failing of the *nafs* such as vanity, anger and pride. It is this which will be the subject of the second module on *'Towards a Tranquil soul.'*

---

[25] *al-Jawi, Maraqi al-Ubudiyyah Sharh Bidayat ul-Hidayah, pg 271*

'The first rank on the journey of servitude (ubudiyah) is awakening, which is alarming and stirring up of the heart from the sleep of heedlessness (ghaflah). By God, how priceless is that revitalising alarm! How valuable and indispensable for the journey!

Whoever experiences it has indeed experienced the breeze of success. Without experiencing it, everyone is lost in heedlessness (ghaflah). His hearing is asleep while his eyes appear awake. It is this blessed alarm that wakes one up and makes him a seeker of God. The seeker now rolls up his sleeves and musters up courage to set out on the journey to God, station by station.' [Ibn Qayyim al-Jawziyyah, Madraj as-Salikin, V1 [4] pg 240]

4.1 Importance of gradual change

The Prophet ﷺ said: 'The most beloved act to God is one that a person does consistently even if it is small.' [Muslim, 2723]

Cultivating good habits and leaving wrong actions can take time to habituate oneself to, so it is important to persevere with corrective measures. The time required to rid oneself of bad habits varies from person to person and it is never possible to completely free oneself of wrong action. One should also take a graded and balanced approach to rectifying one's conduct and focus first on eliminating what is clearly *haram*, and once addressed one should move on to that which is disapproved of.

'Training the nafs by doing and leaving things in a gradual manner is the most efficient way of achieving the desired disciplining [of the nafs]. This is why it is said: 'Leaving wrong actions is easier than seeking (true) repentance'. One who leaves a prohibited desire seven times in such a manner that it is resisted every time it reappears will never again be tested [by God] through it, as God is more generous than to punish a heart due to a desire that has been left for His sake alone.

Hence al-Muhasabi said when describing [the manner of doing] taubah (repentance): 'One should repent in a general way [first] but then follow this up by leaving each [prohibited] thing one at a time. This method will be more stable and enduring for the person.' This is correct. Ultimately it is only God that knows best.' [al-Zarruq, Qawaid at-Tassuwwuf, no.105]

In making a change, it is important that one is realistic and does not fall into the trap of being overzealous by trying to do everything at once. The Prophet ﷺ warned against a person taking on more than they can manage:

'This religion is solid/tough (mat̲in), so deal with it with caution, and do not make the worship of God repulsive to your soul, since one that is over-exuberant will neither cover any distance, nor be left with a mount.' [Musnad Ahmed, v3, pg 197]

4.2 Prerequisite of spiritual change: The three R's of Tawba.

At the heart of spiritual change is the move to repair one's connection to God, done by focusing on sincerely turning towards God in a state of abject need and humility. This is the basic meaning of the Arabic word *Tawba*: *'to turn back to something'*. This, in turn, has conditions which may be referred to as the three R's of *Tawba*: **removing** oneself (*iqlah*) from the prohibited act; **remorse** (*nadm*) over one's previous conduct and lastly **resolve** (*azm*) not to return back to one's former ways[26].

When a person takes it upon themselves to make a change and travel to God, then not only does God help them in doing so, but He also provides them with certitude to pursue spiritual perfection. In the hadith mentioned previously of the man who killed ninety-nine people and who displayed a yearning to make amends, it is noted that he seeks advice from those whom he imagines to have a special connection with God.

On enquiring from a worshipper/monk, he is told in no uncertain terms that there is not, and so the man also kills him. However, he does not give up and enquires from a person given knowledge. He is advised by him to set out for a certain towns-people, where he would find the fulfillment of his need. It happens that the man dies on the way there, but having taken steps to remove himself from wrong, with a feeling of remorse over what came to pass previously and resolving not to fall foul of his previous ways, he is granted the enveloping mercy of God, and the angels who dispute over his fate are told to grant him an abode in paradise.

---

[26] As mentioned by al-Ghazali, this is if it relates to the rights owed exclusively to God. If the wrong action relates to a right owed to creation, such as in the case of usurping another persons wealth, a fourth condition is required: to **return** any rights owed or **rectify** any outstanding issue than can reasonably be discharged.

Understanding the Sunnah

Investigating the preservation, importance and terminology of Prophetic guidance

Module Asl 2.02.D

iSyllabus
islam · iman · ihsan

Lesson One - Hadith: authority and preservation

Lesson One

Aim: In this lesson, students will be introduced to the detailed meanings of the terms hadith and *sunnah* as well as the evidences given for the authority of the prophetic sunnah. Students will also appreciate the factors that aided in preserving the sunnah and the high degree of diligence the Companions displayed in carrying out this task.

Objectives: By the end of this lesson, students should be able to display the ability to:
1. **Define** what is meant by hadith and how the word *sunnah* is used by different sets of scholars.
2. **Provide** examples of hadith which convey words, actions, tacit approval, and description of the Messenger (may God bless and grant him peace) .
3. **Summarise** the main evidences for the authoritativeness of the sunnah, both Qur'anic as well as from the Prophetic norm.
4. **Detail** the main factors that aided the Companions in preserving the Prophetic norm.
5. **Mention** the different stylistic methods used by the Prophet (may God bless and grant him peace) to aid people in preserving his advice.
6. **Provide** an example of the faithfulness by which the Companions transmitted Prophetic hadith.

---

1. Hadith and sunnah: What do they mean?

1.1 The word *hadith.*

While the Arabic word *hadith (pl. ahadith)* is used in a general sense to convey the meaning of *story, message, conversation* and adjectivally to mean *something new*, the word has developed a specific lexical meaning amongst scholars for **'any reports relating to the Messenger** ﷺ **, be they about his words, actions, tacit approval, or else matters relating to the blessed physical or moral characteristics of the Prophet of God** ﷺ **.'**

1.2 The word *sunnah*

The word *sunnah* literally means conduct or a path that is taken, regardless of whether it is praiseworthy or not. An example of this usage in Prophetic hadith is his ﷺ saying: *'Whoever carves out a path (sanna) in Islam that is praiseworthy, he will have the reward of it, and whoever acts upon it after him without it decreasing in reward in any way; and whoever carves out a path (sanna) in Islam that is evil, then upon him will be the sin of it and whoever acts upon it.' [Muslim, 2351]*

1.2.1 The use of the word *sunnah in the different Islamic sciences*

1.2.1.1 The hadith scholars have defined the *sunnah* as being largely synonymous with the word *hadith.* However the word *sunnah* conveys a sense of actual practice and established action as opposed to the word *hadith.* More specifically, the word *sunnah* is used to denote a practice that is still acted upon, whereas what is recorded in a hadith may no longer be acted upon for various reasons.
An example of this is the saying of the Prophet ﷺ : *'Whoever drinks shall be lashed, and if he repeats it four times, shall be killed.' [al-Tirmidhi and Abu Dawud].* Although this is referred to as a hadith, it is not the *sunnah* i.e. the exemplary Prophetic path, as it has, by the consensus of scholars, been annulled. As Imam Nawawi said: *'Consensus indicates that this has been abrogated, even if Ibn Hazm dissented in this regard, as the dissenting voice of the Dhahiriyyah (those that take religious text literally) is of no consequence in this regard.' [al-Suyuti, Tadrib al-Rawi, pg 472]*
1.2.1.2 The scholars of fiqh use the word *sunnah* to refer to any action for which one receives a reward for performing and for which one is not blamed for leaving.
1.2.1.3 The scholars of jurisprudence [*I.e. Islamic Legal theory (usul-al-fiqh)*] use the word *sunnah* as a reference for one of the principal sources of Islamic law, like the Qur'an and Consensus (*'ijma*). They include therein the words, actions and tacit approval of the Prophet ﷺ , but not that of the physical descriptions and character traits of the Prophet ﷺ , as these have no direct bearing in reaching legal rulings.[27]

---

[27] Another word used in this context of Prophetic traditions is *athar*, which means *a report*. The majority of scholars used this as a synonym for *hadith*, though some scholars restrict the word *athar* to refer to the words of the Companions of the Prophet ﷺ . *[See 'Itr, Minhaj an-Naqd, p.28]*

2. Different types of hadith

2.1 Words *(qawl)*: *'Actions are but by intention.' [al-Bukhari]*

2.2 Action *(fi'il)* : The words of 'Aishah regarding the voluntary fast of the Prophet ﷺ : *'He used to fast until we would say: 'He will not break his fast,' and he would break his fast until we would say: 'He will not fast.' [al-Bukhari]*

2.3 Tacit approval *(taqrir)*: The hadith of Ibn Umar in which the Prophet ﷺ said to the Companions: *'Let none of you pray 'Asr until you reach the habitation of Bani Qurayzah.'* Some of the Companions were still travelling at the time of *'Asr* prayer and so some of them prayed *'Asr* before arriving at Bani Qurayzah, while the others waited until they arrived there. When this was mentioned to the Prophet ﷺ , he did not censure or reprimand either party. *[al-Bukhari]*

2.4 A description *(wasf)*: *'The Prophet ﷺ was the most generous of all people and he was the most generous in the month of Ramadan.' [al-Bukhari]*

3. The role and authority of the Prophetic sunnah

The authority of the words and actions of the Prophet ﷺ in the Islamic tradition is something proven through even a cursory reading of primary religious sources. The Qur'an establishes in no uncertain terms the role of the Prophet ﷺ as teacher, leader and spiritual guide for the Muslim community. Therefore the general injunctions contained in the Qur'an are left to be explained by the Prophetic norm. The acts of worship, for example, are nowhere in the Qur'an detailed in the way that the early Muslim community or indeed the present one now performs these acts. It is the sunnah that sheds light on these issues and acts as the most authoritative commentary to the Divine Text.

3.1 The Qur'anic authority for the sunnah

> *'Your Companion is neither astray nor being misled, nor does he utter speech out of (his own) desire. It is no less than a divinely inspired revelation.' [53:2-4]*

> *'No, by your Lord, they shall not believe until they make you judge of what is in dispute between them and find within themselves no dislike of that which you decide, and submit with full conviction.' [4:65]*

The great scholar and jurist Imam al-Shafi'i comments on the latter verse and its emphasis on the authority of the Prophet ﷺ thus:

> *'According to what has reached us - and God knows best - this verse was revealed about a man who disputed with al-Zubayr [ibn Awwam] over a piece of land. The Prophet ﷺ ruled in favour of al-Zubayr. This judgement was thus a sunnah of God's Messenger ﷺ and not a ruling stipulated in the Qur'an. The Qur'an shows – and God knows best – what I have just mentioned. If it had been a judgment based upon the Qur'an, it would have been a ruling stipulated in God's Book, in which case they, in refusing to submit to a ruling in God's Book, would not have been considered to be believers without any difficulty, simply for rejecting the ruling that had been revealed and refusing to submit to it.' [Al-Shafi'i, al-Risalah, p83]*

3.2 The Prophetic authority for the sunnah

> *Abdullah ibn 'Amr said: 'I used to write down everything that I heard from God's Messenger ﷺ intending to memorise it. The Quraysh forbade me saying: 'Do you write everything you hear from God's Messenger ﷺ , knowing that he is a human who speaks sometimes in anger and sometimes when content?' Thereupon I stopped writing. I mentioned this to God's Messenger ﷺ and he said: 'Write! By Him in Whose Hand is my soul! Nothing comes out of this but truth,' and he indicated to his mouth.'*

It is clear from a survey of early traditions that the Prophet ﷺ himself was aware of his role in explaining the Divine revelation to mankind. Numerous hadith, reaching the degree of *mutawatir*, point to the fact that he saw his own sunnah as the second most authoritative source of religious teachings after the Qur'an.

> *Mu'adh ibn Jabal said: 'When God's Messenger ﷺ sent me to Yemen, he said: 'How will you pass judgement if a judgement is asked of you?' I replied: 'I shall pass judgement on the basis of God's Book.' He said: 'What if it is not in God's Book?' I replied: ' Then on the basis of the sunnah of God's Messenger.' He said: 'What if it is not in the sunnah of God's Messenger?' I*

replied: 'Then I will make a personal effort and I will not fall short therein.' Upon this, the Prophet ﷺ slapped my chest and said: 'Praise to God Who has graced the Messenger of God's Messenger with what pleases God's Messenger.' [Abu Dawud & al-Tirmidhi]

Abdullah ibn Rawahah heard the Prophet ﷺ say: "Sit!" Whereupon he sat in the middle of the road. The Prophet ﷺ passed by him and said: "What are you doing?" He replied: 'I heard you say: 'Sit,' so I sat.' The Prophet ﷺ said: 'May God increase you in obedience.' [Abd al-Razzaq, al-Musanaf, 3/211]

4. The preservation of the Prophetic sunnah

The preservation of the words and actions of the Prophet ﷺ went through a number of phases in order for later generations to be able to clearly access the Prophetic guidance.

The most important of these phases was the historical period of his Companions. They have a special status in hadith studies as they are the only generation that saw the practical application of the prophetic sunnah. This phase is critical in understanding why Muslim scholars hold that hadith literature, and particularly the sunnah, has been preserved to a high degree of accuracy.

Being the generation that was blessed with the honour of having the close companionship of the final Messenger of God ﷺ , the Companions were the most eager of all generations in acting and passing on what they were taught by the Prophet ﷺ .

4.1 Factors that aided the Companions in preserving the Prophetic hadith

4.1.1 Memorisation capability of the Arabs: The Arabs at that time had an exemplary oral tradition. This aided in preserving knowledge based on an extraordinary capacity to memorise and relate narratives pertaining to elements of their culture, such as history and literature. They in turn utilised this ability to preserve the Prophetic norm. In a culture where it was second nature to be able to recall through memory long poems and sermons, it is no surprise that the Companions found no difficulty in taking it upon themselves to transmit all the knowledge that the Prophet ﷺ conveyed to them.

4.1.2 Religious fervour: The Companions were imbued with a sense of the utmost sanctity for the Prophetic sunnah, making its preservation central to their religious convictions.

4.1.3 Importance of hadith in the Islamic faith: The sunnah was at the core of religious teaching at their time and as such whenever the Companions would hear the words of the Prophet ﷺ they realised the importance of preserving, transmitting and acting upon the prophetic reports.

4.1.4 The Prophet ﷺ would use different stylistic methods to ensure that the audience was able to precisely hear and memorise what he said to them:

4.1.4.1 He ﷺ spoke in a measured way, pausing so as to be understood. 'Aishah said: *'The Prophet ﷺ would not speak without pausing like you do, but would speak in a way that was clear and considered so that whoever sat with him would be able to remember it.' [al-Tirmidhi]*
4.1.4.2 He would not speak aimlessly. His speech would have a specific intent. This is indicated by the hadith of 'Aishah in which she said: *'He would speak in a way that if one wanted to count his words, one could do so.' [al-Bukhari].*
4.1.4.3 The Prophet ﷺ would often repeat what he had said. Anas said: *'The Prophet ﷺ used to repeat his words three times in order for it to be understood from him.' [al-Bukhari]*

5. The faithfulness of the Companions in ensuring the precise transmission of hadith

One of the greatest tasks, if not the greatest, that the Companions were charged with was the faithful transmission of the sunnah of the Prophet ﷺ to mankind. They were well aware of this and strove to relate exactly what they saw and heard from him having verified the matter beforehand. The Prophet ﷺ had warned them of relating anything from him that was incorrect or false and so they took extra precautions to ensure that no errors were committed in this regard.
In one of the few examples of a hadith which is *mutawatir* in terms of the wording used, the Prophet ﷺ said: *'Whoever lies about me knowingly, let him take his seat in the Fire!' [al-Bukhari and Muslim]*

A number of instances help to demonstrate that the first generation saw it as their duty to ensure that what they related was faithful to what was said or done by the Prophet ﷺ , even if this meant that they would have to correct one another in the process. *'It is important to note here that this was done on their part out* of a duty to being precise in relating hadith and not out of accusation of impropriety or having a bad opinion of one another.' [`Ittr, Minhaj al-Naqd, pg54]

5.1 Hadith verification at the time of the Companions.

The wife of the Prophet ﷺ , 'Aishah was particularly notable for doing this. She would correct more senior companions in the rare lapses they did make in relating aspects of the life of the Prophet ﷺ . The eighth century scholar al-Zarkashi penned a work entitled *'al-Ijabah'*, collecting the instances in which she took others to task for imprecise narrations of Prophetic hadith.

5.1.1 A case in point is the hadith related by Abu Hurayrah in which he reports that the Prophet ﷺ is reported to have said: *'The evil omen exists in three things: Women, one's mount [or means of transport (dabbah)] and one's dwelling.'* A person entered to visit 'Aishah and told her of this, at which point she became extremely annoyed. *'By the One who revealed the Qur'an upon Abu Qasim! This is not what he said. Rather he said* **'The pre-Islamic Arabs used to say**: *'The evil omen exists in three things: Women, one's mount (dabbah) and one's dwelling.'* She then recited the verse: **'No affliction occurs in the earth nor in yourselves, without it first being in a Book before it happens.' [57:22]** *[Ahmed 6/246]. In another version she said: 'Abu Hurayrah did not memorise the instance well [...] as he heard the end of the words and not their beginning.' [Abu Dawud al-Tayalisi, Musnad, §1537].*

What we can deduce from this is that not only did she measure what was related in the light of the Qur'an, she was also acutely aware of the effect of the context in understanding the words of the Prophet ﷺ .

She understood that the hadith was actually a refutation of the beliefs of the *Jahili* Arabs rather than a teaching of Islam. Since it is recorded through different variants by other Companions, some scholars, while rejecting a misogynistic and fatalist understandings of the hadith, have given explanations for the version of the hadith related by Abu Hurayrah. Al-Zarkashi leaves the issue undecided, initially saying the opinion of 'Aishah should be given precedence because she provided extra circumstantial evidence for her view, quoting in support of her a divergent tradition from Abu Hurayrah recorded by Imam Ahmed. He then quotes possible interpretations given for the narration of Abu Hurayrah. *[al-Zarkashi, al-Ijabah, pg104-107]*

5.1.2 'Umar ibn al-Khattab was also known for ensuring that people faithfully reported the sunnah and did not become lax in transmitting the sunnah. *It is reported that Abu Musa called upon Umar's house and left after having called for him three times, waiting for a response after each time. 'Umar called out to him, whereupon Abu Musa replied: 'I heard the Prophet* ﷺ *say: 'If one of you sends greetings upon someone [from outside the house while knocking] three times and no-one replies back, then they should leave.' It is related that 'Umar did not accept the hadith from him, but rather said: 'You either bring me a witness for what you are saying or else...!' Abu Musa went to the Companions and explained the situation to them and enquired if any of them heard these same words. They replied that they had, whereupon one of them accompanied Abu Musa to see 'Umar and report the hadith to him.' ['Ittr, Minhaj an-Naqd, pg35]*

Lesson Two - Recording of hadith and the *isnad* system

Lesson Two

Aim: Through this lesson, students will look at the manner by which different Companions set out to record the sunnah, and how this is understood in the context of the initial prohibition of writing down the sunnah. They will also be provided with an overview of the *isnad* system and the status of the Companions in terms of their uprightness (*adalah*).

Objectives: By the end of this lesson, students should be able to display the ability to:
1. Describe the three main methods used by different Companions to preserve hadith.
2. Discuss whether the Prophet (may God bless and grant him peace) ever forbade people from recording his words and, if so, why?
3. Analyse a report permitting the recording of hadith and what this tells us of the underlying reason for the initial prohibition.
4. Summarise, with a brief example, the two main elements of a hadith (*matn* and *isnad*).
5. Discuss the main issues relating the legal probity (*adalah*) and uprightness of the Companions and stating clearly why this is important.

---

1. The Companions and the recording of hadith

The companions had differing methods by which to preserve the prophetic teachings. Some, such as Abdullah ibn 'Amr ibn al-A'as and Jabir ibn Abdillah, were known to have written down and preserved what they had heard, while others, such as Abu Hurayrah, did not.

1.1 Those that compiled their own recordings of ahadith

Early reports mention that a number of companions had their own personal record of the actions of the Prophet ﷺ . For example Jabir b. Abdillah had parchments which contained his own hadith which he had heard from the Messenger ﷺ . It is well known that there are many hadith from the companions related to the Hajj performed by the Messenger of God ﷺ . However none are so inclusive, detailed and pivotal in understanding the rulings of Hajj as the hadith preserved by Jabir. Qadi Iyad states: *'Scholars have made profuse commentaries on this one hadith [of Jabir]. Abu Bakr ibn Mundhir alone wrote a large work on it covering over one hundred and fifty types of rulings, while it is easy to extend this to that amount again...'.* [al-Nawawi, Sharh Muslim, 8:402-3]

This description was so well regarded that people would travel to him to hear this account directly from him. Qatadah (d. 118 H), knew it so well he once remarked: *'I remember the record of Jabir better than Surah al-Baqarah.'*

More well known than the personal collection of Jabir is that which was collected by *Abdullah b. Amr b. al-Aas.*

> *"One of the best known collections of ahadith that was written during the Prophet's ﷺ lifetime was al-Sahifah al-Sadiqah (the true collection) by Abdullah b. Amr b. al-Aas (d. 65 H). It contained one thousand ahadith, and although the actual manuscript has not reached us, its contents have been quoted almost entirely in the musnad of Imam Ahmad b. Hanbal. This has often been described as one of the 'most reliable historical documents to prove the writing of ahadith during the Prophet's lifetime'. [Kamali, A Textbook of Hadith Studies, p25]*

1.2 Those that did not set down ahadith in writing, but their students did.

The fact that certain Companions did not themselves record what they had heard from the Prophet ﷺ does not mean that their knowledge of the Prophetic sunnah was not preserved in written form in their lifetime.

As an example, the *Sahifah* collection of one the students of Abu Hurayrah contains some 138 ahadith collected around the middle of the 1st century *Hijri*. The collector, Hammam ibn Munabbih, gathered the material, saying that Abu Hurayrah had heard them from the Prophet ﷺ . One can also conclude from this instance that the systematic writing of ahadith began at a very early stage of Islam, thus the Orientalist claim that the recording of ahadith only took place in the 2nd century after the Hijra can be seen to be dubious.

1.3 Those that recorded important hadith.

Certain Companions relied primarily on their memory to preserve what they had heard from the Prophet ﷺ , only writing the ahadith pertaining to the most important of matters.

> *'Abu Juhayfa has thus stated, "I asked 'Ali, 'Do you have anything written with you, and he said 'No, except for the Book of God… or what is in this sahifah.' I asked, 'What is in this sahifah then?' He said, '(It is about the rules of) blood money, release of war prisoners, and (the hadith to the effect) that a Muslim is not executed for killing a disbeliever'." [Kamali, A Textbook of Hadith Studies, p26]*

2. Did the Prophet ﷺ permit his Companions to write down his words?

We know that certain Companions, such as 'Umar ibn al-Khattab, Ibn Mas'ud and Abu Sa'id al-Khudri were not in favour of recording in writing of Prophetic ahadith. *[Ibn Salah, Muqadimmah, 103].* Why did they hold to this opinion? Was it an unchangeable opinion, or one based on the context and circumstances at the time?

Paradoxically, there are indeed ahadith that prohibit the writing down of ahadith. Abu Sa'id al-Khudri relates that the Prophet ﷺ is reported to have said, *"Do not write from me anything except the Qur'an, and whoever has written anything from me other than the Qur'an, should erase it". [Muslim § 7510]*

2.1 Discussion regarding certain hadith:

2.1.1 Some scholars, such as al-Bukhari, believed that these are actually the words of the narrator of the hadith, Abu Sa'id al Khudri and not the words of the Prophet ﷺ himself. Others have said that this relates to the prohibition of writing anything on the same piece of material as that used for the recording of the Qur'an.

2.1.2 Others still say that the prohibition relates to the early period of Islam when people had yet to differentiate between the Qur'anic text and the words of the Prophet ﷺ . Once this distinction had been made, there was no longer any need for the prohibition.

2.1.3 The general scarcity of writing material at the time of the Qur'anic revelation also meant that priority had to be given to channeling any available writing material to ensuring that the Qur'an was not only preserved through memorisation, but also through writing.

> *'It seems that the prohibition preceded the permission to write. It has been said that the only reason that people were forbidden from writing hadith together with the Qur'an on one document was so that they would not become intermingled to such a point that it would become confusing upon the reader. However, if the document itself is guarded well and the knowledge is preserved through writing that prevents this, then there is no [intrinsic] problem in writing ahadith.' [al-Khattabi, Ma'alim as-Sunan, 5/246]*

2.2 Reports permitting the recording of ahadith

Ibn Salah reports that the Prophet ﷺ gave specific permission to individuals to record his sayings on account of need. Abu Shah al-Yamani, who had a weak memory, was given permission to record what he had heard and convey it to his countrymen [al-Bukhari]. Similarly, Abdullah ibn 'Amr ibn al-A'as was exhorted by the Prophet ﷺ to collect his sayings. A cursory look at the early recording of hadith shows that the Companions took it upon themselves to preserve and promote the Prophetic sunnah and teach others what they had heard in the presence of the Prophet ﷺ . Some did so orally, while others enlisted the aid of written records to ensure that their knowledge was suitably preserved.

2.3 What was the underlying reason for this difference?

> *"It is established that the initial disapproval of the written preservation [of ahadith] was only so that nothing may vie with the Qur'an [in terms of importance], or out of fear that people become preoccupied with anything else." [al-Khattib, Taqyid al-Ilm, 57]*

> *"Based upon this, there is no getting away from the fact that there has to be an underlying reason why it was both permitted and forbidden to record ahadith. In our opinion, the underlying reason which holds true in this regard is the fear of people rushing to attend to other than the Qur'an, thereby leaving aside the Qur'an, relying instead on other things." ['Itr, Minhaj an-Naqd, 43]*

3. The *isnad* system – Safeguarding against forgery

> *"The isnad is integral to this religion. If it were not for the isnad, everyone could say what they wanted." [Ibn Mubarak, Sahih Muslim, § 32]*

In order to ensure that people did not falsely attribute words or actions to the Prophet ﷺ , scholars developed one of the most intricate and precise sciences known to the scholarship of History. That system is known as the *isnad* system of verifying traditions and narrations. Not only were individuals required to be attentive and mindful of what they related, they also had to provide a valid reference for their information: an earlier authority from whom they related what they were now relating. Any discrepancies would render the information questionable, if not outright rejected.

While the *isnad* system was not fully needed at the time of the first few generations, once the trustworthiness and veracity of people declined, scholars increasingly insisted on the chain of authorities through which the text of a hadith was being related. Ibn Sirin remarked: *"They never enquired regarding the isnad, but once discord appeared, they started to say 'Name your authorities.'" [Imam Muslim, Muqadimah as-Sahih, § 27]*

3.1 The two elements of a hadith

Any narration relating to religious texts is made up of two elements.

3.1.1 The *isnad*: a chain of transmission of the narrators who relate the hadith from their teachers back to the source of the hadith, which is usually the Prophet ﷺ .
3.1.2 The *matn*: the text of the hadith.

3.2 Example

Isnad: 'Imam al-Bukhari relates that Sulayman Abu ar-Rabi' informed him, saying that Ismail b. Ja'far said that Nafi b. Malik informed him on the authority of his father that Abu Hurayrah related that the Prophet ﷺ said:

[Matn] *'The signs of a hypocrite are three: whenever he speaks, he tells a lie; whenever he makes a promise, he breaks it; and whenever entrusted with something, he proves to be dishonest.' [al-Bukhari § 33]*

3.2.1 The people in the *isnad*

From the above example we see that al-Bukhari (d. 256 Hijri) records a hadith (in this case in his Sahih collection in *Book of Faith, Chapter: 'The signs of the hypocrite'*) which he heard with the following *isnad*:

Abu ar-Rabi Sulayman ibn Dawud ibn Rushyd (d. 231). Originally from Basra, he became a resident of Baghdad. Shahin ibn al-Musaydi' said: *"I heard Ahmed ibn Hanbal heap praise on Abi Rabi".* Al-Khatib al Baghdadi said about him: *"He was trustworthy (thiqah)." [Ibn Hajar, Tahdhib, 2/401 §2983]*

Ismail Ibn Ja'far ibn Abi Kathir Al-Ansari (d. 180 Hijri). He related ahadith **from** Ja'far as-Sadiq, Imam Malik, and Nafi ibn Malik amongst others. Those that relate **from him** include Abu ar-Rabi Sulaiman ibn Dawud (mentioned above). Ibn Sa'd said about him: *'He is trustworthy (thiqah) and from the people of Madinah'.* He later moved to Baghdad, where he died. He knew 500 ahadith, which he had heard from others. Ibn Ma'in said about him *"He is trustworthy (thiqah) and safe (ma'mun), and as well as being extremely truthful (suduq) and commits mistakes only rarely." [Ibn Hajar, Tahdhib, 1/183 § 534]*

Nafi b. Malik ibn Abi 'Amir al Madani (d. c.140 Hijri) He was the paternal uncle of Imam Malik. He related ahadith **from** Anas ibn Malik, his father (mentioned below) as well as Sa'id ibn Musayyab amongst others. Those that relate **from him** include Imam az-Zuhri as well his nephew, Imam Malik. Ibn Kharash said about him: *"He was extremely truthful (suduq)." [Ibn Hajar, Tahdhib, 5/604 § 8216]*

Malik ibn Abi 'Amir al Madani Al-Asbahi (d. 74 Hijri). He related ahadith from many Companions, including Ibn 'Umar, 'Uthman and Abu Hurayrah. Those that relate **from him** include Sulayman ibn Yasar as well as his sons Anas, Nafi' (see above) and ar-Rabiah. All later scholars are unanimous as to his credentials in relating hadith. For example, Imam an-Nisai simply said about him: *"He is trustworthy (thiqah)." [Ibn Hajar, Tahdhib, 5/359 § 7505]*

Abu Hurayrah ad-Dawsi al-Yamani, the Companion. He embraced Islam in the year of Khaybar (7 AH). Scholars differ as to what was his original name. Some say it was Abd ur-Rahman ibn Sakhr, others that it was Abdullah ibn A'idh, Sikin ibn Razmah or Amir ibn Abd as-Shams. It is also said that his name, in Jahiliyyah, was Abu Aswad Abd as-Shams and that the Prophet ﷺ subsequently changed his name and he was given the nickname Abu Hurayrah on account of the fact that he was fond of kittens. Al-Bukhari said *"Over 800 individuals related ahadith from him." [Ibn Hajar, Tahdhib, 6/479-482, § 10353]*

4. The legal probity (adalah) and uprightness of the Companions of the Prophet ﷺ

The scholars of hadith are unanimous as to the need to verify the truthfulness and uprightness of every individual that reports a narration from the Prophet ﷺ . The search for the probity (*adalah*) or uprightness of the narrator (*rawi*) is essential in verifying the strength of hadith. Questions such as the truthfulness, veracity and character of an individual are the main areas that are examined in order to ascertain that the person relating words of the Prophet ﷺ is reliable. The question arises: Do the Companions of the Prophet ﷺ have to go through the same degree of inspection as later generations of narrators?

> *"What has preceded relating to the conditional probity of the narrator only relates to those other than the Companions. As for them, this is not the case since, according to us, the basic ruling regarding them is that they are all upright based upon the words of God, **'You are indeed the best community to have been raised up for mankind' [3:110]**. And the authentic hadith, **'The best generation is my generation'**."*

> *Therefore, their narrations are accepted without having to ascertain their individual status. Al-Qadi [al-Baqilani] said: 'This is the position of the Salaf and the vast majority of the Khalaf [28].' [az-Zarkashi al-Bahar Muhit, 4/299]*

4.1 Why is this the case?

This general consensus is based on them having been selected by God to convey the message of Islam to mankind. Any suggestion that they would wilfully lie regarding a hadith of the Prophet ﷺ , and could do so with impunity, undermines the wisdom of God in choosing them as the Companions of His final Prophet ﷺ . They were given a status that no other direct followers of any other Prophet were blessed with.

As Imam al-Juwayni says: *'This is established by consensus [...]. It is as if the underlying reason is that they transmitted the Shari'ah down to us. If one were to hesitate in accepting their narrations, [knowledge of] the Shari'ah would have been restricted to the era of the Prophet ﷺ and it would not have filtered down to later eras [with any degree of certainty]." [al-Zarkashi al-Bahar Muhit, 4/299].*

In summary, if we were to question their transmission of the prophetic teachings, no one from later generations would be sure of having the pristine teachings of the Prophet ﷺ , as the only way to achieve that would be to be alive during his lifetime and learn directly from him. As this is impossible for latter generations, the sunnah was preserved by the generation of the Companions as a whole. Those coming later could rest assured that whatever teachings they received passed down from him ﷺ genuinely represent his ﷺ sunnah.

There are, however, a minority of scholars who hold that this ruling does not apply to all of the Companions.

> *'Al-Mazari held that this uprightness was only established for the famous amongst the Companions and not those whose period of companionship was short or fleeting, or who only caught a glimpse of the Prophet ﷺ . He said: 'Who we mean by the Companions in this context are those that kept his company and defended him and helped him and followed the light with which he was sent.'*

> Al-Zarkashi comments: *"This is a strange position since it removes many of those that are famous as being Companions such as Wa'il ibn Hujr, Malik ibn al-Huwayrith and the like, who travelled in delegations to the Prophet ﷺ and only remained with him for a few days, after which they returned back to their tribes.' [al-Zarkashi al-Bahar Muhit, 4/299]*

Whatever the theoretical discussion around the legal probity (*adalah*) of the Companions, the issue has no practical ramifications, as no person of ill-repute is recorded as having related hadith from the Prophet ﷺ . We can therefore be sure that any hadith on the authority of a Companion is faithfully related by them in the context that they recollect it. In this regard, the words of the hadith master Al-Hafidh Jamal al-Din al-Mizzi [author of *Tahdhib al-Kamal fi Asma' al-Rijal* (d. 742)] is of relevance. He said: *'One cannot find even a single narration from individuals that were implicated in hypocrisy from amongst [those classed] as Companions.' [al-Zarkashi al-Bahar Muhit, 4/300]*

---

[28] *The text of the Arabic original has 'salaf' which is a typographic mistake.*

Lesson Three - Hadith classification

Lesson Three

Aim: In this lesson, students will be introduced to two of the main methods of classifying hadith. The first is based on studying the frequency in which the *isnad* occurs and deal with *mutawatir* and *ahad* hadith. The other is based upon a study of breaks in the *isnad* of a hadith. This will include a comprehensive look at the status of *mursal* hadith.

Objectives: By the end of this lesson, students should be able to display the ability to:
1. Define what is meant by *mutawatir* hadith and what criteria are used in classifying *ahadith* as such.
2. Mention, with examples, what is meant by '*Mutawatir by wording (Lafdhi)*' and '*Mutawatir by meaning (Ma'nawi)*'.
3. Define what is meant by a solitary (*ahad*) hadith as well as mention its three main subcategories.
4. Discuss the proof-status of *Mutawatir* and *Ahad* hadith and why it is of importance today.
5. Define and recognise each of the five classes of hadith related to breaks in the *isnad*.
6. Explain how *mursal* hadith came into being and summarise the position of scholars on their use.

---

1. Hadith classification with reference to the number of narrators - *Mutawatir* and *Ahad*

The most important classification of *ahadith* is based on the frequency with which the *isnad* occurs. This is of particular importance in the science of *usul al-fiqh*, which looks at how to derive Shari'ah rulings from the detailed proofs of the Qur'an and Sunnah. They may, for example, look at the frequency of variant hadith in order to give priority to one over others in cases where there appears to be mutual contradiction between them. In general, what is narrated by a large group of individuals naturally conveys a stronger degree of certainty and knowledge than what is narrated by a few.

1.1 *Mutawatir* hadith and its conditions

> '[This is any] report of an occurrence from a large number of narrators whose agreement upon a lie, on account of their number, is inconceivable.' [al-Zarkashi, al-Bahr, 4/231].

1.1.1 What are the criteria placed on individuals narrating a *mutawatir* narration?

It is not a condition that all individuals be legally upright (*adil*) and neither that they be Muslims, since a *mutawatir* narration is defined simply as one which gives rise to definitive knowledge. What is important is not the personal traits of the individuals, but their being of such a large number that it conveys definitive knowledge. Once this is achieved, it is of no consequence that the individual narrators be of the calibre required for a solitary hadith (*ahad*) to be acceptable or not. [al-Kittani, Nadhm al-Mutanathir, 18]

1.1.2 Does *mutawatir* require a minimum number of narrators?

Al-Ghazali (d. 505) states that for a hadith to qualify as a *mutawatir* narration, it must be conveyed by a large number of reporters equally at the **beginning**, **middle** and **end** of the chain of narration. There is no exact number of narrators that is required for a hadith to be considered *mutawatir*.

> "The criteria is the provision of definitive knowledge (al-ilm al-qat'i), so that whenever such a group narrate it, and their narration conveys definitive knowledge, we will come to know that it is mutawatir. If this is not the case, then we cannot." [al-Zarkashi, al-Bahr, 4/232]

Those that put a precise number on what constitutes *mutawatir*, differ as to what that number is. Different circumstances can give rise to certain knowledge without it being dependent on a specific number of narrators. Al-Qadi Abu at-Tayyib said that there should be more than four people because, in certain cases of defamation, four people in a court of law are not deemed to provide certain knowledge until they have been further investigated for their outward uprightness (*adalah*). Therefore the criteria for a *mutawatir* hadith should be more stringent than this.

Al-Istakhri said there should be at least ten people at each stage of the *isnad*, since anything less than ten is considered arithmetically singular. It is said that they should be at least twelve based on the verse *"...and We sent with them twelve leaders." [5:12]*. Others held it to be twenty, based on the verse *"and if there are twenty patient amongst you, they will overcome two hundred," [8:65]*. Some have insisted on forty individuals, while others insisted on far more. Imam al-Haramayn concludes: 'These are all weak positions as they mutually contradict one another, with no one position being preferable over the other." [al-Subqi, Jam'al-Jawami', 2/182-4; al-Zarkashi, al-Bahr, 4/233]

1.1.3 Mutawatir by wording (lafdhi) and meaning (ma'nawi)

There are very few *ahadith* that are classed as *mutawatir* based on the wording of the *matn* alone. On the other hand, there are many *ahadith* that fulfill the criteria of *mutawatir* based on a shared meaning. Sayyid Abi Abdillah al-Kittani in his work on the topic of *mutawatir* hadith collected around 310 hadith as being *mutawatir*, the vast majority, such as raising one's hands when supplicating, being of this latter type.

An example of a narration that is *mutawatir* by wording *(lafdhi)* is the hadith: *'Whoever intentionally lies concerning me let him take his seat in the Fire"*. According to one estimation this hadith, with this exact wording, has been related on the authority of 75 Companions of the Prophet ﷺ , while Hafidh al-'Iraqi in his poem '*al-Alfiyyah* puts the number at closer to one hundred.

1.2 The solitary hadith (al-ahad)

> *'As for the solitary hadith, it is defined as one that does not fulfill the conditions of mutawatir, regardless of whether it is narrated by one or more individuals.' [al-Nawawi, Sharh Sahih Muslim, 1/131]* [29]

1.2.1 The status of solitary hadith

> *'These [solitary ahadith] encompass accepted as well as rejected [reports], since using them as evidence rests upon investigating the status of the narrators.' [Ibn Hajr, Nukhbah]*

2. The proof status of *Mutawatir* and *Ahad*: Qati ath-thabut versus Dhanni ath-thabut

> *Al-Shafi'i: "Consensus is greater than a solitary hadith.' [al-Dhahabi, Siyar 'Alam, 10/20]*

Scholars have discussed the relative strengths of both types of narrations and their role in establishing both belief and practice. Can we establish a tenet of belief based solely on a solitary hadith, without recourse to any other proof? What is the ruling of one who rejects a solitary hadith? Is it tantamount to rejecting a Qur'anic verse or *mutawatir* hadith? Ibn Abd al-Barr explains.

> *"The sunnah is divided into two types. **The first [mutawatir]** is a narration transmitted through consensus from masses to masses. This is the type of proof that leaves no room for denial and as such, there is no disagreement concerning such narrations. Whoever rejects this consensus has rejected one of God's textual stipulations, thereby committing apostasy.*
>
> ***The second [ahad]** consists of reports from verifiable, trustworthy solitary narrators with uninterrupted chains. The congregation of scholars of the ummah have said that this second type conveys an obligation in terms of practice. Some of them said that it makes both knowledge and practice obligatory." [Ibn Abd al-Barr, Jami' Bayan, 2/33]*

He goes on to clarify the majority position elsewhere by saying:

> *"What we uphold is that solitary hadith (ahad) make practice obligatory **but not** knowledge. This is the position of most jurists and hadith scholars." [Ibn 'Abd al-Barr, al-Tamhid, 1:7]*

There is a vast array of proofs to indicate that the Companions of the Prophet ﷺ did not consider a solitary hadith to convey definitive knowledge unless corroborated by other factors. For example 'Ali ﷺ said:

---

[29] *Ahad* hadith divided further depending on the number of narrators of hadith.
Mushhur (well-known report): *A hadith transmitted by three or more narrators in every stage of the isnad.*
Anas relates that 'The Prophet ﷺ made du'a (qunut) for one month against (the tribes of) Ra'al and Dhakwan.' [al-Bukhari]. This has been related by numerous numbers of narrators from Anas at all stages of the isnad, never falling below three narrators, but it does not fulfill the mutawatir criteria.' [al Sakhawi Fath al-Mughith, Alfiyyah [v4, pg 13]
Aziz (rare report): *A hadith where the number of narrators does not drop below two. "None of you (truly) believes until I become more beloved to him than his father, his son, and all the people."*
Anas relates this hadith from the Messenger ﷺ , and **two** reporters, Qatadah and 'Abdul 'Aziz b. Shu'aib, report this hadith from Anas. In the next level of narrators, two others narrate from each of them. Shu'bah and Sa'id report from Qatada, while Isma'il b. Ulayyah and 'Abd al-Warith narrate from 'Abd al-'Aziz; after which the chain of narration continues. *[al-Qari, Sharh sharh Nukhbah, pg 2007-8]*
Gharib (singular report). *A hadith transmitted by only a single reporter at some stage of the isnad."Indeed actions are only by intentions" [al-Bukhari, 1]*
This hadith was related by the 'Umar ibn al-Khattab. This was heard from him by 'Alqamah ibn Waqqas alone. He related the hadith to Muhammed ibn Ibrahim from whom Yahya ibn Sa'id received the hadith; he then transmitted it to over a hundred students. Obviously, a hadith being classified as a singular report does not necessarily have any bearing on the status of the hadith itself in terms of authenticity *[Ibn Salah, Muqadimah, 77, 271]*.

"When I heard something from the Messenger of God ﷺ , God would benefit me with it as He wished; but when someone other than him ﷺ narrated it to me, I would make him swear to it; if he took an oath, I would believe him."

The famous Shafi'i jurist (*faqih*) and traditionist (*muhaddith*) al-Bayhaqi says:

"Those of an investigative disposition (tahqiq) from among our companions left using solitary reports as proofs in the area of the Divine Attributes (sifat) if such reports did not have a supporting basis in either the Qur'an or scholarly consensus ('ijma). Instead, they interpreted them figuratively." [Al-Bayhaqi, al-Asma' wa al-Sifat p.357]

Perhaps the most conclusive statement on the status of solitary *ahadith* is that of the commentator on Sahih Muslim, Imam an-Nawawi. He says:

"Scholars have differed as to its ruling. The position of the vast majority (jamahir) of Muslims, whether it be the Companions or those that followed them (tabi`in), those that came after them, be they hadith experts, scholars of jurisprudence and law, is that a solitary hadith from a reliable source (thiqah) is a legal proof which obligates one to act but provides conjectural, not definitive knowledge." [al-Nawawi, Sharh Sahih Muslim, 1/131]

2.1 The majority position regarding solitary ahadith

2.1.1 In cases where a solitary hadith contradicts a *mutawatir* text, be it a hadith or a Qur'anic verse, preference is given to the *mutawatir* text.

2.1.2 It is obligatory to act in accordance with a solitary hadith because it provides the degree of surety that makes applying it necessary.

2.1.3 They do not convey certain knowledge due to the possibility of error in the transmission of the hadith and therefore are only conditionally used in establishing creed (*aqidah*).

2.1.4 Secondary tenets of belief may be established on the basis of a solitary hadith if it does not conflict with more conclusive proofs. An example of this would be the Sunni creedal belief in the punishment of the grave. However, one denying such a belief would not exit the fold of Islam. *[see az-Zarkashi, al-Bahr, 4/262-266]*

2.2 A minority position regarding solitary ahadith

A few scholars of the past took a view that went against the majority consensus, holding that solitary hadith convey definitive knowledge (*al-'ilm al-qat'i*) in the same way that *mutawatir ahadith* do. Some individuals in the modern age have also championed this position, leading to confusion and aberrant views amongst some contemporary Muslims which are not in accordance with accepted doctrines and beliefs as understood by the majority of Sunni scholars through the ages. The problem with this approach to religious text rests in two underlying issues:

2.2.1 Epistemic contradiction. Those that hold this view accept that a solitary hadith is conjectural in terms of the *isnad* (due to the need to verify each and every narrator in the chain), while at the same time they state that they convey definitive knowledge. This is clearly contradictory.

2.2.2 Blurring of the lines. Equating *Mutawatir* with *Ahad* blurs the vital distinction between the strength of definitive knowledge on the one hand, and that which is conjectural on the other. Such a distinction is vitally important in cases where there is a conflict with the meaning of a solitary hadith and a religious source that imparts definitive knowledge. Examples of a religious source that imparts definitive knowledge are clear Qur'anic verses, *mutawatir* hadith or consensus ('ijma).

3. Hadith classification according to breaks in the chain.

3.1 *Marfu'* (lit. raised)– reports ascribed to the Prophet ﷺ , regardless of whether or not there is a break in the chain.

3.2 *Musnad* (lit. connected) - hadith that are related to the Prophet ﷺ , without a break in the chain.

3.3 *Mawquf* - a narration relating words of the Companions, such as the words of 'Umar: *'Acquire understanding before you are made leaders".*

3.4 *Maqtu'* (lit. severed) – a narration relating words of the followers of the Companions such as the words of Mujahid: *'Knowledge is not attained by one that is shy nor one that is arrogant".*

3.5 *Mursal* (lit. sent forth) - when a follower (*tabi'i*) relates a hadith from the Prophet ﷺ but does not mention the missing link from whom he received the hadith. For example Hasan al-Basri, who was a follower, said that the Prophet ﷺ said: *"Fortify your wealth through giving zakat, treat your sick through* *giving extra charity (sadaqah) and face the waves of tribulation with supplication and humbleness." [Abu Dawud, Kitab al-Marasil, §96, p.133]*

Another example of this is what is related by Yazid ibn Abi Habib that the Messenger ﷺ passed by two women who were praying. He said: '*When you prostrate, let part of your body cling to the earth, for women are unlike men in this regard.'* [Abu Dawud, al-Marasil §81, pg 130].[30]

4. Text in focus - The authenticity of *mursal* ahadith

Since one of the most important issues in authenticating a hadith is an uninterrupted chain of narrators, any break in the *isnad* causes the text of the hadith to be of questionable authenticity. One type of break in the chain that has been the subject of particularly heated debate amongst scholars: that of the *mursal ahadith*. The existence of this particular category of hadith has to do with the history of recording of hadith itself.

In the early period of hadith transmission, before the spread of suspicion as to veracity and truthfulness of narrators, the generation of followers (*tabi'un*) used to narrate hadith ascribing them directly to the Prophet ﷺ . Given that they were not going to be asked who the Companion from whom they had received the hadith was, they would frequently omit mentioning of the Companion. As Ibn Sirin said: '*They never used to enquire regarding the isnad, but once discord appeared, they started to say: 'Name your authorities...'* [Imam Muslim, Muqadimah, § 27].

As *hadith* were codified and the science of hadith criticism developed, the practice of omitting the name of the companion, acceptable at a time of relative truthfulness and integrity, came under scrutiny. The stringent rules that had been set up in order for hadith scholars to ensure hadith were reported faithfully were now used retrospectively by some to reject *mursal* hadith.

4.1 Opinions regarding the use of *mursal* ahadith:

4.1.1 Imam Malik, Imam Abu Hanifah and Imam Ahmad b. Hanbal[31]

The *mursal* of a trustworthy person is a valid as proof just like a *musnad* hadith. This is because if the follower (*tabi'i*) is an authority and well-known, they will be known to only relate on the authority of trustworthy sources. If the follower is not trustworthy, then any hadith related by them will not be accepted anyway. The logic being that they would only leave mentioning the source of their information if it was credible in the first instance. Ibn Abdul Barr explains:

> '*The one who reports a musnad hadith leaves you with the names of the reporters for further investigation and scrutiny. The one who narrates a mursal hadith, being knowledgeable and trustworthy, has already done the investigative work and found the hadith to be sound.' [Ibn Abdul Barr, al-Tamhid , 1/2: al-Lakanwi, Dhafar al-Amani, 351-2]*

4.1.2 Imam Muslim and the majority of traditionalists (*muhadithun*)

They take the position that this is a weak (*da'if*) narration based on the break in the *isnad* which could be a companion, but could also be another Tabi' who may be weak. '*Mursal narrations are, in our view and that of those conversant with the science of narrations (akhbar), not a binding proof.*' [Muslim, Muqadimah]

4.1.3 Imam ash-Shafi'i

He placed conditions upon the acceptance of *mursal ahadith*. Amongst these are:

> **4.1.3.1** That it be reported as a *musnad* hadith through another *isnad*.
> **4.1.3.2** That most scholars act in accordance with the information contained within it.
> **4.1.3.3** That the one narrating it be a senior follower (*tabi'i*). Upon investigation, the *mursal hadith* of people like Sa'id ibn Musayyab and 'Ata' ibn Abi Rabah have been found to come directly from the Companions, thereby giving them the status of *musnad* hadith. [Siraj ud-Din, Sharh Bayquniyyah, 108-109]

---

[30] See Prayer module 2 lesson 3. Yazid (d 128 h.) was one of the most knowledgeable people of his day in Egypt but never met the Prophet ﷺ so is considered a *tabi'i (follower)*.

[31] Ahmad accepts *mursal* hadith if nothing opposing them is found on an issue preferring them over *qiyas* (analogy).

Lesson Four - Hadith classification according to authenticity - 1

> **Aim:** Students will be introduced to how hadith are classified as rigorously authenticated (*sahih*) or not. The conditions for this will be explained through examples, and the student will be shown how falling short of any of the conditions leads to the hadith being classed as 'sound' (*hasan*) or 'weak' (*da'if*).
>
> **Objectives:** By the end of this lesson, students should be able to display the ability to:
> 1. Define what a *sahih* hadith is, marking out clearly the five conditions of a *sahih* hadith.
> 2. Mention what is meant by the uprightness of the narrator (*adalah*) and how this is ascertained.
> 3. Mention what is meant by a person having a high degree of accuracy (*dabt*) in terms of what they narrate and how this is ascertained.
> 4. Identify what is meant when a hadith is said to be irregular (*shadh*).
> 5. Identify, with an example, what is meant by a hadith not having any hidden defects (*ma'lul*).
> 6. Discuss whether Imam al-Bukhari set out to record all *sahih* hadith.
> 7. Mention what is meant by the '*golden chain*'.
> 8. Define, with an example, what a *hasan* (sound) hadith is and how it differs from a *sahih* hadith.
> 9. Summarise the two main types of *hasan* hadith.
> 10. Mention when a weak hadith *cannot* be raised to the status of being sound based on supporting evidences (*hasan li-ghayrihi*).
> 11. Mention when the classification into *sahih* - *hasan* - *da'if* came into being and why is this

1. *Sahih* (rigorously authenticated) hadith defined.

> '*A sahih hadith is one which has a continuous isnad of narrators of reliable memory who in turn narrate from comparable authorities, and which is found to be free from any irregularities or defects [in the isnad].*" [Ibn Salah, Muqadimah, 11-12]

2. What are the conditions of a *sahih* hadith?

Scholars have put down five conditions for a hadith to be classified as vigorously authenticated (*sahih*): continuity of the chain of narration (*ittisal*); the uprightness of the narrator (*adalah*); the person having a high degree of accuracy (*dabt*) of what they narrate; that the hadith not be irregular (*shadh*); that it not be anomalous (*ma'lul*)

2.1 Continuity of the chain of narration (*ittisal*)

The first condition (*ittisal*) necessitates that the person narrating the hadith met and narrated from their source who is likewise required to have done the same from his source and so on, *without break,* until the end of the chain.

2.2 The uprightness of the narrator (*adalah*)

> "*O you who believe, if one of ill repute comes to you with information, verify it.*" [49:6]

Uprightness in this context implies that the person narrating the hadith be free of *moral corruption (fisq)* in terms of committing major wrong actions or continually committing smaller ones. It also requires the individual having the quality of '*Maruwah*' (lit. chivalry).

> **2.2.1 '*Maruwah*'** is a term used to describe an individual that conforms what is generally acceptable to people and shuns that which they despise. It also implies that the person protects themselves from socially reprehensible activities which would lower their standing amongst people.[32]

The importance of this type of uprightness is emphasised in a number of traditions. Al-Hafiz Al-Khatib narrates that the Prophet ﷺ said to Ibn 'Umar: "*O Ibn Umar, be wary for your religion, be wary for your religion, for indeed it is your very flesh and blood. Look from whom you acquire it, take it from those that are upright – not from those that are of questionable standing.*" It is also narrated that 'Ali said, "*Be careful of whom you take this knowledge from, for indeed it is religion itself.*"

---

[32] Scholars do not accept narrations that are related by children as it is difficult to ascertain whether or not they are speaking the truth. Also included in this category are those that do not belong to the Muslim faith tradition, due to the possibility of them harbouring a degree of animosity that would move them to dissimulate the truth.

2.2.2 How does one ascertain the uprightness of a narrator?

Scholars have given a number of indicators of a persons uprightness: A reputation amongst those of knowledge for being upright; unremitting praise given to the person as is the case with the four Imams (of Islamic law) and their like; and specific mention of them being upright by scholars.

2.3 The person having a high degree of accuracy *(dabt)*[33] of what they narrate

This is when the narrator is: ***aware*** what he/she is narrating; ***memorised*** what they are narrating such that they are able to recollect it whenever they want, or have suitably ***guarded*** and authenticated the books from which they narrate such that they can assure that they have not been altered or tampered with; ***know*** what they are narrating and be aware of how the meaning may change through a change in wording.

2.3.1 How does one ascertain the accuracy *(dabt)* of a narrator?

This is known through the agreement of scholars of hadith who are proficient in *hadith* science. One or two scholars going against a wider scholarly agreement on the accuracy of a narrator is of little consequence here, as this will not generally lead to the *sanad* dropping below the quality of *sahih*.

2.4 The hadith not be irregular *(shadh)*

The issue of irregularity is a relative term and simply means that the person in question, even if they have a high standard of reliability in narrating hadith, does not narrate something that contradicts the narration of a person more who is more proficient. Irregularity can affect both the *sanad* and the text *(matn)*.

An example of this is the hadith recorded by Imam al-Daraqutni on the authority of 'Aishah. *'The Prophet ﷺ used to shorten his prayers as well as complete them, fast and break his fast while travelling.'* [Daraqutni, Sunan, 2/189].

Al-Daraqutni rules on the hadith saying: *'This sanad is sahih'*. However, others have questioned this classification as the hadith in question is said to be **irregular** *(shadh)*, both in terms of its *sanad* and its text *(matn)*. The *sanad* is **irregular** since other chains of the hadith from trustworthy narrators agree in narrating this as the practice of 'Aishah and not the Prophet ﷺ . As for the text of the hadith, it is **irregular** because what is established is that he ☒would shorten his prayers while travelling. Ibn Hajr says in his hadith law manual *Balugh al-Maram*: *'What is preserved is that this was in fact her habit.'* ['Ittr, *Minhaj, 428*].

2.5 It is not anomalous *(ma'lul)* having hidden defects

For a hadith to be declared *sahih* it should also be clear of any hidden defects. A hidden defect *('illah)* occurs in a hadith when a proficient scholar of hadith discovers a critical hidden defect in its authenticity while it outwardly appears to be free of any weakness. As Ibn Hajr says, this is *'one of the most elusive sciences of hadith as well as the most precise, which none can excel in except one that God has blessed with a piercing intellect, extensive memory coupled with a complete knowledge of the different classes of hadith narrators, not to mention a strong acquaintance with different sanad channels and text of ahadith.'*

One example of this is where a *mursal* (disconnected) hadith is inadvertently added on to a *musnad* (complete isnad) hadith thus ending a *mursal [hadith]* with a *musnad* [hadith]. An example of this is the hadith narrated by Abu Qulabah (a Follower), that the Prophet ﷺ said: *"The most compassionate of my Ummah is Abu Bakr, and the most stringent in God's religion is 'Umar; the most truly modest is 'Uthman; the most proficient in recitation is Ubayy b. Ka`b and the most knowledgeable on halal and haram is Mu'adh b. Jabal. Verily every ummah has a trustee and the trustee of this ummah is Abu 'Ubaydah"*.

The larger part of this hadith is *mursal*, as it is said that Abu Qulaba may have heard it from Anas b. Malik, but this is uncertain. Only the last sentence of the hadith concerning Abu 'Ubaydah is *musnad* (as known from other reports). Hence this is a separate hadith which is joined to a larger [*mursal*] hadith, thus ending a *mursal* with a *musnad*. The separate hadith here is: *"Verily every ummah has a trustee, and the trustee of this ummah is Abu Ubaydah."* [Kamali, p.100, quoting Nisaburi, Marifah 114-115]

---

[33] This condition of accuracy *(dabt)* is of central importance in classifying a hadith as *sahih*, as any laxity in this condition will lead to the hadith being classified in the lower category known as *hasan*.

3. Example of a *sahih* hadith

The aforementioned five conditions of a *sahih* hadith exist in the following narration. Al-Bukhari relates that Sulayman Abu ar-Rabi informed him saying that Ismail b. Ja'far said that Nafi b. Malik informed him on the authority of his father that Abu Hurayrah related that the Prophet ﷺ said: *"The signs of a hypocrite are three: whenever he speaks, he tells a lie; whenever he makes a promise, he breaks it; and whenever entrusted with something, he proves to be dishonest.' [al-Bukhari § 33]*

4. Did scholars such as al-Bukhari set out to record every single *sahih* hadith?

Some people contend that if a hadith does not exist in the collections of Muslim or al-Bukhari, then the hadith must necessarily be below the level of *sahih*. This implies that [1] these Imams set out to collect **all** the *sahih* hadith in their collections; [2] only what is contained within these collections is *sahih* and [3] hadith in other collections are of a lower standard of authenticity than those in the collections of al-Bukhari and Muslim.

4.1 Discussion :

4.1.1 The statements of al-Bukhari as well as Imam Muslim indicate that they never set out to collect every single hadith that is *sahih*. Al-Bukhari said: *'I have not included in this book of mine except that which is sahih, but I have left out other sahih ahadith out of fear of it becoming voluminous.'*
Imam Muslim similarly said: *'Not all that I consider to be sahih have I included here. I have only included here that which scholars have agreed about.' [Ibn Salah, Muqadimah, 19-20]*

4.1.2 Scholars unanimously agree that other collections contain hadith that are vigorously authenticated (*sahih*). *'More sahih ahadith, over and above that contained in the two sahih collections, can be found by one who sets out to seek them in what is contained in one of the famous established collections of the Imams of hadith, such as Abu Dawud as-Sijistani, Abi 'Isa at-Tirmidhi, Abd al-Rahman an-Nisa'i, Abu Bakr ibn Khuzaymah, Abi Hasan al-Daraqutni and others who explicitly state the vigorously authentic (sahih) nature of the ahadith.' [Ibn Salah, Muqadimah, 21]*

4.1.3 Scholars are unanimous that what classifies a hadith as being *sahih* is the individual *isnad* related to the text, and not that it exists in any collection in particular. Therefore each hadith is investigated on its own according to the quality of the narrators. In fact, *ahadith* in the collections of al-Bukhari and Muslim have also been questioned by some scholars that lived during their time and later. Al-Daraqutni and others questioned the *sahih* classification of over 200 *ahadith* in the two collections. 32 of these are shared by both of the *sahih* collections, while 78 are specific to al-Bukhari and around 100 in the collection of Imam Muslim. [*Shaykh Abdulah Siraj ud-Din, Sharh al-Bayquniyyah, 47*]

5. Different levels of *sahih* hadith

Not all *sahih* hadith are of the same strength. Some, known as those with the 'golden chain', are marked by the exceptional level of moral standing and accuracy of the narrators. Foremost amongst this is the *isnad* of Imam Malik when he relates from his teacher Nafi', who in turn narrates a hadith from Abdullah b. 'Umar from the Prophet ﷺ . This is called a *"golden isnad"* because of its illustrious reporters.

6. *Hasan* (sound) hadith[34]

This is a hadith which falls between the categories of *sahih* and *da'if*. There only one difference between this type of hadith and the *sahih*, *that of accuracy (dabt)*. While the hadith in question has no break in the *sanad*, the narrators of the hadith are all trustworthy, with there being no hidden defects (*'illah*) or irregularity (*shadh*), there is nevertheless a question mark over the degree of accuracy (dabt) of one or more narrators of the hadith.

6.1 Example of a *hasan* hadith

al-Tirmidhi relates that Bundar relates that Yahya ibn Said at-Qattan relates that *Bahz ibn Hakim* said: 'My father related to me on the authority of my grandfather that he said: *'I asked the Prophet* ﷺ *: Messenger of God, who should I show best companionship?' He said, 'Your mother.' I said, 'Then whom?' and he said, 'Your mother?' I said, 'Then whom?' and he said, 'Your mother.' I said, 'And then whom?' and he said, 'Then*

---

[34] The origins of the tripartite division of ahadith into *sahih - hasan – da'if* comes from the work of Imam at-Tirmidhi. Prior to this, hadith were loosely classified into two broad categories only: *sahih* and *da'if*. Based on this, it is important that the ruling of early hadith scholars be put in the correct context, as what they are relating to when they say *da'if* may not be weak at all, but rather *hasan* in the usage of later hadith scholars.

your father and thereafter your next in kin and so on.' Al-Tirmidhi said: *'This hadith is hasan since Shu'bah spoke (critically) about the status of Bahz ibn Hakim [in terms of his accuracy]. However, he is trustworthy according to the scholars of hadith."*

We can see from this that the narrator in question did not have the requisite *degree of accuracy* of a *sahih* narrator. Nevertheless, there is no question with regards to his trustworthiness, so the hadith is classified as *hasan*. This chain containing Bahz, is also considered the highest type of *hasan* chain. *['Ittr, Minhaj, 266]*

6.2 Types of *hasan* – intrinsically sound or sound on account of supporting evidence

There are two types of hadith that are classified as *hasan*: Intrinsically sound (*hasan li dhatihi*), an example of which has been provided above and that which is sound due to a supporting evidence (*hasan li ghayrihi*).

This second type of hadith is originally a weak (*da'if*) narration where the weakness is not critical. This may be either because it is related by an unknown narrator or because of some other inconsistency in the *sanad* that is disputed amongst scholars. Mildly weak hadith may be strengthened by other chains of narrations such that the text of the hadith has supporting evidences increasing the classification from weak to *hasan*.

6.3 Example of a hadith that is sound based on a supporting evidence (*hasan li ghayrihi*)

Imam at-Tirmidhi *[§1113]* relates on the authority of Shu'bah who relates from Asim ibn Ubaydillah on the authority of Abdullah ibn Amir ibn Rabi'ah on the authority of his father that a woman from the Fazarah tribe married upon a dowry of a pair of sandals. The Prophet ﷺ said: *'Are you pleased to give yourself in marriage for the dowry of a pair of sandals?'* She said, *'Yes,'* and the Prophet ﷺ permitted the marriage.

6.3.1 The status of Asim ibn Ubaydillah

Asim ibn Ubaydillah, who is one of the narrators of hadith has been criticised as being weak on account of his poor memory. Imam Malik relates one hadith on his authority in the Muwatta.

Some scholars, such as Shu'bah, were scathing in their criticism of Asim. He said about him: *'If one were to ask him who built the mosque in Basra he would narrate a hadith saying that 'so and so' relates on the authority of 'so and so' that the Prophet ﷺ said that he built it[!]"* Abu Hatim ar-Razi said: *'His ahadith are reprehensible (munkar al-hadith), relating confused narrations (mudtarib al-hadith); he has no hadith anyone can rely on."*

Others were slightly less critical of him. Ibn Khuzaymah said: *'I do not use him as a proof on account of his poor memory. Ibn Hibban said about him: 'He has a bad memory, imagines a lot (kathir al-wahm) and makes some glaring mistakes, and has been left on account of his numerous mistakes.' [Ibn Hajr, Tahdhib at-Tahdhib v3, 35-36]*

Imam Tirmidhi qualified the hadith as being *hasan* on account of it being related from a number of different routes. He says: *'This topic also contains hadith on the authority of 'Umar, Abu Hurayrah, Sahl ibn Sa'd, Abi Sai'd, Anas, 'Aishah, Jabir and Abi Hadrad al-Aslami."*

6.4 When can a weak hadith not be strengthened?

A weak hadith cannot be raised in rank if the weakness in the hadith is due to serious discrepancies such as:
  6.4.1 The moral corruption (*fisq*) of the narrator, or
  6.4.2 The narrator being known *unanimously* as a liar.

[Summarised from Shaykh Siraj ud-Din, Sharh al-Bayquniyyah unless otherwise stated]

Lesson Five - Hadith classification according to authenticity -2

Aim: Through this lesson, students will complete their understanding of hadith classification by looking at how a hadith is classed as either *da'if* (weak) or *mawdu* (fabricated) as well as the issues related to how to interact with such hadith.

Objectives:
By the end of this lesson a student should be able to display the ability to:
1. Define, with an example, what a *da'if* hadith is.
2. Mention the main categories of weak hadith in as much as this relates to the conditions outlined previously for a *sahih* hadith.
3. Summarise the discussion amongst scholars regarding acting upon 'weak' hadith, mentioning the position preferred by Imam al-Nawawi in this regard.
4. Define what a *mawdu* hadith is.
5. Discuss the main reasons why people fabricated hadith.
6. Summarise the methods used by hadith scholars to combat fabrication of hadith.
7. Mention the main signs of a fabricated hadith.
8. List the three rulings concerning fabricated hadith.
9. Understand orientalist criticisms of the *isnad* system and the response to these by scholars.

1. Weak hadith

This is defined as a hadith which does not reach the conditions required for a hadith to be *hasan* or *sahih*.

1.1 Example

The Prophet ﷺ is reported to have said to a woman from the Fazarah tribe: *"Are you pleased to give yourself in marriage for the dowry of a pair of sandals?" She said, 'Yes,' and the Prophet permitted the marriage".* [Imam al-Tirmidhi, 1113]

As has been stated before, this hadith is classed **on its own** as weak *(da'if)* because one of the narrators, Asim ibn Ubaydillah, is criticised by hadith scholars for his general laxity in relating hadith.

2. Types of weak hadith

There are many types of weak *ahadith*, some of which have a specific title, while others do not. Ibn Salah states that weak *ahadith* are classified according to the lack of one or more of the conditions mentioned for a hadith to be *sahih*, and therefore stated the existence of 42 classes of weak hadith. Some have identified as many as 129 different types of weak *hadith*, but according to ibn Hajr this is of little practical importance. In general weak *ahadith* can be classified into three main categories:

2.1 Where the condition of a continuous chain *(ittisal)* is not met.
2.2 Where the condition of uprightness *(adalah)* is not met; either due to lack of knowledge of a narrator, or due to the narrator being referred to by an unknown name. A lack of biographical information usually leads scholars to suspend making a judgement on the uprightness of a narrator and classing it as *da'if*.
2.3 Where the required degree of accuracy *(dabt)* for it to be *hasan* is not met.

3. The ruling of acting upon weak *ahadith*.

> *'Ibn Mahdi said: If we relate something from the Prophet ﷺ regarding the halal and haram and religious rulings, we are strict in ascertaining the sanad and taking narrators to task. However, when we narrate ahadith related to good actions, punishment and reward, we are lenient in our assessment of the sanad and would overlook the status of the narrators.'*

There are a number of views on this issue and these can be summarised as follows:

3.1 One is not allowed to use weak hadith under any conditions. This is upheld by al-Qadi Abu Bakr ibn al-Arabi and is the position of the hadith master, Yahya ibn Ma'in[35].

---

[35] The assertion that this was their actual position is open to debate.

3.2 One may act in accordance with them without restriction: This has been narrated from Abu Dawud as well as Imam Ahmed.

3.3 They may be used for meritorious acts as well as exhorting people to good actions. However, they cannot be used in the branch of belief and creed, nor in establishing shari'ah rulings. This is the majority opinion.

> "Scholars from amongst the muhaddithin and jurists have said that it is permitted, and even recommended, that one act in accordance with weak hadith in areas of good actions and exhortation to such acts, **as long as the ahadith are not fabricated**. As for legal rulings such as halal and haram, financial transactions, marriage, divorce and other such matters, it is not permitted to act, except with sahih or hasan ahadith, unless of course this be due to precautionary measures in these issues, such as if there exists a hadith relating to the reprehensibility of certain types of financial transactions or types of marriage. In such cases it is recommended that one leave aside such actions. However, it is not obligatory." [al-Nawawi, Kitab al-Adhkar] [Summarised from Shaykh Abdullah Siraj ud-Din Sharh al-Bayquniyyah unless otherwise stated]

4. Fabricated hadith (*Mawdu*)

This is a made up *hadith* falsely attributed by somebody as being the words of the Messenger ﷺ .

> "The goodness of a dinar is known when it is measured against another. Thus, if it differs in redness and purity, it will be known that it is a fake. The diamond is examined through measuring it with another one. If it differs in sparkle and firmness it will be known to be glass. The authenticity of a hadith is known by its coming from reliable narrators and the statement itself must be worthy of being the statement of Prophethood." [Abu Hatim al-Razi, al-Jarh wa Ta'dil 1/351]

4.1 Underlying reasons for the fabrication of hadith

> Ibn 'Adi relates that Abu Asim al-Nabil said: 'I have never seen pious people lie more than in the subject of hadith'

4.1.1 Internal sectarian strife in the community after the death of the Prophet ﷺ . This led to the proliferation of fabricated *ahadith* that spoke of the merits of certain individuals such as: 'Abu Bakr will lead the community after me," and "Ali is the best of mankind and whoever doubts this has disbelieved". Other fabricated *ahadith* were related to doctrinal issues such as: 'The Qur'an is uncreated.'

4.1.2 Enmity towards Islam and the intent to misrepresent it. Hammad ibn Zayid said: 'Heretics falsely attributed 14,000 ahadith to the Prophet ﷺ ". For example, a tradition, 'Indeed God, when He becomes angry, expands and becomes enraged upon the throne to the point that it becomes heavy for those that carry it,' is recorded by Ibn Hibban. The narrator of the hadith, Ayyub ibn Salaam, is known to be a liar. Another example of this type of hadith is that related by Muhammad ibn Sa'id ash-Shami, the heretic, who related that the Prophet ﷺ said: "I am the seal of the Prophets and there is no Prophet after me **except if Allah wills**". The last section of this hadith was fabricated by him in order to support his claim to Prophecy.

4.1.3 To exhort people to acts of goodness and worship. A case in point is the majority of *ahadith* regarding the benefits of reciting certain suras of the Qur'an. Abu 'Ismah Nuh ibn Abi Maryam was asked: 'From where do you narrate all these ahadith on the authority of Ikrimah from ibn Abbas when we know that other Companions of Ikrimah do not have [knowledge of] these?' He said: 'I saw people turn their backs on the Qur'an and concern themselves with the fiqh of Abu Hanifah and the maghazi (sirah) of Ibn Ishaq, so I fabricated these hadith seeking to receive reward thereby."[36]

Ibn Rajab al-Hanbali mentions in his commentary of 'Ilal al-Tirmidhi:

> 'Those that are engaged in worship whose hadith are abandoned are of two types:
> Those who were unable to preserve what they have in terms of hadith and so they started imagining things, to the point that they attributed a saying of a Companion directly to the

---

[36] Given that Nuh ibn Ibrahim was and remained a close student of Abu Hanifah, this narrative shows that even such clear examples of an admittance of fabrication need to be researched to verify that they themselves are not fabricated to discredit particular individuals, schools of law or theological positions. In this case it is clearly an attempt to both discredit Imam Abu Hanifah, but also one of his foremost students, thereby discrediting the whole school.

Prophet ﷺ and complete an otherwise broken chain of narration (wasala al-mursal); [The other are] those who intentionally fabricate a hadith and sought to gain reward through this.'

4.1.4 To gain a worldly benefit. This is particularly so in the case of storytellers and popular preachers who create fantastic stories in order to gain the attention of their listeners.

4.2 Signs of fabricated hadith

'Rabiah ibn Khuthaym said: 'Surely, there are ahadith which have a light like that of daylight through which we know them and there are ahadith which have a darkness like the darkness of the night through which we know them.'

One of the signs of a hadith being fabricated is the unbefitting *(raqiq),* spurious language and meanings associated with the hadith. Ibn Hajr said: *'The central point of a hadith being forged is the existence of an unbefitting meaning, as this religion is based upon fine meanings (mahasin). Anything unbefitting (raqiq) returns back to lowliness."* Imam al-Baka'i said: *'An 'unbefitting meaning' can be an exaggerated threat for a trivial act, or a promise of great reward for a small action. This is well known in the tales of storytellers."*

4.3 Rulings related to fabricated hadith[37]

4.3.1 It has already been mentioned that the Prophet ﷺ said: *'Whoever intentionally fabricates a lie and attributes it to me, let them take their seat in the fire of Hell".* Therefore, it is one of the gravest sins to fabricate a hadith.

4.3.2 Scholars have agreed that a fabricated hadith cannot be used in any way to inform a Muslim concerning what constitutes proper faith and practice in Islam.

4.3.3 It is forbidden to narrate fabricated hadith, regardless of the intentions for doing so unless done to inform of the fabricated nature of the report.

To this end, scholars have collected fabricated *ahadith* in separate books to make known hadith that are spurious. Those that have written on this topic include al-Jawzaqani who wrote *Kitab al-Abatil,* Ibn al-Jawzi in *Al-Maudu'at,* al-Suyuti in *Al-La'ali al-Masnu'ah fi 'l-Ahadith al-Maudu`ah,* and 'Ali al-Qari who put together *Kitab Al-Maudu'at. [Taken from: 'Itr, Minhaj an-Naqd, 301-319]*

5. Orientalist criticism of the *isnad* system

Some Orientalists who study or write on Islam have questioned the numbers of *ahadith* that are reported to have been known and memorised by the scholars of hadith. Imam Ahmad, whose Musnad collection contains over 40,000 hadith, including 10,000 repetitions from over 700 Companions, selected his material from over 750,000 *ahadith [Abu Zahra, Imam Ahmed, 170].* Al-Bukhari and Imam Muslim had received over 600,000 and 300,000 hadith respectively. The large numbers of *ahadith* involved is reflected in hadith scholars reserving the title *'Hafidh'* for an individual who has memorised over one hundred thousand hadith.

Given that the numbers of traditions recorded in hadith collections is far smaller, some early Orientalists ventured to question the authenticity of all *ahadith.* If hadith scholars were wary of the majority of *ahadith,* how could one ascertain the authentic from the spurious. They further asked: If there were so many hadith known to scholars, *where have all these ahadith gone?*

5.1 Important facts related to Orientalist criticisms

There are two main issues that need to be understood to respond to these points:

5.1.1 As has already been shown, the Imams did not set out to record all vigorously authenticated or sound *ahadith* in their collections but only a representative selection.

---

[37] **There were special methods used by hadith scholars to combat hadith fabrication: Researching the status of narrators**: This is one of the most striking elements of hadith scholarship and has assured the quality in the gradation of *ahadith* for later generations; **Giving warning of fabricators and making their status public.** It is reported that Ja'far ibn Zubayr and Imran ibn Hudayr were in a mosque praying and people crowded round Ja'far, while nobody paid any attention to Imran. Shu'bah, who was a well known authority in hadith, passed by them and explained to the people how strange it was that people had crowded around the greatest liar in preference to the most truthful of men! A little while later, everyone had crowded around Imran and left Ja'far; **Investigating the nature of the *isnad*.** Hadith with no *isnad* was rejected outright; **To test the hadith by comparing it to those from other narrators; Establishing ground rules in order to uncover fabricated hadith; Authoring collections that bring together fabricated ahadith in order to warn people of their status.**

5.1.2 The numbers quoted are not based on the number of hadith texts (*matn*). Instead they refer to each chain of narration as each one is classified as a separate hadith according to the scholars.

The example below shows **one hadith text which has at least 13 different chains (isnad)** that are *sahih*, six of which are mentioned in just one hadith collection, that of Imam Muslim. In other words this **one matn** counts for at least **12 separate hadith** as far as scholars are concerned. The reason for this is that each separate *sanad* would be given an individual grading and classification in keeping with the rules of hadith science.

The benefit of this is obvious. Scholars preserving all chains of one *matn* made the process of hadith criticism more proficient and accurate, as each separate *sanad* was thoroughly investigated. As N. Abbott notes:

> "[...] the traditions of Muhammad, as transmitted by his Companions and their successors were, as a rule, scrupulously scrutinised at each step of the transmission, and that the so-called phenomenal growth of tradition in the second and third centuries of Islam was not primarily growth of content, so far as the hadith of Muhammad and the hadith of the Companions are concerned, but represents largely the progressive increase in parallel and multiple chains of transmission. [N. Abbott, Studies In Arabic Literary Papyri, Volume II, 1967, The University Of Chicago Press, p.2]

This simple mathematics that underlies the *isnad* system points a natural transmission of knowledge from the Prophet ﷺ to the Companions and then to their students and would easily produce the sort of figures quoted in classical sources.

> '[...] using geometric progression, we find that one to two thousand Companions and senior successors transmitting two to five traditions each would bring us well within the range of the total number of traditions credited to the exhaustive collections of the third century. Once it is realised that the isnad did, indeed, initiate a chain reaction that resulted in an explosive increase in the number of traditions, the huge numbers that are credited to Ibn Hanbal, Muslim and Bukhari seem not so fantastic after all.' [Ibid, p.72]

Recent research as to the number of *isnad* contained in the main hadith collections shows the way in which the number of *ahadith* fluctuates when one takes into account the different channels and chains of narration for one individual hadith text (*matn*). For example, the collection of al-Bukhari is said to contain only 2,202 separate texts (*matn*) whereas the number of *isnad* channels is much higher: 10,315 (a 500% increase).[38]

5.2 Schacht's 'Projecting-back' hypothesis

One of the most influential critics of Muslim hadith scholarship was Joseph Schacht, who, in his '*Origins Of Muhammadan Jurisprudence*', forwarded a number of theories that he believed would undermine the religion of Islam by questioning the very foundations of how Muslims received their knowledge, namely through the chain of transmission (*isnad*).

His main thesis was that early scholars fabricated chains of transmission in support of their own legal and doctrinal claims. In other words, a hadith was fabricated to support a particular claim, an *isnad* constructed for it and this was then projected forward to the time of the one that fabricated it.

5.2.1 The problem with Schacht's hypothesis

The problem with his theory is quite clear. As can be seen in the example below, for this to be even slightly plausible it would:

- Require a community-wide conspiracy involving different generations of otherwise scrupulous scholars seeking to cover up the intentional fabrication of Prophetic hadith by others.
- Require them to communicate in a way unthinkable without modern day technology, to corroborate information on these fabricated chains.
- Mean that individuals, who may never have met, **being part of a separate chain of the same matn**, would have to ensure that the information as to the earlier authorities matched up with those other chains – without it being found out by other scholars. [*For more details on this topic see al-Azami, On Schacht's Origins Of Muhammadan Jurisprudence*]

---

[38] *Number of isnad mentioned in hadith books including repetition: Al-Bukhari: 10,315. Muslim: 14,188. Abu Dawud: 7,865. Al-Tirmidhi: 6,530. Al-Nisa'i: 7,130. Ibn Majah: 5,991. Al-Muwatta: 2,140. Total: 54,160 [source: Hadith Encyclopedia of the Thesaurus, Islamicus Foundation]*

The Prophet ﷺ said: 'Whenever you pray Jumah prayer, pray four rakah after it.'

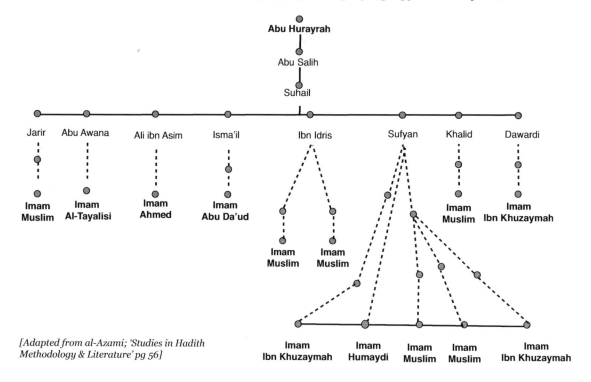

[Adapted from al-Azami; 'Studies in Hadith Methodology & Literature' pg 56]

Main Narrators:

1. Abu Hurayrah: *al-Dawsi al-Yamani, the Companion.*

2. Abu Salih: He is Dhakwan Ibn Abdillah al-Saman. *'Exemplary authority in hadith and one of the leading scholars of Madinah. He used to export oils and fats (samn) to Kufah as a profession and hence his title. Abu Hatim al-Razi says of him: A reliable authority in hadith whose hadith are used as proofs.'* [al-Dhahabi, Siyar al-'Alam, 5,37]

3. Suhail: He is Abu Yazid Suhail ibn Dhakwan Ibn Abdillah al-Madani[39]. *'Al-Nisa says of him: 'There is no problem with him.' Ibn Adi' mentions: 'Suhail had manuscripts and the Imams related from him. According to me he is an established authority and there is no problem with him.' Abu Abd al-Rahman al-Sulami said: I asked al-Daraqutni: Why did al-Bukhari not relate from Suhail in his 'Sahih'? He replied: 'I can find no reason for this and al-Nisa'i, when he used to relates from Suhail, would say: 'By Allah, Suhail is better than Abi Yaman, Yahya ibn Bukayr (one of the narrators of the Muwatta) and others. Al-Bukhari relates profusely from them. He relates from Falih ibn Sulayman and I know not why.'* [al-Mizzi, Tahdhib al-Kamal]

---

[39] All authorities agree on his originally proficient nature as narrator, though it is known that this status deteriorated rapidly. What is known is one of his brothers died as a result of which both his recollection of hadith as well as his precision was badly affected. *Al-Bukhari relates that he heard Ali [Al-Madini] state, 'One of bothers died and as a result he became forgetful of many of his hadith.' Abu Hatim al-Razi said 'His hadith are recorded but are not used as proofs.'*

Lesson Six - Narrator authentication, methods of transmission and the etiquette of narrating hadith

Aim: Through this lesson, students will come to understand the methods used by hadith scholars to ensure the truthfulness and accuracy of those that narrate the hadith of the Prophet (may God bless and grant him peace). They will also be introduced to the unique way in which hadith are passed from teacher to student in an unbroken chain going back to the Prophet (may God bless and grant him peace), as well as the etiquette this entails.

Objectives: By the end of this lesson, students should be able to display the ability to:
1. Define what is meant by *impugnment* and *validation* (*al-jarh* and *al-ta'dil*) and why this is important.
2. List the twelve categories of impugnment and validation worked out by Ibn Hajr.
3. Summarise how these twelve categories relate to the classification of hadith into *sahih*, *hasan* and *da'if*.
4. Discuss the varying methods of scholars in arriving at a judgement concerning a narrator of hadith.
5. List the eight methods of receiving hadith (*turuq tahamul al-hadith*).
6. Discuss scholars' opinions as to which is superior: hearing or reciting hadith.
7. Mention what the *'ijaza* is and what conditions it has.

1. Impugnment and validation: [Al-jarh and al-ta'dil]

> 'The honour of the believers is like a pit from the pits of Hell. Two parties stand on its precipice: Hadith scholars and the Judges.' [Ibn Daqiq al-Iid, al-Iqtrah]

Al-jarh is mentioning the shortcomings in terms of uprightness (*adalah*) and precision (*dabt*) of a narrator on account of which their ahadith are questioned or rejected. *At-ta'dil* is the opposite.

> 'While Ibn Abi Hatim ar-Razi was narrating his book (on the biographical sketches of individuals who related hadith), he was told of the saying of Yahya Ibn Ma'in: 'We critically analyse people who may well have already put down their bags in paradise over two hundred years ago.' At this he started to quake and the book fell from Ibn Abi Hatim's hand and he started to weep.' [Ibn Salah, Muqaddimah, 238]

The science which looks at this aspect of hadith classification is rightly seen as one of the greatest achievements of Muslim scholarship. The development of detailed and precise biographical sketches on individuals who related *ahadith* made verification of the prophetic sunnah a less subjective task. The reason behind this move by Muslim scholars was clear: to ensure the authenticity of all reports claiming to be from the Prophet ﷺ . Detailed records of every individual who was recorded as having narrated a Prophetic hadith preserved all the relevant information for it to be possible to assess the suitability of the individual as a reliable authority. The task was difficult and challenging as it required a balance to be struck between having a good opinion of fellow believers and being detached and objective on the other.

> 'It is related that Abu Bakr ibn Khalad said to Yahya ibn Sa'id: 'Do you not fear that these individuals whose ahadith you have rejected (on account of their character) will take you to task in front of God (in the hereafter)?'' Yahya replied: 'That these people take me to task in front of God is preferable to me than being taken to task by the Prophet ﷺ . If he were to say: 'Why did you not protect my ahadith from the lies of people?''' [Ibn Salah, Muqadimah, 237; Al-Suyuti, Tadrib ar-Rawi p.520]

2. Categories of impugnment and validation: [al-Jarh and ta'dil]

The general rule set down was this: **The narration of an individual who is considered trustworthy (adil) in his religion and is precise (dabt) in terms of what he relates is accepted by hadith scholars**. As has already been discussed, they focused on two main criteria: **uprightness** and **precision**. Individuals were then placed into different levels based on these criteria. Hafiz ibn Hajr mentions the different levels of narrators in his biographical dictionary *Taqrib al-Tahdhib,* classifying them into twelve different categories depending on their degree of trustworthiness and precision. *[Summarised from Shaykh Abdullah Siraj al-Din Sharh al-Bayquniyyah unless otherwise stated]*

2.1 Ibn Hajr on the 12 levels of narrators of ahadith

The sahih category of narrators of ahadith

1. The Companions of the Prophet ﷺ . They are, by consensus, the highest rank in terms of *adalah*.

2. Individuals who have been praised by hadith scholars on account of the proficiency of their hadith narrations through descriptions that use the superlative form, such as the **"most trustworthy of people"** or **"the most precise of people"** or else through the repetition of a description of commendation such as **"the person is trustworthy, trustworthy"** or **"the individual is trustworthy, proficient of memory."**

3. A person described by one distinguishing characteristic such as **"trustworthy"**, **"proficient"** or **"established"**, and the like.

The hasan category of narrators of ahadith

4. An individual whose stature is below those mentioned above, such as a description of **"truthful"** or **"there is no problem with him"** and the like.

The moderately da'if category of narrators of ahadith

5. An individual who is slightly lower than those in the status above him; such people are referred to by terms such as **"truthful but bad of memory"** or **"truthful but imagines things"**, or **"truthful but detrimentally affected towards the end of his life"**. Included in this category are sometimes those accused of general heresy such as individuals from the *Qadariyah* and the *Rawafid* sect.

6. Those that only have a few hadith related from them and who have no reasons given for their hadith to be rejected. Such individuals are referred to by phrases such as **"acceptable in situations where they have a supporting reference (mutaba'a)"**. If no such reference is found then they are considered to be weak.

The da'if category of narrators of ahadith

7. A known person, from whom more than one person has related *ahadith*, but for whom there is no record of validation by hadith scholars. Such an individual is referred to by terms such as **"hidden"** or **"of an unknown status (majhul al-hal)"** due to a scarcity of information regarding their uprightness.

8. An individual who has not been commended by an established authority and who has also been declared as weak by others. Such an individual is referred to by the simple term **"weak"**.

9. An unknown individual from whom only one person narrates *ahadith* about whom no commendation has been reported. Scholars refer to such an individual by the terms **"individually unknown (majhul al-'ayn)"**, meaning that he is not known amongst hadith scholars;

10. An individual who has not been commended by anybody. Moreover, they have also been declared weak on account of a specific accusation or discrepancy. Such an individual is referred to by terms such as **"abandoned"** or **"extremely weak in hadith"** or **"disregarded"**.

11. An individual who has been accused of lying. Terms such as **"under accusation of lying"** are used to refer to such an individual. This does not mean that the person has intentionally lied. Rather, discrepancies occur with such frequency that they are accused of having intentionally lied.

12. An individual who is referred specifically by the name **'the liar'** or **'intentional fabricator.'**

2.2 The effect of these categories on the gradation of a hadith

Scholars have made general rulings in relation to the aforementioned categories.
The first three categories are acceptable and strong, with the majority coming into the category of narrators in the collections of al-Bukhari and Muslim. **The fourth category** is made up of individuals whose *ahadith* are acceptable to a lesser degree than the first. These are people that Imam at-Tirmidhi has referred to using the term **'hasan'** (sound) and who Imam Abu Dawud has remained silent about. The hadith from **categories five and six** are inherently weak but if strengthened through supporting evidences and chains of narration, are declared as being *hasan li'ghayrhi* i.e. sound on account of supporting evidences. **The remaining six categories** are those of individuals whose *ahadith* are weak, with the degree of weakness increasing the further one travels down the categories.

3. Arriving at a judgement concerning a narrator of hadith

Although the categories listed above are the product of later scholarship, the general method followed by Ibn Hajr is accepted by all. This does not mean that there was unanimity with regards to an individual's standing amongst hadith masters. Rarely has an individual received universal praise or criticism. Hence, scholars differed in their assessment of individual hadith narrators, some being critical while others being lenient.

In such a situation, preference is usually given to the more critical position *unless this has been taken into account by those that state the narrator as being acceptable.* An example would be certain types of heretics who disowned their heresy and thereby were deemed later to be acceptable. Some scholars hold that if the number of people stating the trustworthiness of the narrator of hadith is more than those critical of him/her then those who report acceptability of the narrator are given precedence.

Suffice it to say that all opinions as to the reliability of a hadith narrator have to be investigated before a definitive statement can be made as to an individual's status. Al-Lacknawi says: '*It is important that one does not pre-empt judgement regarding a narrator of hadith due to the existence of judgements passed by scholars of al-jarh and al-tadil. It is important that one investigates the matter further as this issue is one of grave importance and danger. It is not permitted for one to take on face value criticisms of a narrator of hadith. Many a time one finds that there is an issue that disqualifies one from accepting such a criticism. This has many forms which are not hidden from those that are well versed.*'

The person criticising the integrity of a narrator may himself be criticised by others. Ibn Hajr says in his biography of Ahmad ibn Shabib, after having recorded al-Azadi's criticism of him as not being an acceptable narrator: '*Nobody took any notice of this statement. Al-Azadi himself is not acceptable!*'

3.1 Strict and lenient hadith scholars

Another factor to be taken into consideration is when the one criticising is excessively harsh in demoting the status of a narrator of hadith. It is well known amongst scholars that hadith authorities were not equally stringent in their assessment of narrators of hadith.

Imam al-Nisapuri and al-Tirmidhi were considered to be slightly lenient in their assessment of hadith narrators, whereas the two Yahyas, namely Ibn Ma'in and Ibn Sa'id al-Qattan were extremely strict in theirs as were Abu Hatim ar-Razi and al-Nasa'i. Imam al-Bukhari and Muslim are considered to be moderate in this regard, as was Imam Ahmad ibn Hanbal. [*al-Dhahabi, al-Muqidhah, 83; 'Itr, Naqd, p.96-97*]

4. Methods of receiving hadith (*turuq tahamul al-hadith*)

Not all hadith have been received and recorded in the same way; sometimes an authority will have heard the hadith directly from their teacher. In other instances it was written for them in a letter and received on the authority of the one that relates the hadith. Scholars laid down different categories through which *ahadith* have been passed down to us based on the method used. Hadith authorities were meticulous in verifying which method was used by each narrator as a means of uncovering deception and slackness in hadith preservation and scholarship. Sometimes an individual who discovered the handwriting of a shaykh relating a hadith would venture to use words such as "My teacher informed me" or "*I heard him say*", whereas this is considered deception by hadith scholars.

The modern age has seen an explosion of would-be hadith scholars who have not even achieved the lowest conditions of relating hadith. They venture to report Prophetic reports with little regard for both the verification process involved in ascertaining the status of a hadith, or the degree of care taken in recording it.

It is interesting that most people's knowledge of Prophetic traditions in this age is through no recognised method of transmission. This is indicative of the poor state of the knowledge tradition at the present time.[40]

5. Etiquettes of hadith narration

Scholars have emphasised the importance given to the spiritual state of the students of hadith and have set down guidelines which should be followed for those that seek to collect and narrate the sayings of the Prophet ﷺ . The most important of these is:

5.1 Sincerity towards God.

> *Abu Jafar ibn Hamdan was asked: 'With what intention should one write down hadith?' He said 'Do you not relate that when one makes mention of the pious, God's mercy descends?' He said: 'Why, yes!' He then said: 'The Messenger of God ﷺ is the fountain-head of the pious.'*

5.2 To act in accordance with one's knowledge.

> *The Qur'an says, "The example of those that sought to uphold the Torah and then fell short is like the example of the donkey laden with books…"[62:5]*

> *It is related that Waqi' ibn Al-Jarah, the teacher of Imam Shafi'i, said: 'If you want to memorise hadith, then act in accordance with them".*

5.3 Respecting one's hadith teachers and showing them honour.

In seeking knowledge, one should not be afflicted by embarrassment or shyness. Mujahid said: *'Knowledge is not gained by one that is either shy or arrogant'*. This may also mean that one seek knowledge from an individual that appears to have a lower rank in knowledge. Waqi' said: *'A person will not be considered from amongst the proficient authorities of hadith until he records knowledge from one that is superior than them, of a similar rank to them, and also one who is below them in rank.'*

5.4 Sharing knowledge benefits with other students.

> *Imam Malik said, "Part of the blessing of hadith is students benefitting from one another".*
> *[Selected and summarised from Dr. Ittr', Minhaj al-Naqd, Pg 189-196]*

---

[40] There are eight methods of receiving *ahadith* mentioned by scholars:

1. Direct hearing (*as-sam'a*): the recipient of the hadith, according to this method, has received a hadith through directly hearing the hadith from a teacher, who has recited it either from memory or from a written record. In such a situation one can use the phrase *"I heard so and so"* or *"such and such spoke to me or informed me."*

2. Recitation or rehearsal (*al-qira'a 'ala al-shaykh*): The disciple in this case reads back to the shaykh, from memory or record, the hadith which he has known from his shaykh or someone else, and wants the shaykh to verify its accuracy. In such a situation one says *"I read this to so-and-so"*. However, scholars disagree as to whether the narrator of hadith can say that they were 'directly informed of' or 'were narrated' the hadith by the shaykh. Abu Hanifah considered this second type of receiving hadith to be the strongest, on account of the fact that it entails repetition from the students, whereas others, such as Imam Malik, have considered the first and second type to be of equal standing.

3. Permission (*al-'ijazah*): This is when the teacher grants permission to transmit from him ahadith in a specified or unspecified context, even without direct hearing or recitation. Scholars of hadith are known to have employed this method with their disciples and the '*ijazah* so granted was equivalent to a license that they gave. The condition for the student to relate hadith on account of the '*ijazah* given is that they have the necessary scholarly qualifications to do so, namely a sound understanding of the classical Arabic language and accuracy in relating the hadith in question. Imam Malik held that it is a condition of the validity of an '*ijazah* that the one to whom it is given is suitably competent.

4. Presentation (*al-munawala*): This is when the teacher/shaykh presents his own manuscript he himself has originally received from his source and tells him that *"these are what I have heard or received from so and so"*. This may be combined with permission ('*ijazah*) for the disciple to transmit what the teacher gives him.

5. Correspondence (*al-mukataba*): This is when the hadith teacher writes the hadith in his own handwriting, or asks someone else to write it, and then hands it over or sends it personally to his disciple, with approval for the latter to transmit what the teacher wrote.

6. Declaration (*al-i'lan*): This is when the teacher merely declares to his disciple that *"this hadith or collection thereof is what I have heard from so and so, or I received it from so and so"*, without saying anything regarding permission for the disciple to transmit it.

7. Bequest (*al-wasiyya*): what is meant by this is that a hadith teacher leaves instructions, upon departing on a journey or at the time of death, addressed to someone, asking him to transmit the contents of a particular collection or book from him.

8. Finding (*al-wijada*): This is where a person finds a hadith in the handwriting of his teacher, or under his instruction, which he has not heard from his teacher. The one who has found the materials may then transmit them to others provided that he recognises the handwriting is of his teacher, or when he is assured of the reliability of his finding.

[See Kamali, A Textbook of Hadith Studies, p14-20]

Appendix of sample texts of impugnment and validation: (*al-jarh* and *ta'dil*)

1. Ahmad ibn al-Hasan ibn al-Qasim ibn Samura al-Kufi died in Egypt in 262 AH. Al-Daraqutni and others said concerning him that he was *"matrook" (abandoned)* and Ibn Hibban said that he was a liar *"kadhaab"*. A so-called hadith that is reported by him from Waki', from Sufyan, from Ibn Jurayj, from Amr ibn Dinar from Ibn Abbas, labelled as a *marfu`* (elevated) hadith, says, *"On the Day of Resurrection, a caller will call from beneath the Throne (`Arsh) and will mention the names of Abu Bakr, 'Umar, 'Uthman, and 'Ali,"* [An example of a lower-end category ten-eleven da'if narrator].

2. Habib ibn Ali Habib (d. 280 AH), whose father's name is Zariq, or some said to be Marzuq Abu Muhammad al-Misri. Ahmed ibn Hanbal said of him that he was *"unreliable (laysa bi-thiqah)"*, whereas Abu Dawud went so far as to say that he was *"the greatest of liars (akdhab al-nas)"*. Abu Hatim ar-Razi said that he pretentiously narrated hadith from his nephew al-Zuhri which he actually fabricated. Ibn Adi (d. 315) said that virtually all of his ahadith were forgeries. Ibn Hibban said concerning him that he attributed ahadith to reliable people and chains of transmitters, such as Malik-Nafi-Ibn Umar, which were forgeries. One such forgery by him was the so called hadith: *"The beauty of this world would be lost as of the year 225 AH"* [This is an example of a category twelve narrator]. [Kamali, A Textbook of Hadith studies, p94-95]

3. *Al-Rabiah ibn Yahya ibn Muqsim.* One of the narrators that al-Bukhari relates from in his Sahih. Ibn Abi Hatim said that he was *"trustworthy and well-grounded (thiqatun thabt)"*, while Ibn Hibban mentions him in his book *ath-Thiqat* on trustworthy narrators. However, the hadith scholar Ibn Qani' holds him to be *"weak"*, while ad-Daraqutni says *"Weak – not solid – makes many mistakes. He narrated from ath-Thawri on the authority of Ibn al-Munkadar from Jabir (ibn Abdullah) that 'the Prophet ﷺ combined two prayers together'. This hadith is not associated to Ibn al-Munkadar under any stretch of the imagination. This mistake alone is enough to disqualify one hundred thousand hadith!"*

Scholars have paid little attention to these two criticisms, as Ibn Qani' provides no supporting evidence for his judgement, while ad-Daraqutni's exaggerated claim that one single mistake can lead to a total rejection of all his ahadith has not been accepted by others. Furthermore, ar-Rabiah ibn Yahya has been declared trustworthy by none other than Ibn Abi Hatim, considered one of the most stringent and meticulous critics of hadith narrators. [Ibn Abdul Mun'im, Taysir, p.91. This is an example of a category three narrator that is disputed]

4. Bahz ibn Hakim [see Lesson Four in example of a category four narrator of a sound (hasan) hadith]

5. Asim ibn Ubaydillah [see Lesson Four, where Imam at-Tirmidhi is extremely liberal in raising the hadith to hasan li ghayrihi]

Setting the base for Worship

Understanding the law and spirituality of Prayer 1

Module Fqh 2.02.D

Lesson One - Meaning, importance and types of prayer

Aim: Through this lesson, students will develop an understanding of the word used for prayer *(salah)* in Arabic as well as a brief history of prayer in earlier manifestations of Islam. The importance of the prayer as well as the basic types of prayers will also be covered along with a look at *khushu'* (humility) in prayer.

Objectives: By the end of this lesson a student should be able to display the ability to:
1. **Explain** the meaning of *salah* in Islamic law and where this is derived from.
2. **Summarise** the history of the prayer and the stages through which the daily prayer went through until it was set at five daily prayers.
3. **Discuss** the main reasons why prayer is important in Islam.
4. **List** the conditions that make the prayer an individual obligation.
5. **Detail** the various types of prayers and how these types differ.
6. **Appreciate** the spiritual aspect of praying with particular reference to '*khushu*'.

1. What does the word '*salah*' mean?

1.1 In the **Arabic language,** the word *salah* is taken from a linguistic root which means *any type of supplication which is done intending good thereby*. In the Qur'an, God says to the Prophet ﷺ :

> **"and supplicate for them (salli alayhim), for indeed your supplication is a source of consolation for them" [9:103]**.

Here, it is taken to mean a prayer or *du'a* made for the good of the community and his ﷺ followers.

It is also said that the word comes from the root meaning '*to heat and burn*', as in the Arabic saying '*to straighten the spear-staff in the fire*'. Crooked branches were used to make spears and would be straightened through the use of heat to make them supple and then gently bent until they became straight. Upon cooling they would retain their straightness. This word was then used in Islam for the ritual prayer as the prayer straightens and rectifies the one who prays from indecency and wrong actions in the same way that the spear-staff is straightened from crookedness by applying heat.

1.2 In **Islamic law (*fiqh*),** Prayer is defined simply as: '*A type of worship which consists of recitation, bowing and prostration.*' *[al-Qarafi, adh-Dhakhirah, V1, pg384; al-Qastalani, Marasid al-Salah, pg53]*

2. A short history of the prayer

The actions that make up the prayer have remained largely unchanged throughout human history, and consist of the simple act of bowing and prostration out of reverence to God. It was the practice of all those who sought to draw near to their Creator and has altered little in basic form and substance. We find it mentioned many times in the Old and New Testaments in a form that is recognisable to Muslims.

> *"Ezra praised the Lord! The great God; and all the people lifted their hands and responded, "Amen! Amen!" Then they bowed down and worshipped the Lord with their faces to the ground [Nehemiah 8:6]*

The Qur'an emphasises this when relating the stories of previous Prophets, mentioning the act of bowing and prostrating as being the common thread of worship.

> **"And the angels said: "O Mary! Behold, God has elected you and made you pure, and raised you above all the women of the world. O Mary! Remain truly devout to your Sustainer, and prostrate yourself in worship, and bow down with those who bow down [before Him]."[3:42-43]**

2.1 The five prayers made obligatory

One of the many blessings of the night journey and heavenly ascension *(al-Isra' wal Mi'raj)* that the Prophet ﷺ was taken on was that the five daily prayers were given to his community.

Before that time, it is related that the prayer was two units *(rakah)* in the late afternoon and two at daybreak *(fajr)* and Imam al-Muzani, one of the students of Imam al-Shafi'i, mentioned that before the night journey, the early Muslims prayed twice every day. Once before the setting of the sun and the other just before daybreak. This is the meaning given to the verse ***"and glorify the praises of your Lord in the evening and the early morning' [40:55].***

Ibn Hajr on the other hand narrates that some scholars held that the only prayer required initially in Makkah was the night prayer. *[Al-Suhayli, Rawd al-'Unf, 2:284; al-Qurtubi 15:310; Ibn-Hajr, Fath al-Bari 1:603]*

The narrations surrounding the instance of the *al-Isra' wal Mi'raj* are well authenticated, detailing how the initial number of prayers made obligatory was fifty in a day and night and that this was gradually reduced for the Prophet ﷺ to just five prayers, which nevertheless equated in reward to fifty.

> *"....Then Jibril (A.S) ascended with me to a place where I heard the creaking of the pens. Then God enjoined fifty prayers on my followers. When I returned with this order of God, I passed by Musa (A.S) who asked me: "What has God enjoined on your followers? I replied: "He has enjoined fifty prayers on them". Musa (A.S) said: "Go back to your Lord, for your followers will not be able to bear it". So I returned to God and requested a reduction, and He reduced it to half. When I passed by Musa (A.S) again and informed him of it, he said: "Go back to your Lord as your followers will not be able to bear it". So I returned to God and requested a further reduction, and half of it was reduced. I again passed by Musa (A.S) and he said to me: "Return to your Lord, for your followers will not be able to bear it". So I returned to God and He said: "These are five prayers and they are equal to fifty in reward, for My word does not change'.*
>
> *I returned to Musa (A.S) and he told me to go back again. I replied: "I feel shy of asking my Lord again". Then Jibril (A.S) took me until we reached Sidrat al-Muntaha (the Lote-tree) which was shrouded in colours, indescribable. Then I was admitted into Paradise, where I found small tents or walls made of pearls and its earth was musk". [al-Bukhari]*

2.2 The importance of Prayer

The importance of the prayer can be understood from two of the main benefits that it affords humans. **Firstly**, the prayer helps to nurture a connection with God in the midst of our busy and hectic lives.

> ***"Guard your prayers, especially the middle Prayer, and stand up with devotion to God". [2: 238]***

Secondly, by keeping us mindful of God for the majority of the day, it also aids in the wider social function of preventing irreligious behaviour by creating the habit of good conduct in society.

> ***"Establish prayer at the two ends of the day and in some hours of the night. Verily, the good deeds remove the evil deeds. This is a reminder for the mindful". [11:114]***

On account of its many benefits, it is the act most recommended in the Qur'an, and will be the first act of worship that will be taken to account on the Day of Judgement.

Abdullah ibn Qart related that the Messenger of God ﷺ said: *"The first act that the slave will be accountable for on the Day of Judgement will be the prayer. If it is good, then the rest of his acts will be good. If it falls short, then the rest of his acts will fall short." [Al-Tabarani]*

3. The conditions that make the prayer an individual obligation

> Ali ibn Abi Talib related that the Messenger of God ﷺ said: *"The pen is raised for three: the one who is sleeping until he wakens; the child until he becomes an adult; and one who is insane until he becomes sane." [Abu Dawud]*

An individual is obliged to pray, upon the fulfillment of the following conditions:

3.1 Islam.

3.2 Sanity. This is where an individual is able to distinguish between fair and foul as well as understand the consequences of their actions.

3.3 Maturity. This is ascertained either by:
    3.3.1 Physical changes, such as menstruation in the case of a female or seminal discharge for males
    3.3.2 reaching 15 years of age, whichever occurs first.

4. Types of prayers

Are all prayers equally important and emphasized? What happens if one cannot perform some prayers due to an excuse? To answer this question it is necessary to understand how different prayers have been given different rulings by scholars based on their study of the Qur'an and Sunnah.There are four basic types of prayer:

4.1 Compulsory (*fard*) prayers which are so classified because they have been established through the use of indisputable strong proofs. These prayers are broken down into two types:

    4.1.1 *Fard 'ayn* which are prayers that are compulsory on all individuals. Examples are the *Jumah* (Friday) and five daily prayers. Leaving such prayers is considered a major wrong action (*kabirah*).

    4.1.2 *Fard kifayah* are prayers which are compulsory on the community as a whole. If such prayers, like the funeral prayer, are performed by a section of the community, the rest of the community is absolved of blame for not performing them.

4.2 Obligatory (*wajib*) prayers are those prayers that are less emphasised than *fard* prayers and so entail less blame if left unperformed. They are, however, more emphasised than the *sunnah* prayers mentioned below. Examples of this type of prayer are the *witr* prayer, as well as a *nafl* prayer that after having been started was spoiled or broken off incomplete.

4.3 Recommended through a Prophetic norm (*sunnah*). These are of two types:

    4.3.1 *Mu'akadah* (emphasised) are those prayers performed alongside the five daily prayers and whose importance is stressed more than other sunnah prayers.

    4.3.2 *Ghayr mu'akadah*, (non-emphasised) which are the other prayers established by the Prophetic example, such as the two rakah prayed when entering a *masjid*.

4.4 Supererogatory (*nafl*) which are prayers that are neither *fard*, *wajib* or *sunnah*.

5. The number of compulsory prayers

It has been established by sound and incontrovertible proofs that there are five prayers each day and night. This has been the practice of the Muslim community since the time it was first made an obligation, and continues to this day.

> *Talha ibn Ubaydullah narrated: "A Bedouin with scattered hair came to the Messenger ﷺ and said: "O Messenger of God, inform me of what God has made obligatory on me with regards to prayers?" He replied: "Five prayers, unless you do more voluntarily". [al-Bukhari]*

6. Reconnecting with the spirit:

6.1 Khushu - Humility in the prayer

> *Jubayr ibn Nufayr related on the authority of 'Awf ibn Malik that one day the Messenger ﷺ looked to the sky and said: "This is the abode to which knowledge will be raised". Ziyad ibn Labid , who was from the Ansar said to him: "O Messenger, how is it that knowledge will be raised while it has now become so well established and hearts have preserved it? He replied: "I thought you were amongst the most intelligent people of Madinah!" He ﷺ went on to mention the misguidance of previous nations in spite of them having revelation from God. Jubayr went on to say: 'So I met Shaddad ibn 'Aws and related this instance to him and he said: "Awf has told the truth. Should I not tell you the first part of knowledge to be raised? I replied 'Why of course! He replied: "Khushu', such that the time will come that you will not be able to find even a single soul having it'. [Al-Hakim, § 337]*

> *Ubadah Ibn Samit said: "I will relate to you of the first knowledge to be raised up from amongst people - khushu' such that a time will soon come when one enters a large masjid and finds not a single soul with it" [Al-Hakim, 338]*

> *"Al-Rabi ibn Khuthaym used to say: "When engaged in prayer, I never pay attention to anything, except what I am saying and what is being said to me" [...]*

> *[...] Amir ibn Abdullah was one of those who were humble in his prayers. He would sometimes pray while his daughter was playing the tambourine and the women of the house were chatting freely, but he was quite oblivious to the noise and did not hear it. They once asked him: "Does anything come to your mind when you are in the prayer?" He said, "Yes, the thought that I am standing in the presence of God, and that I am bound for Paradise or Hell...."*

"[...] Some of them kept their prayers short, fearing the whisperings of the Devil. We are told that on a certain occasion Ammar bin Yasir finished his prayer quickly. When someone commented on this he said "Did you see me skip any of the essentials?'

[...] It is related that Umar ibn al-Khattab said from the pulpit: "A man's hair may turn grey while in Islam without having completed one prayer for God. When people asked him how this could be, he said: 'Because he never achieves perfect humility, submissiveness and devotion to God in any of his prayers". [al-Ghazali, al-Ihya]

6.2 The metaphor of the prayer - Blowing spirit into the outward form

"The prayer is composed in a wondrous way, made up of the acts of standing, reciting, bowing and prostrating, and it is as if each pillar of the prayer corresponds to the bricks and wood used in a building. Whereas in Paradise, palaces are described as having building blocks of gold and silver and the cement is made of musk, the prayer is made up of building blocks of standing and reciting, bowing and prostrating for which the cement is the glorifying, praising and exalting of God. This whole structure of the prayer corresponds to a structure for which sincerity is like the spirit.

*In the same way that God created Adam (A.S.) in the best form and then blew into him the spirit that he may become alive, Adam (A.S.) and his progeny were ordered to establish the outward form of the prayer out of these actions and then told to blow into it the spirit of sincerity. He created Adam (A.S.) "**from dried clay formed of altered black mud" [15:26]** and his outward form had no value until the spirit was blown into him. In the same way, the outward form of the prayer has no value if it does not have the spirit of sincerity in it.*

*Sincerity is the spirit in every form of worship. Praise be to the One who is able to create both the outward forms as well as the spirit, order his servants to acquire the form of worship, then commands them to give it life by blowing into it the spirit of sincerity. He did not leave His servants without an aim [in life]. Rather he made them deserving of being addressed by Him and brought them close to Him as a subtle gift (lutf) and grace (fadl) and said: "**prostrate and draw close" [96:20]** [Abi Abdillah al-Bukhari, Mahasin al-Islam, p8]*

Lesson Two - Making up missed prayers (*qada'*)

> **Lesson Aim:** By the end of this lesson students will appreciate the gravity of intentionally missing the five prayers as well as how to make amends for this. They will also become well-versed in the main arguments surrounding the issue of whether one needs to make such prayers up or not.
>
> **Objectives:** By the end of this lesson students should be able to display the ability to:
> 1. **Discuss** the difference of opinion regarding the one intentionally neglecting the prayer.
> 2. **Detail** whether it is necessary to make up prayers (*qada'*) missed out of forgetfulness or sleep.
> 3. **Explain** how one makes up missed prayers and **list** the three situations where one does not have to perform missed prayers in their original sequence.
> 4. **Summarise** the difference of opinion relating to making up prayers missed intentionally.
> 5. **List** the main proofs provided by Ibn Hazm supporting his position and what one point this can be summarised to.
> 6. **List** the main proofs used by the four schools of Sunni law supporting their position.
> 7. **Mention** the response of the four schools to the points made by Ibn Hazm.

1. Neglecting the Prayer

> *Jabir relates that the Messenger ﷺ said: "[What lies] between a person and disbelief is discarding the prayer." [Muslim]*

Given the importance and associated benefits of the five daily prayers, it is no wonder that the gravity of neglecting the prayer has led to some scholars holding that such a person ceases to remain a Muslim. However, the overwhelming majority of the schools of Islamic law do not extend this ruling to one who, while affirming the obligatory nature of the five prayers, neglects them out of laziness.

Needless to say, anyone who claims to be Muslim and yet denies that the prayer is an obligation, as set out clearly in the Qur'an, denies a matter known to be an essential part of this religion and thereby ceases to be part of that very community.

> *Abdullah ibn 'Amr al-A'as reported that the Prophet ﷺ one day mentioned the prayer and said: 'Whoever guards their prayer, it will be a light, proof and salvation for them on the Day of Resurrection. For whoever does not guard it, there will be no light, no proof and no salvation for them. On the Day of Resurrection they will be with Qarun, Fir'awn, Haman, and Ubayy ibn Khalaf'. [Ahmad, §6576]*

2. The making up of missed Prayers (*qada'*)

> *Abu Qatadah narrated that the Prophet ﷺ said: "There is no negligence [recorded] while one is asleep. Rather negligence occurs when one is awake. If one of you forgets the prayer or sleeps through its time, he should do the prayer when he recalls it." [al-Tirmidhi, §177]*

It is obligatory to make up any missed *salah*, whether missed knowingly, due to forgetfulness or sleep. Missing a prayer knowingly is a major wrong action (*kabirah*) and one should make sincere repentance immediately. As for prayers missed unintentionally due to sleep or forgetfulness, they should be made up as soon as one wakes or remembers.

Abu Hurayrah reported: *"The Messenger of God ﷺ returned from the battle of Khaybar travelling by night. When we were overcome with sleep, he halted to rest. He addressed Bilal saying: "Keep watch at night for us". But Bilal, who was leaning against the saddle of his mount, was overcome by sleep. Neither the Prophet ﷺ , Bilal, nor any of the other Companions woke until the sun struck them.*

The Messenger of God ﷺ was the first to rise. He called out: "O Bilal!" He replied: "Messenger of God, may my parents be sacrificed for you! He who held captive your soul, held captive mine". Then they drove their mounts a short distance. The Prophet ﷺ did wudu' and commanded Bilal to give the call to prayer and led them in prayer. When he ﷺ finished the prayer, he said: "If anyone forgets praying the prayer, he should do it when he recalls it, for God has said **"Establish prayer for My remembrance"**. *[Abu Dawud]*

3. Chronological order and making up prayers

It is necessary to make up missed prayers in their correct sequence. This means that, when making up prayers that have been missed, one starts by performing the first prayer that was missed before moving on to the next.

3.1 Does one always have to make up prayers in chronological order?

There are three situations in which performing missed prayers in sequence is not necessary and one may pray the prayer at hand and delay the makeup of missed prayers.

3.1.1 Shortage of time. When there is not enough time for the performance of anything other than the prayer at hand.

3.1.2 Forgetfulness. This is when one has forgotten that previous prayers have been missed. Any prayers done in this state of forgetfulness are valid.

3.1.3 When the number of prayers missed becomes six or more in number.

4. Text in Focus - Should one make up prayers missed intentionally?

One issue that has recently been the subject of ongoing confusion and debate is whether or not one is required to make up prayers missed intentionally due to laziness or neglect. Some say that this is not necessary because such a person has in fact left Islam through such negligence, so how can they be asked to make up something they neglected while no longer a Muslim?

Others held that while such an action is one of the most grievous of major wrong actions, a person in such a situation has to make up (*qada'*) such prayers.

Qada' is defined as the performance of an obligatory act after its original time has elapsed. God says in the Qur'an: **"And when you have attained serenity, establish the prayer, for indeed the prayer has been established at fixed times for the believers"**. **[4:103]** This verse shows that there are specific times assigned for each obligatory prayer; it is the duty of believers to perform their prayers within the prescribed times.

4.1 The areas of agreement

It is useful to summarise the areas of agreement amongst scholars first, so that one is better placed to see what the question of debate is. There are two scenarios upon which scholars agree.

4.1.1 There is a consensus amongst scholars that a person who misses a prayer due to sleep or forgetfulness should repeat the prayer when they remember [*Ibn Rushd, Bidayah*]. This is based on the hadith in which the Prophet ﷺ said: *"There is no negligence [recorded] while one is asleep. Rather negligence occurs when one is awake. If one of you forgets the prayer or sleeps through its time, then he should do the prayer when he recalls it"* [*al-Tirmidhi, 177*]

4.1.2 They also agree that there is no *qada* upon a woman who misses prayers due to menstruation, one suffering from post natal bleeding, or a non-Muslim for prayers they missed before they enter Islam.

4.2 The areas of disagreement

Scholars differed concerning an individual who misses out prayers intentionally through laziness or general neglect.

All four schools of Sunni law (namely the Maliki, Hanafi, Shafi'i and Hanbali schools) consider it obligatory for a person who intentionally misses the obligatory five prayers to perform *qada'* as atonement for missing these out.

However, the Andalusian scholar Ibn Hazm broke with this consensus, stating in his book '*al-Muhallah'* [*Question no. 279*] that there was no basis for such a ruling. He argued that a person that misses prayers intentionally is not obliged to make up these prayers. He was followed later by Ibn Taymiyyah and his student Ibn Qayyim al-Jawziyyah in championing this position.

4.2.1 What is at the root of the disagreement?

The basis of this controversy is the fact that there is no conclusive legal text in either the Qur'an or the Prophetic sunnah concerning an individual who misses out prayers intentionally through laziness or general neglect. This issue therefore serves as an excellent case study on the methodologies used by different scholars in arriving at a ruling in cases of law where there is no specific text in the Quran or Sunnah on a topic.

4.3 How did the minority arrive at their position and what were their proofs?

> *"As for one that intentionally leaves the prayer until its time has elapsed, such a person will never be able to make up this prayer, but rather he should extend himself in performing good acts and non-obligatory prayers so that his scales become heavy on the Day of Judgement. Let him repent and ask forgiveness from God" [Ibn Hazm, Al-Muhallah]*

4.3.1 What are the evidences he forwarded in support of this view?

4.3.1.1 *'If it was obligatory then God would not have left out the mention of this in the Qur'an. God says: '**And indeed your Lord is not forgetful.' [19:64]***

4.3.1.2 *'The Prophet* ﷺ *said: 'Whoever misses the 'Asr prayer, it is as if they have been bereaved of their family and lost their wealth.'*

4.3.1.3 *'It is related that Umar said in one of his sermons: "Indeed the prayer has a time which God has made a condition for its performance, and it is not proper except in such a time.'*

4.3.2 Summary of Ibn Hazm's proof.

The basic proof used by Ibn Hazm is that the lack of any direct legal text to the contrary indicates that it is not obligatory to make up the prayers missed intentionally out of laziness.

This is known as *al-Baraa'at al-Asliyyah (The original state of freedom from obligation),* where in the case of a lack of proofs to the contrary, one resorts back to the original ruling, which is the freedom from any obligation. This is sometimes also referred to as *al-Istishab (Presumption of Continuity).* Hence, it is not permitted to formulate a ruling unless there is a clear text to support it. *[See Shari'ah Module 1, Lesson 3].*

4.4 How did the majority arrive at their position and what were their proofs?

The position of the majority of scholars is represented by Imam an-Nawawi when he states:

> *"Scholars who are given importance in such matters have reached a consensus that whoever leaves a prayer intentionally is obliged to perform qada'. [Only] Abu Mohammed Ali ibn Hazm opposed them. What he has stated, as well as being against the scholarly consensus ('ijma), is invalid in terms of the proofs furnished. He extended himself in trying to prove otherwise, and in all that which he mentioned there is in fact no binding proof.*
>
> *Amongst the things that point towards the obligation of qada are:*
>
> **4.4.1** *The tradition related by Abu Hurayrah that the Prophet* ﷺ *ordered those that engaged in sexual intercourse during the daylight hours of Ramadan to fast a day, as well as also give the [set] expiation for the act. In other words, [fast] in place of the day that had been [intentionally] nullified through intentional intercourse. This has been related by Al-Bayhaqi with a sound chain (isnad), and Abu Dawud has related likewise.*
> **4.4.1** *If it is deemed obligatory to perform qada for what has been missed due to forgetfulness, then it is **more proper** that somebody that misses it out intentionally does so as well"*[41] *[Al-Nawawi, al-Mujmu' , v3, p54]*

4.4.1.1 Summary of the Majority proof:

The majority of scholars have made use of a self-evident analogy *(the 'a fortiori' argument; Ar. mafhum al-muwafaqah)* to establish the ruling for this issue. If one has to make up prayers missed out of forgetfulness, then more so if this was intentional. *[Al-Maziri, al-Mu'lim; Al-Qarafi, al-Dhakhirah].*

4.5 Response to the points of Ibn Hazm

The majority of scholars have rejected the proofs put forward by Ibn Hazm as being of no direct relevance to the issue at hand, based on the following reasons:

---

[41] *See Qur'an module lesson 3, under Mafhum or implied meaning, for use of this type of reasoning.*

- The vast majority of fiqh rulings do not have directly corresponding primary legal texts from the Qur'an and Sunnah providing a ruling for them, therefore the use of the Qur'anic verse: **"And indeed your Lord is not forgetful"** [19:64] is misplaced.

- The majority do not deny the enormity of the wrong action entailed when missing a prayer intentionally. This, however, has no bearing on whether the person should make up the prayer or not.

- The statement of 'Umar regarding the nature of the prayer times has no relevance to the question of *qada*, as prayer is like a debt owed to God which needs to be paid even if done in a belated manner.

5. Reconnecting with the spirit: Bring to mind the greatness of God during the prayer

"It befits the one praying that he bring to mind that which demonstrates to his heart that he is in a state of fear during the **recitation** *of the Qur'an, and [bring to mind] during the* **bowing** *that which provides evidence of his humbleness (khudu') and need (inabah), and [bring to mind] during his* **prostrating** *that through which he proves to himself the presence of extreme abasement, lowliness, poverty and destitution in that lowly state.*

[All this] so as to challenge what man aspires to in terms of arrogance, haughtiness and a feeling of self-sufficiency from the guiding help (imdad) of God. This [reflection only] comes through His grace and generosity.

He should bear witness as to the exalted station of God, may He be praised, on account of His lofty nature and independence from His creation due to His elevated nature and the might of His dominion." *[al-Qastalani, Marasid as-Salah, pg124]*

Lesson Three - Prayer timings and the Call to prayer

> **Lesson Aim:** Through this lesson students will be given an insight into the timings of the five daily prayers as well as the issues related to praying at different times of the day. The call to prayer and its relevance and rulings will also be covered.
>
> **Objectives:** By the end of this lesson the student should be able to display the ability to:
> 1. **Mention** how and by whom the times for the prayers were established.
> 2. **Identify and explain clearly** the start and finishing times of the five daily prayers.
> 3. **Explain** the difference of opinion regarding the starting time of *'Asr* and *'Isha* respectively.
> 4. **List** the three times when it is prohibited to pray as well as the times it is disliked to do so.
> 5. **Mention** the way in which the Muslim call to prayer was decided and the wording used.
> 6. **List** some of the *sunnah* acts of the *adhan*.
> 7. **Explain** who should perform the *adhan* and *iqamah* and when this should be done.

1. Establishing the times of the prayers

> *"Verily, the prayer has been enjoined on the believers at fixed times"* [4:103]

> *Umar ibn Abd al-Aziz delayed the prayer one day and Urwah ibn al-Zubayr went to him and said: "Once in Iraq, al-Mughirah ibn Shu'bah delayed his prayer and Abu Mas'ud al-Ansari went to him and said, "O Mughirah, what is this? Don't you know that Jibril came and offered the prayer (Fajr) and God's Messenger ﷺ prayed too, then he prayed again and so did God's Messenger and again he prayed and God's messenger did the same: again he prayed and so did God's Messenger and again he prayed and so did God's Messenger?".*
> *Then Jibril said: "I was ordered to do so to demonstrate the prayers prescribed to you." Umar [ibn Abd al-Aziz] said to Urwah "Be sure of what you say! Did Jibril lead God's Messenger at the stated times of the prayers?" Urwah replied: "Bashir ibn Abi Mas'ud narrated like this on the authority of his father" [Malik, al-Muwatta, Bab Waqt al-Salah]*

> Abdullah ibn Abbas said: *"A prayer is not missed until the call to prayer (adhan) of another is said"* [Ibn Abi Shaybah]

1.1 The time of the *Fajr* (early morning) prayer

The time of the *Fajr* prayer extends from the start of true dawn which is marked by light lying along horizon, and extends until sunrise.

It is related by Anas ibn Malik that a man came to the Prophet ﷺ and asked him about the time of the *fajr* prayer. The Prophet ordered that the prayer be established just when true dawn broke. The next day, when dawn became clear, he ordered that the prayer be established. He then asked: *"Where is the person asking about the prayer time? It is between these two."* [al-Nasa'i, 545].

It should be remembered that true dawn is preceded by a vertical light, known as the lying dawn *(fajr al-kadhib),* that extends into the sky before disappearing. This can be mistaken for the actual daybreak.[42]

1.2 The time of the *Dhuhr* (mid-afternoon) prayer

The time for *Dhuhr* prayer extends from just after the sun has gone past its highest point in the sky (the zenith) and extends until the shadow of an object becomes twice its own length. This is according to the position of Abu Hanifah. His students Imam Abu Yusuf and Muhammad ibn Hassan al-Shaybani hold that it extends only until the shadow of an object is equal to its own length[43].

1.3 The time of the *'Asr* (late-afternoon) prayer

The time for *'Asr* prayer extends from the end of *Dhuhr* until the beginning of *Maghrib,* however the preferred time to pray the *'Asr* ends when the sun becomes yellowish on the horizon. To delay it till the sun becomes yellowish without genuine excuse is disliked. 'Ala ibn Abd al-Rahman said: *"We came to Anas ibn*

---

[42] The time between the two varies, but is approximated to just over 10 minutes in equatorial latitudes.

[43] In both situations this excludes the length of any residual shadow that may exists when the sun is at its highest point (zenith) before the shadow begins to then lengthen.

Malik after Dhuhr. He stood up for the 'Asr prayer. When he finished, we or he himself mentioned performing the prayer at such an early time. He said: "The prayer of the hypocrite [is that] he waits until the sun is between the two horns of satan, then he gets up and prays four rak'ahs quickly, remembering God therein but a little." [Muslim, 1412].

On a cloudy day, *'Asr* should be prayed within its time but slightly earlier than normal. Buraydah al-Aslami reported: *"We were with the Messenger of God ﷺ during a battle and he said: "Hasten to pray on a cloudy day, for one who misses the prayer has destroyed all of his [good] deeds." [Ibn Majah, 694]*

1.4 The time of the *Maghrib* (early evening) prayer

The time for *Maghrib* extends from when the sun has set until the *shafaq* (twilight) disappears. Abdullah ibn 'Amr reported that the Prophet ﷺ said: *"The time for Maghrib is when the sun has disappeared [continuing] until the shafaq has not yet gone." [Muslim, 1388]*

1.4.1 What is the *shafaq*?

Umar ibn Abd al-Aziz said: "Do not pray 'Isha until the whiteness has disappeared from the horizon." [Ibn Abi Shaybah, v2, 264]

There is a disagreement amongst scholars as to what the word *shafaq* refers to. Abu Yusuf and Muhammad ibn Hassan and most others hold that *shafaq* refers to the remnants of redness in the horizon, while according to Abu Hanifah, it is the whiteness in the horizon after this initial redness disappears.

1.5 The time of the *'Isha* (late evening) prayer

The time for *'isha* extends from when the *shafaq* has disappeared, and it lasts until the time *fajr* starts.

'Aishah reported: *"One night the Prophet ﷺ prayed 'Isha after most of the night had passed and most people in the masjid had been overtaken by sleep. He came out, prayed and later said: 'This would be the proper time if it were not a hardship on my nation.' [Muslim, 1445]*

It is preferred that *'Isha* be prayed at around the time that the first third of the night has elapsed. 'Aishah said: *"They used to pray the 'isha between the disappearance of the shafaq and the final third of the night beginning." [al-Bukhari]*

2. The three prohibited times[44]

Uqbah ibn 'Amir relates 'There are three times in which the Messenger ﷺ used to forbid us from praying or burying our dead. When the sun appears fully radiant until it has risen; when a person standing in the intensity of the midday sun [produces no shadow] till the sun starts to decline [from the meridian]; and when the sun inclines to set until it sets.' [Muslim]

This hadith sets down the following times when it is not permitted to pray, including missed prayers.

2.1 While the sun is rising
2.2 At midday when the sun is at its peak (*istiwah*) (around 10 minutes before *Dhuhr* time starts)
2.3 At sunset (except for *'Asr* of the same day, which one may pray until the sun sets)

3. Disapproved of times

3.1 To perform anything after true dawn other than the two *sunnah rak'ah* of *Fajr*.
3.2 To pray after having performed the *Fajr* prayer until after the sun has risen, or after performing the *'Asr* prayer until after the sun has set. Abu Hurayrah reported that the Prophet ﷺ said: *"Whoever catches one rak'ah of the 'Asr before the sun sets, he has caught the 'Asr" [al-Bukhari, 554]*

It is however allowed to make up missed prayers in these disapproved times, as well as making the *sajdah* for recitation *(sajdah tilawah)* or perform the funeral prayer.

---

[44] These prohibited times are also applicable to the funeral prayer, though if for some reason it was performed, the funeral prayer would be valid. The type of prohibition entailed above is technically referred to as *makruh tahrimi (strongly disliked)* and so no *nafl* prayers may be said during such times without exception.

4. The *Adhan*- More than a call to prayer

> *"God, in His infinite wisdom, did not intend the adhan to be merely an announcement and warning but also to form part of the essential practices of Islam, that its status for those negligent [of the prayer] be not only an announcement or sign [for the prayer time], but also be made a symbol of loyalty and devotion. It was necessary that the adhan include the name of God, the articles of the testification to faith over and above just 'a call to prayer', so that the wisdom underlying the call be served as well."* [Al-Dihlawi, Hujjat-Ullah al-Balighah]

4.1 The history of the call to prayer

Although the five daily prayers were made compulsory in Makkah, there was no call to prayer (*adhan*) at that time and the *adhan* was instituted during the first year after the *Hijrah* after consultation amongst the community there, and '*some people suggested the use of a bell like the Christians, while others proposed a trumpet like the horn used by the Jews, but Umar was the first to suggest that a person should make the call to prayer. The Messenger* ﷺ *then ordered Bilal to stand and pronounce the adhan for the prayers."* [al-Bukhari]

More detail behind this is provided by the following report in which it is related that Abdullah ibn Zayd said:

> *"When the Messenger of God* ﷺ *ordered the use of a bell to gather people for the prayer, in my sleep a man came to me carrying a bell. I said to him: "Slave of God! Will you sell me that bell?" He said: "What would you do with it?" I replied: "We shall use it to call the people to prayer." He said: "Shall I not guide you to something better than that?" I said: "Certainly". He said: "Call out:*
>
>
>
> *Allahu akbar, Allahu akbar, Allahu akbar, Allahu akbar.*
> *Ashhadu alla ilaha illal-lah, ashhadu alla ilaha illa-llah,*
> *Ashhadu anna Muhammad ar-Rasullal-lah, ashhadu anna Muhammadar-Rasullal-lah.*
> *Hayya 'alas-salah, hayyah 'alas-salah. Hayya 'alal-falah, hayya 'alal-falah.*
> *Allahu akbar, Allahu akbar. La ilaha illal-lah."*
>
>
>
> *When the morning broke, I went to the Messenger* ﷺ *to tell him what I had seen. He said, "Your dream is true, God willing. Go to Bilal, tell him what you have seen, and tell him to make the call to prayer as he has the best voice amongst you".* [Abu Dawud, 499]

4.2 The virtue of performing *Adhan*

Making the call to prayer comes just behind that of leading the prayer in terms of virtue.

> *Abu Hurayrah reported that the Prophet* ﷺ *said: "The one making the call to prayer is forgiven for as far as his voice reaches and whoever hears him confirms what he says.'* [Abu Dawud]

> *'Uqba ibn 'Amir said he heard the Prophet* ﷺ *say: "Your Lord, the Exalted, is amazed by one who, shepherding a flock of sheep, climbs a mountain crevice to make the call to prayer then prays. God, the Exalted, say: 'Look at my servant who makes the call to prayer and establishes the prayer out of awe of Me. I have forgiven my servant and admitted him to Paradise.'"* [Ahmad]

4.3 Time of the *Adhan*

The *adhan* is to be made when the time for prayer enters. If it is said before its time, it should be repeated.

4.4 The *sunnah* of the *Adhan*

The Prophetic norms for the *adhan* are many, and are all related to the way in which the *adhan* was performed in the presence of the Messenger of God ﷺ .

All actions done by those making the *adhan* in his blessed presence which he ﷺ approved of are considered part of the Prophetic sunnah with regards to how to perform the *adhan*. These are:

4.4.1 Raising one's voice[45]: *"Go to Bilal as he has the best voice amongst you."* [Abu Dawud]

4.4.2 Pausing between the phrases: The Prophet ﷺ said to Bilal: *"When you perform the adhan then pause, and when you perform the iqamah, be quick."* [at-Tirmidhi]

4.4.3 Facing the qiblah: Ibn Sirin said: *"When the Mu'adhdhin performs adhan, he should face the qiblah."* [Ibn Abi Shaybah]

4.4.4 Turning right and left: Abu Juhayfah narrated: *"Bilal performed the adhan, and I saw the movement of his head from this side..."* [al-Bukhari]

4.4.5 The Mu'adhin should be male: Ali ibn Abi Talib said: *"Women neither perform the adhan nor the iqamah."* [Ibn Abi Shaybah]

4.4.6 The placing of one's fingers in one's ears: Abu Juhayfah said about Bilal: *"He put his index fingers into his ears."* [Al-Tirmidhi]

4.4.7 Purification: Abu Hurayrah narrated that the Prophet ﷺ said: *"The adhan should be performed by someone who has wudu' (Al-Tirmidhi)* though the *adhan performed* without *wudu'* is valid. Moreover, it is disliked for the one calling the *adhan* to be in a state of major ritual impurity *(janabah)*.

4.4.8 Whoever calls the *adhan* should also call the iqamah: Al-Tirmidhi said: *"The practice of most scholars is that whosoever performs the adhan performs the iqamah."*

4.5 Responding to the *adhan*

"When you listen to the adhan, you should repeat the words of the caller" [al-Bukhari].

The one listening to the *adhan* should repeat what the caller is saying, except for the two phrases *hayya 'ala salah, hayya 'alal-falah,* to which one should both be responded to with: *'la haula wa la quwatah illa billah' (There is no power or might save through God).*

4.6 The supplication after the *adhan*[46]

The Prophet ﷺ said: "Supplication made between the adhan and iqamah is not rejected". [Abu Dawud]

Abdullah ibn 'Amr related that the Messenger of God ﷺ said: "If you hear the call to prayer, repeat what is said. Then supplicate for me, for whoever supplicates for me, God supplicates tenfold for him. Then ask God to grant me al-Wasilah - a rank in Paradise reserved for only one servant of God. I hope to be that one, and whoever asks God to grant me the rank of al-Wasilah, it becomes incumbent upon me to intercede for such a person." [Muslim]

5. The shorter call to prayer (*Iqamah*)

This is called immediately before the prayer is to be performed. The first takbir is recited four times, and everything else twice, except for the last statement of *'la ilaha illal-lah',* which is said once.

Abu Mahdhurah said that the Prophet ﷺ taught him the *iqamah* consisting of seventeen phrases: *Allahu akbar (4 times), ashhadu alla ilaha illal-lah (twice), ashhaduanna Muhammad ar-Rasul-lal-lah (twice), hayya 'alas-salah (twice), hayya 'alal-falah (twice), qad qamatis-salah (twice), Allahu akbar, Allahu akbar. La ilaha illal-lah. [al-Nisa'i]*

Did you know?
It is an emphasised sunnah (*mu'akkada*) for men to give both the *adhan* and *iqama* for obligatory prayers, even when praying alone, whether for current prayers or prayers being made up afterwards, whether on a journey or at home. As a minimum, the *iqamah* should be performed. *[Shurunbulali, Maraqi al-Falah, pg 194-195]*

---

[45] To sing the adhan or to mispronounce its words is disliked as it should be done according to the general rules of recitation *(tajwid)*. It is related that Umar ibn Abd Al-Aziz heard someone singing the *adhan*, so he said to him: *"Perform it in the normal way, otherwise leave us."* [Ibn Abi Shaybah]

[46] See attached appendix for the Arabic *dua'*.

Lesson Four - Preconditions, pillars and invalidators of the prayer.

> **Lesson Aim:** Through this lesson, students will gain a clear understanding as to which actions are essential (*fard*) for the validity of the prayer and why. This covers the preconditions (*shurut*) as well as the pillars of the prayer (*arkan*). From this students will also understand what invalidates the prayer.
>
> **Objectives:** By the end of this lesson the student should be able to display the ability to:
> 1. **Explain** the two guidelines which are used to determine if an act is *fard* or not.
> 2. **Define** the two categories of *fard* in terms of what actions are done before the prayer (*shurut*) and that which are performed during it (*arkan*).
> 3. **List** and **explain** the six preconditions (*shurut*) of the prayer .
> 4. **List** and **explain** the five pillars (*arkan*) of the prayer.
> 5. **List** and **explain** what immediately invalidates the prayer and how this relates to *fard* acts.

1. The essential elements (*fard*) of the prayer

The essential elements (*fard*) of the prayer are those components of the prayer without which the prayer is not valid. This means that if missed out, the prayer cannot be rectified except by repeating the full prayer. Leaving out a *fard* act also therefore entails the highest degree of censure and blame *(isa'a)*.

1.1 How do scholars decide what is *fard*?

All *fard* acts are established by means of proofs and evidences that leave no room for doubt as to the essential nature of the act in question. This is deciphered from the textual sources of the Qur'an and the Prophetic *sunnah* by looking at two main questions:

1.1.1 The authenticity of the text (*al-thabut*). For an action to be classed as *fard* it must have reached us in such a way that leaves no doubt as to its authenticity. A text of this nature is referred to in Arabic as *qati'i al-thubut*. In practice, this means that it has to be established by either a verse of the Qur'an or a *mutawatir* hadith.

1.1.2 The meaning of the text (*al-dalalah*). For an action to be classed as *fard* it must also provide a clear meaning, such that it leaves no doubt as to the bare minimum of what is meant. A text of this nature is referred to in Arabic as *qati'i al-dalalah*.

By using such a methodology, scholars can differentiate between the different components of the prayer. The *fard* acts are therefore established in a manner more stringent than both *wajib* and *sunnah* acts, as both of the latter are not established to such a high level of certainty. The *fard* components of prayer are broken down further into **two categories,** depending on whether the action is internal or external to the prayer.

The first are the preconditions of the prayer (*shurut*). This refer to those elements of the prayer that are essential to its performance, yet exist outside the prayer. The second are the pillars of the prayer (*rukn, pl. arkan*). This refers to those elements of the prayer that are essential to its performance, *and exist as an integral part of the prayer.*

2. The six preconditions of the prayer (*shurut*).

2.1 Time

> *"Verily, the prayer has been enjoined on the believers at fixed hours"* [4:103]

A prayer started before its time, regardless of excuse, is deemed invalid and requires to be repeated.

2.2 Purity

This refers to the attainment of *haqiqi* purity (with regards to the place and clothing of the worshipper) as well as *hukmi* purity (such as ablution and the ritual bath) before starting the prayer. A prayer performed while not having either type of purity is therefore invalid.

2.3 Covering one's nakedness (*awrah*)

> *"O Children of Adam, take your adornment for every masjid"* [7:31]

It is reported by way of *tafsir al-ma'thur* that the word *adornment* (*zinah*) in the verse means *clothing* while '*masjid*' refers to the prayer itself. The *awrah* is a word used to describe the area of the male and female body that must be covered while in the state of prayer.

2.3.1 The *awrah* of a male

The minimum that must be covered extends from the area from the navel up to and including the knee.

> *Muhammad ibn Jahsh relates that the Messenger* ﷺ *passed by Ma'mar while his thighs were uncovered. He said to him: 'Ma'mar, cover your thighs, for they are the 'awrah."* [al-Bukhari]

2.3.2 The *awrah* of a female

The *awrah* of a female while in prayer is the whole of the body except for the face, hands and feet.

> *'Aishah states that the Prophet* ﷺ *said: "God does not accept the prayer of a woman unless she is wearing a head covering (khimar)."* [Abu Dawud]

Clothes worn by both men and women must not only cover the *awrah* but must also not be so tight as to cling to the body. If clothes are so thin that one's skin colour is seen, the *awrah* is not deemed as covered. If nakedness required to be covered becomes uncovered during prayer, one should immediate rectify this. If more than a quarter of any body part that is *awrah* is exposed by mistake during prayer and remains so for the time it takes to complete a pillar (*rukn*) of the prayer (approximated as the time it takes to say '*Subhan Allah*' three times), one's prayer becomes invalid. *(Al-Shurbunbulali, Maraqih al-Falah)*

2.4 Facing the direction of the Qibla.

> *Amir ibn Rabiah stated 'We were travelling with the Prophet* ﷺ *during a pitch-dark night and we did not know the direction of the qiblah. We then prayed. When morning broke, we noticed that we had prayed in a direction other than the Qiblah, so we mentioned this to the Prophet* ﷺ *, after which the verse '....and wherever you turn to, there is the countenance of God' was revealed'.* [Related by al-Tirmidhi]

2.4.1 The wisdom in facing the Ka'bah

> *"Since the Ka'bah is amongst the signs of God, it is incumbent that we hold it in reverence, the greatest token of which is that the face should turn towards it in the best and most elevated state we have [...] its objective is that the attributes of fear, repentance and concentration may develop in the one worshipping [...]. As attentiveness of the heart is a hidden matter, turning of face to the Ka'bah has been prescribed as an evidence of attentiveness itself - an essential part of the prayer - just like wudu', purity and the covering of [one's] nakedness [...] therefore the physical acts and mannerisms generally carried out in the presence of kings and regarded as part of courtly protocol have been enjoined as an outward proof and expression of this [attentiveness]."* [Al-Dihlawi, Hujjat Ullah al-Balighah]

2.4.2 Rulings related to facing the direction of the *qibla*

This condition differs according to where one is. For those in the immediate vicinity of the Ka'bah, the direction of *qibla* is the Ka'bah itself. For others it is the general direction of the city of Makkah. For those not in its vicinity, the '*direction*' of the qibla is deemed to be within 45 ° either side of the Ka'bah.

It is a requirement that a person who is unaware of the direction of the *qibla* strive to determine its direction. If thereafter one is unable to ascertain its approximate direction and performs the prayer in a direction which turns out to be wrong and one is still in prayer, one must change direction accordingly. Even if this comes to be known afterwards, the prayer will be valid and need not be repeated since the person made an attempt to find its direction. Praying without striving to find the direction of *qibla* renders the prayer invalid in all cases.

Exceptions: There are circumstances in which one is not obliged to face the *qibla*. In the case of illness[47] or genuine fear for one's safety, it is allowed to pray the *fard* prayers in any direction one is able to. Moreover, the obligation to face the *qiblah* does not apply to one performing *nafl* prayer while classed as a traveler.[48]

---

[47] For an outline of what constitutes '*illness*' in Islamic law, refer to Lesson 6 of the 'Seeking Purity module.

[48] Meaning a person defined as a traveller in Sacred law while traveling on a vehicle.

'Amr ibn Rabi'ah said: "I saw the Messenger of God ﷺ pray while riding, and he faced the direction in which he was going." [Muslim]

2.5 Intention

"Every action is based upon intention." [al-Bukhari, 1]

With the five daily prayers, it is necessary that one makes the intention for the specific prayer being performed, as well as the intention of following the imam if the prayer is congregational.

2.6 Pronouncing the initial *takbir* the beginning of the prayer

Ali reported that the Prophet ﷺ said: "The key to prayer is purity. The takbir enters one into the inviolable sanctity of the prayer, and the final salam releases one from it." [Abu Dawud]

3. The Five Pillars (*arkan*) of the prayer

As mentioned previously, the *arkan* are those components of the prayer that are essential to its performance, and exist as an integral part of the prayer. Failure to perform them renders the prayer invalid.

3.1 Standing

"Guard the prayers and the mid-most prayer, and stand for God with utmost devotion." [2:238]

'Umar ibn Hussain said: "I had a physical ailment, so I asked the Prophet ⊠ about the prayer and he said: 'Pray standing, if you are not able to pray sitting, if you are not able to then pray (lying) on your side." [al-Bukhari]

It is necessary that one stand for the amount of time it takes to perform the Qur'anic recitation of the prayer.

3.2 The recitation of Qur'an

'Therefore recite of the Qur'an so much as is easy for you ' [73:20]

The Messenger of God ﷺ said to one to whom he was teaching the way to perform the basics of the prayer: "When you stand for the prayer say Allahu Akbar, then read what is easy for you to read from the Qur'an, then bow down" [al-Bukhari]

It is important to note that the recitation should be such that it is audible to the one reciting, otherwise it is not classed as recitation. The bare minimum that need be recited for the prayer is one verse in each of two *rakah* of the daily prayers. Abu Yusuf and Muhammed al-Shaybani hold that the minimum is three short verses or one long verse.

3.2.1 What if one cannot recite the Qur'an?

If one cannot learn a part of Qur'an, one should say the *tasbih (Subhan Allah - glory be to God)*, the tamhid *(al-hamdu lillah - all praise is due to God)*, and tahlil *(La ilaha illal-lah - there is no god except God)*.

The Messenger ﷺ said "If you have something from the Qur'an, recite it. If not, then say the tamhid, takbir and the tahlil and then bow." [Abu Dawud]

3.3 Bowing (ruku)

"Believers! Bow down and prostrate yourselves." [22:77]
The bare essential is accomplished by bending forward so that one is closer to bowing than standing, achieved when one's hands reach to one's knees while extending the arms. *[al-Tahtawi, Hashiyyah, pg 229]*

3.4 Prostrating

"Believers! Bow down and prostrate yourselves." [22:77]

The bare essential of the prostration is to place the forehead on the ground. If prostrating on anything other than bare ground, the place upon which the prostration is being made should be such that the firmness of the ground below be felt.

3.5 The final sitting

> *The Prophet* ﷺ *said to the Bedouin man while teaching him the prayer: "When you raise your head from the last prostration and have sat for the final sitting, you have completed your prayer" [al-Bukhari]*

The bare minimum for this sitting is the amount of time it would take for one to recite the *tashahud*.

4. Actions that invalidate the prayer

The sacred law has singled out a number of actions that lead to the immediate invalidation of the prayer, as they either directly or indirectly run counter to the preconditions and pillars of the prayer mentioned above.

4.1 Leaving a precondition or pillar of the prayer

> *"There is an agreement that if one prays and is not in a state of purity, it is obligatory to repeat the prayer, whether this be intentional or out of forgetfulness. The same is also true of one who prays not facing the qibla, intentionally or due to forgetfulness. In general, if any of the conditions for the correct performance of the prayer are absent, it becomes obligatory to repeat the prayer.' [Ibn Rushd, Bidayah al-Mujtahid]*

Therefore, acts such as turning one's chest away from the *qibla* invalidate the prayer.

4.2 Speaking

> *Zayd ibn Arqam relates 'We used to speak and mention our daily needs to one another while in prayer during the time of the Prophet* ﷺ *until the verse 'Protect over the prayers and particularly the middle prayer and stand in utter reverence for God' [2:238] was revealed. At that point we were told to remain silent and forbidden from speaking. [Agreed upon]*

4.3 Eating or drinking

What is meant by eating is introducing something into the mouth from outside it while in prayer. It also includes swallowing the remnants of what is in one's mouth from before entering the prayer, approximated by scholars as the amount of a chick pea or more.

4.4 Excessive movement

> *Abu Qatadah relates that the Prophet* ﷺ *used to offer prayers while carrying Umamah bint Zainab . When he* ﷺ *prostrated, he* ﷺ *put her down, and when he* ﷺ *got up from his prostration, he* ﷺ *would carry he again." [Agreed upon]*

There is no difference of opinion that if a person performs excessive movements that are not part of the prayer, this invalidates the prayer. If the acts are few, then they do not invalidate the prayer and, on this point, there is also no difference of opinion. Most scholars have explained the hadith above by pointing out that it did not entail consecutive movement [such that it would affect the validity of the prayer] as stillness was achieved when the pillars of the prayer were being performed.

However, there does exist a difference of opinion over what exactly constitutes excessive actions. The exact definitions of too much and too little are subjective. The difference between excessive and minimal movement is said to be that excessive movement is that where an external observer would not consider the person to be in a state of prayer. Others judge it by the number of movements one makes, where three consecutive moves during one component of the prayer would be deemed excessive.

Did you know?

The Prophet (may God bless and grant him peace) would make use of every situation to make important wider points and so commenting on the carrying of Umamah in prayer, Imam al-Fakihani said *'The purpose behind the Prophet* (may God bless and grant him peace) *carrying Umamah in the prayer was to make a point to the Arabs, who considered having daughters and carrying them around as something shameful. The Prophet* (may God bless and grant him peace) *acted counter to them, and carried a girl on his neck during the prayer. Demonstrating by example is more effective than a mere precept'. [al-'Ayni, Umdat al-Qari, 1/608]*

Lesson Five - The obligatory actions of Prayer

Lesson Aim: Through this lesson students will gain a clear understanding as to which actions of the prayer are obligatory (*wajib*) and why. The way that these differ from the essentials (*arkan*) will be demonstrated through a case-study on the ruling given by scholars to the reciting of the '*Fatihah*'.

Objectives: By the end of this lesson students should be able to display the ability to:
1. **Mention** the central hadith from which the obligatory (*wajib*) elements of the prayer are derived, providing a short back ground to the text.
2. **Explain** why scholars did not make the actions mentioned in this hadith essential elements (*arkan*) of the prayer.
3. **Distinguish** between the essential (*arkan*) and obligatory (*wajib*) elements of the prayer.
4. **List** the obligatory elements of the prayer.
5. **Discuss** the difference over the status of reciting the *Fatihah* in the prayer.
6. **Explain** the reasoning of the Hanafi school for their position.
7. **Explain** the reasoning of the other schools regarding reciting *Fatihah* in the prayer.
8. **State** what explanation both sides have given to the hadith: "*There is no prayer...*".

1. What are obligatory (*wajib*) actions, and how are they established?

> *Abu Hurayrah relates that the Messenger ﷺ said 'When you stand to pray then perfect the wudu, then face the Qibah and pronounce 'Allahu Akbar'. Then recite whatever is easy for you from the Quran. Then go into bowing until you come to complete rest bowing, then lift your head till you are standing straight, then prostrate till you come to complete rest in prostrating, then sit up straight till you come to complete rest sitting, then prostrate till you come to complete rest prostrating, then stand till you are standing straight. Thereafter do this in every part of your prayer'.* [Related by the Seven]

The context of this hadith is important for an understanding of the rules of prayer. A Bedouin Arab entered the mosque and hurriedly prayed and the Prophet ﷺ was observing him while he was praying. Upon completing the prayer, the man came to the Prophet ﷺ and greeted him. The Prophet ﷺ did not respond, but rather replied: *"Get up and pray as you have not prayed!"*. The man left and again hurriedly repeated his prayer and returned, whereupon the same thing happened. Finally, the Prophet ﷺ said to him *"When you stand for the prayer..."*

Scholars have given this particular hadith central importance when deciding which acts are obligatory (*wajib*) as opposed to *fard*, stating a general rule (*dabit*): *Everything mentioned in the hadith of the Bedouin is an obligatory (wajib)*. The importance of this one hadith can be gauged by the fact that the eminent Andalusian scholar Qadi Abu Bakr ibn al-Arabi states that it alone contains over forty points of scholarly interest. *[Nur ad-Din 'Ittr, 'Ilam al-Anam]*

As the hadith is solitary (*ahad*) in terms of its chain of transmission from the Prophet ﷺ , being related by the eminent Companion Abu Hurayrah, Hanafi scholars have not taken any of the acts mentioned therein to be pillars of the prayer (unless proven to be otherwise by other evidences). This is because for an action to be held to be a pillar, it must be established through a *mutawatir* chain of narrators, and provide a clear meaning.

1.1 How are Obligatory action established?

From the aforementioned discussion, it can be said that the obligatory (*wajib*) actions of prayer are those that are established in a manner less stringent than that stipulated for an act to be considered an essential elements of the prayer (*fard*). Nevertheless, the level of proof is stronger than that needed for acts to be classified as *sunnah*[49].

2. The ruling related to obligatory actions

If an obligatory action is missed **unintentionally,** the prayer has to be rectified by prostrating twice (by what is referred to as *sajdah al-sahw*) after the final *salam*.

If an obligatory action is missed **intentionally** then the prayer has to be repeated and the one doing so has is also deemed as having acted in a way that is prohibitively disliked (*makruh tahrimi*)

---

[49] How an act is defined as '*sunnah*' will be looked at in the second prayer module.

3. The obligatory acts

The obligatory acts of the prayer can be summarised in the following points:

3.1 Recitation of *surah al-Fatihah*

> The Prophet ﷺ said "There is no prayer for the one that does not recite al-Fatihah." [al-Bukhari].

This is an obligation in the first two *rakah* of the *fard* prayers and every *rakah* of non-obligatory prayers.

3.2 Additional recitation

It is obligatory to recite either a short chapter of the Qur'an or three verses after the recitation of *al-Fatiha*.

> Abu Qatadah said: "The Prophet ﷺ used to recite the Fatiha in the first two rakah of Dhuhr prayer as well as chapters of the Qur'an, making the first recitation longer and the second shorter. Sometimes the verses would be audible. He used to recite al-Fatiha and two other chapters in the 'Asr prayer." [Bukhari]

> It is also related that the Prophet ﷺ said: "The key to the prayer is purification; and the entering into its sacramental state (tahrim) is [through] the takbir; and exiting is through the final salam. There is no prayer for he who does not read the Fatiha as well as another chapter in the obligatory prayers or in others." [Tirmidhi].

3.3 Reciting the Qur'an aloud or in a silent manner.

This refers to the congregational prayer in which the first two *rakah* of prayers are prayed aloud. In such cases the recitation must be audible to others. It is also obligatory for the recitation of the Qur'an to be silent *in those prayers where the recitation should be silent (namely the third and fourth rakah of all prayers and also the whole of the Dhuhr and 'Asr prayers).*

3.4 The perfection of the *ruku* (bowing) and the *sajdah* (prostration).

It is obligatory to completely perform both acts, separating them properly by:

3.4.1 Standing after the act of bowing.

> 'Aishah relates that when the Prophet ﷺ raised his head from ruku, he ﷺ would not prostrate until after his back was straight.' [Muslim].

3.4.2 Prostrating on the seven parts of the body, separating the two prostrations with a sitting in between.

> The Prophet ﷺ said: "I have been ordered to prostrate on the seven parts of the body: the forehead, and he pointed to his nose, hands, knees and the tips of the feet." [al-Bukhari]

> Abu Qatadah related that the Prophet ﷺ said: "The worst people are those who steal part of their prayer." When asked of this he replied: "He does not complete his bowing and prostration" or said: "He does not straighten his back during bowing and prostration.' [Ahmad]

3.5 The first sitting after two *rakah*.

> The Prophet ﷺ said "When you sit in the middle of your prayer, sit properly." [Al-Tabarani v7 /250]

3.6 The recitation of the *tashahud*[50].

This is recited during both sittings. It is related that *Samurah said: "The Prophet ﷺ commanded that when we are in the middle or the end of the prayer that we should recite the tashahud." [Tabarani 7/250]*

---

[50] See attached appendix for Arabic text of the *tashahud*.

3.7 The sequential performance of all acts.

This means that the essential (*fard*) and obligatory (*wajib*) acts of the prayer should be performed in their proper order as demonstrated by the continual habit of the Prophet ﷺ . The Prophet ﷺ always prayed the components of the prayer in a particular order and when he was made to forget the sequence, he would perform a compensatory prostration *(sajdah as-sawh)* at the end of the prayer.

Related to the sequential performance of all acts is that each element of the prayer should be performed without any unnecessary delay between it and the next act.

For example, if somebody delays the performance of the bowing (*ruku*) after having recited the Qur'an, and the delay lasts longer than the time it would take to perform the most basic pillar (*rukn*) of the prayer[51], then the person would need to make a compensatory prostration at the end of the prayer as will be explained later. This is due to the delay in the sequential performance of the acts mentioned above.

3.8 Reciting the *salam* at the end of the prayer.

> *It is related that 'Aishah said "The Prophet ﷺ used to conclude his prayer by performing the salam at the end of the prayer." [Muslim]*

3.9 Calm stillness (*itmi'nan*).

> *Abu Humaid, describing the Prophet's ﷺ prayer, said, 'He would raise his head from bowing, and then stand straight until every bone in his back returned to its place.' [al-Bukhari]*

This means that every act of the prayer should be done properly - without undue haste, allowing the body to come to rest after each act, as described in the hadith:

> *"...then raise your head until you attain calm stillness standing, then prostrate until you attain calm stillness in prostration, then raise your head until you attain calm stillness sitting, then prostrate until you come to calm stillness in prostration. Repeat this in all of your prayer." [Related by all six Canonical collections of hadith]*

4. Text in focus: Reciting the Fatiha in Prayer - The conflict of the *mutawatir* and the *ahad*

> ### *"And so recite whatever is easy of the Qur'an" [73: 20]*

> *Abu Hurayrah related that the Prophet ﷺ said: "...and recite whatever is easy for you from whatever you have of the Qur'an..." [The six collections of hadith]*

> *Ubaydah ibn Samit related that the Prophet ﷺ said: "There is no prayer for the one that does not recite the al-Fatiha." [Bukhari and Muslim]*

4.1 The issue

Scholars have differed over the minimum quantity of Qur'an that needs to be recited for the prayer to be valid. Is *al-Fatihah* as essential a part of the prayer as prostrating and bowing, or is it a less stringently established as part of the prayer?

All scholars agree about the importance of reciting *al-Fatiha*, but differ as to what this specifically means. The basis of the issue revolves around an apparent conflict between two textual proofs on this topic, and the differing methods by which this can be resolved.

4.2 The two groups of scholars

The majority of schools of law, namely the Maliki, Shafi'i and Hanbali, hold that the recitation of *al-Fatiha* is as essential an act of the prayer as standing, bowing and prostrating and so has the same rule as these.
The Hanafi school, on the other hand holds that, though an obligatory part of the prayer, recitation of the *al-Fatiha* cannot be given the same legal status as the more essential acts of the prayer classified as the pillars (*arkan*)[52].

---

[51] Approximated as the time it takes to say *'Subhan Allah'* three times.

[52] The majority of scholars do not differentiate between the word *fard* and *wajib* in most cases, and consider them both to be the same thing. The Hanafi scholars differentiate between them for various reasons, some of which have been previously mentioned.

4.2.1 The proofs of the Hanafi scholars

4.2.1.1 The Qur'an

The verse in the Qur'an stating *"Recite whatever you find easy of the Qur'an"* *[73:20]* does not require any specific portion of the Qur'an, therefore al-Fatiha is not a *rukn* of the prayer.

4.2.1.2 The hadith

It is related by Abu Hurayrah that the Prophet ﷺ said when teaching a person the prayer *"...and recite whatever is easy for you from whatever you have of the Qur'an..."* without specifying whether the Fatiha should be recited. This hadith is related by all six major collections of hadith.

Moreover, there is the hadith of the Prophet ﷺ in which he ﷺ stated: *"If you have anything of the Qur'an memorised then recite it"* *[al-Nisai and Abu Dawud]* which indicates that any portion of the Qur'an is sufficient in achieving the minimum of what is required.

Given this, Hanafi scholars have stated that the bare minimum amount of recitation of Qur'an needed for the prayer to be valid is the amount which is customarily be referred to as *'the Qur'an'*. This may be fulfilled by *al-Fatiha* or even other portions of the Qur'an. This reading also allows for a reconciliation between different proofs since *'the purpose of the hadith of Ubadah is to deny the perfection of the prayer; not its validity, while the purpose of the hadith of Abu Hurayrah is to indicate its validity, as the aim of that hadith was to impart instructions about the obligations of the prayer." [Ibn Rushd, Bidayah, pg 108]*

The summary of the Hanafi argument is that for anything to be classed as a pillar of the prayer, it must be proven through a source which is:

[1] Wholly authentic in terms of the way it is established *[Qati' al-Thabut]*.
This means that it has to be either a verse of the Qur'an or a Prophetic tradition that has been transmitted through a multiple chain of narrators (*mutawatir*), in such a way that we are certain that all those that transmit the tradition could not have conspired to fabricate the report in question.

[2] Definitive in terms of the meaning conveyed *[Qati' al-Dalalah]*.
The religious text in question should have a plain meaning which is not open to interpretation, or have a figurative reading.

If these two elements do not exist, an action cannot be considered to have the status of being a pillar of an act of worship. On the case at hand, the only text that qualifies as living up to these criteria is the verse of the Qur'an, and it does not specify the amount of Qur'an that should be recited in the prayer. Other hadith on this topic support this conclusion as well. As for the hadith of Ubadah mentioning the recitation of *al-Fatiha*, all agree that it is a solitary tradition (*ahad*), and so other proofs are given precedence in situations where there is an apparent conflict (*ta'arud*).

4.2.2 The case of the majority of schools

The majority of scholars took the opinion that the hadith related by Ubadah ibn Samit in which the Prophet ﷺ said *"There is no prayer for who does not recite the Fatiha"* indicates that al-Fatiha is an essential part of the prayer, like standing and prostrating.

4.2.2.1 The basis of the majority position is the fact that this hadith qualifies and explains the meaning of other religious texts on this topic, which in this case is a verse of the Qur'an and also the other hadith used by those that do not consider *al-Fatiha* a pillar (*rukn*).

This majority of scholars held that a solitary (*ahad*) hadith can specify a stronger text, such as a verse of the Qur'an, and alter the meaning conveyed therein. *"These jurists may also argue that the words 'Recite whatever you can from the Qur'an' is ambiguous (mub'ham), while the other hadith [relating to reciting the Fatiha] is explicit (mubayyin) so the explicit hadith takes precedence over the ambiguous" [Ibn Rushd, Bidayah, 108]*

4.3 So what does *'there is no prayer'* mean according to the two groups of scholars?

4.3.1 The majority of scholars have held it to mean *'There is no **valid** prayer without the Fatiha'*. Therefore, they took the words of the Prophet ﷺ - *'There is no prayer'* - to mean that it is invalid and that the prayer does not exist in the eyes of the law and so needs to be repeated.

4.3.2 The Hanafi jurists interpret the hadith in a way that does not conflict with the verse of the Qur'an and other relevant traditions, and took it to mean that *"There is no **'perfect'** prayer without the recitation of al-Fatiha."*

This method of making recourse to a required meaning which is necessarily and logically understood[53] in a religious text, can be seen being used in the hadith related by Imam al-Bukhari in which 'Umar narrates that the Prophet ﷺ said: *"Indeed actions are but by [their] intentions."*

Since actions performed without an intention are still known to come into existence, it is obvious that the literal meaning in the hadith is not intended and there is another required meaning needed for the text to make full sense. The hadith is therefore interpreted and given a meaning that is understood and required from the context. Therefore it is variously explained as *'Indeed actions are but **rewarded/valid/perfected/judged/given value** by [their] intentions.' [see 'Ilam al-Anam, Nur al-Din 'Ittr]*

---

[53] This is technically referred to in *Usul al-Fiqh* as *'Iqtidah al-Nass' or* the *'Required meaning':* a necessary meaning read into a text without which it would remain logically incomplete. Another example of this is the case of the requirement or otherwise to have an intention to fast before first dawn. The Prophet ﷺ said: *'There is no fast for anyone who has not intended it from the night before.' [Ibn Majah].* It is clear that if a person wakes up abstaining from eating and drinking without having made an intention from the night before to do so, they still deem themselves to be fasting. Yet the hadith negates this assumption, which means that it requires to be explained by reading something into the text that is logically required yet missing. The missing element could either be that there is no *'valid fast'* or no *'complete/perfect fast'*. In keeping with the above example, the Hanafi scholars have upheld the meaning to be *'complete/perfect'* whereas the Shafi'i school have read the meaning of *'valid'* into this hadith.

Lesson Six- Rectifying mistakes in the prayer, disliked acts, and the inner state of the one that prays

Lesson Aim: Through this lesson students will cover how to ensure that the prayer is performed in such a way that the validity of the essential elements (*arkan*) and obligatory (*wajib*) acts is ensured. It will look at the function of the prostration for forgetfulness (*sajdah al-sahw*) and the ruling of doubts while in prayer. To finish, the spiritual significance of the components of the prayer will be highlighted.

Objectives: By the end of this lesson the student should be able to display the ability to:
1. **Mention** the ruling regarding *sajdah al-sahw* for one that does not perform an obligatory act either out of forgetfulness or intentionally.
2. **Explain** how the *sajdah al-sahw* is performed.
3. **Understand** the solution to common scenarios that occur in the prayer that need to be rectified.
4. **State** how doubt may affect the prayer and how to deal with different scenarios of doubt in prayer.
5. **Explain** what type of acts are disliked while in the state of prayer and why.
6. **Appreciate** the deeper spiritual significance of the acts of prayer and how these have been explained by scholars.

1. The prostration for forgetfulness (*sajdah al-sahw*)

> The Messenger ﷺ said: "I am only made to forget in order to create a sunnah for you." [Malik, Muwatta bi Riwayah Muhammed al-Shaybani]

> The Messenger ﷺ said: "If one of you has some doubts concerning the prayer and does not recall the number of rakah he has prayed, whether it is three or four, then he should build upon what he was more certain, and then do two prostrations after the salam." [al-Nasa'i]

As has been mentioned in previous lessons, if somebody misses out one of the conditions or pillars of the prayer, the prayer is considered invalid and there is no way to rectify this except by repeating the prayer.

This is not the case if one misses out an obligatory action (*wajib*). If an obligatory action is missed out **intentionally** then one has to repeat the prayer. If it is done **unintentionally** then one can rectify the prayer by prostrating twice after the final *salam*. This is called **sajdah al-sahw** in Arabic.

1.1 How is the *sajdah al-sahw* performed?

> The Prophet ﷺ prayed five rakah and the people asked Him 'Has there been an addition to the prayer?', he asked 'Why do you say that?'. They replied 'You have prayed five rakah'. He ﷺ then made two prostrations after the final salam. [al-Bukhari]

There are a number of ways that *sajdah al-sahw* may be performed. The preferred method by which this is done is that when one comes to the end of the prayer one:

a. performs a *salam* to the right
b. then says the *takbir* and prostrates two extra prostrations *(sajdah al-sahw)*.
c. then recites the *tashahud* a second time as well as the prayer on the Prophet ﷺ and *dua'* before concluding the prayer through the two final *salams*.

1.2 Various scenarios related to *sajdah al-sahw*.

1.2.1 If a person makes an omission (or addition) of an obligatory action such as reciting *al-Fatiha* or sitting for the middle *tashahud*, they must perform *sajdah al-sahw*. In the case of missing the middle sitting for *tashahud*, if one is closer to sitting than standing and notices this, one should return back to the sitting position and complete the obligatory act. Otherwise, one continues the prayer to the standing position (which is *fard*) and performs *sajdah al-sahw* at the end of the prayer.

1.2.2 If a person delays performing an obligatory act for more than the time it takes to say 'Subhan Allah' three times, *sajdah al-sahw* has to be performed.

1.2.3 If a person who is required to perform *sajdah al-sahw* forgets and finishes their prayer by performing the *salams*, they can still rectify the prayer with the prostration for forgetfulness afterwards as long as they remain within the mosque or at their place of prayer, even if there is a delay in performing it.

1.2.4. If the Imam is obliged to perform *sajdah al-sahw* but does not do so, the people following him are not obliged to perform it, as their responsibility is only to follow the Imam. Conversely, if a person praying behind an Imam forgets something obligatory, they do not perform *sajdah al-sahw*.

2. Doubt in the Prayer

2.1 If a person doubts the validity of their prayer after it has been completed, this doubt is ignored, unless they have a strong persistent doubt *(ghalaba al-dhann)* that they have missed something out.

2.2 If this strong persistent doubt *(ghalaba al-dhann)* is during the prayer and relates to the *number of rakah* they have completed then:

2.2.1 If this is the first time they have had this doubt and they are not accustomed to having such doubts, then the prayer becomes invalid and they have to start again. It is related that Ibn Umar said of a person who prays and does not know how much they have prayed: *'He should repeat the prayer until he remembers.' [Ibn Abi Shaybah].*

2.2.2 If the individual is prone to continual doubt, they need only build upon that which they are most certain about having prayed.

3. Acts that are disliked in the prayer

There are many acts that are disliked in the prayer, and though they do not invalidate the prayer, they come close to doing so. Detailed lists of these occur in larger books of *fiqh*. For the purposes of this lesson we will look at the general rule that connects all these acts, thereafter mentioning the most well-known disliked acts.

The general rule (dabit) of disliked acts in prayer is: *'Any act that preoccupies the mind or leads to inattentiveness in the prayer'.*

3.1 Types of dislikes

'Aishah asked the Prophet ﷺ regarding turning here and there in the prayer (ikhtilas) and he replied: 'This is the portion the Satan steals from the servant's prayer.' [al-Bukhari]

Some acts, such as intentionally leaving aside a *wajib* act are more disliked than others and can lead to the invalidation of the prayer. This type of disliked act is called a strongly prohibitive dislike *(al-makruh at-tahrimi)*. This also includes acts that are clearly disapproved of in Prophetic hadith - and are therefore these acts are classed as being *'wajib to avoid'.*

A lesser degree of dislike, called mildly disliked *(al-makruh at-tanzihi)*, is associated with the missing out of a sunnah act, or one that is otherwise termed as recommended *(mandub)*. *[Ibn Abidin, Hashiyyah, 1/89]*

3.2 Examples of disliked acts

3.2.1 *The Prophet ﷺ said 'If the evening meal (asha') is served then start with it before praying Maghrib.' [al-Bukhari].*

3.2.2 *He ﷺ said 'When one of you becomes drowsy while in prayer, they should lie down until refreshed, otherwise he will not know whether he is asking forgiveness or vilifying himself.' [Muslim]*

3.2.3 'Aishah had a curtain to cover the doorway of her house. The Prophet ﷺ said to her *'Remove your curtain, for its pictures distract me during my prayer.' [Al-Bukhari]*

3.2.4 Abu Hurayrah reports that the Messenger ﷺ said; *'Those that raise their gaze to the heavens when in prayer should desist lest their sight be taken from them. [al-Bukhari]*

3.2.5 It is similarly disliked to close one's eyes while in prayer without reason. *The Messenger ﷺ said: 'When one of you stands up in the prayer he should not close his eyes.' [At-Tabarani, 11:29]*

This also holds true for fidgeting with one's clothes or wearing them inappropriately.

3.2.6 *The Messenger ﷺ prohibited 'al-sadl', which is to let one's clothes dangle during the prayer, and he also prohibited a man from covering over his mouth." [Abu Dawud]*

Imam ash-Shaybani said, giving the reason for the prohibition, that this manner of wearing one's clothes is disliked as it resembles the practice of the People of the Book in prayer.

3.2.8 Similarly, designating a specific place for one's prayer in the mosque and praying in a way that is counter to the sunnah, is disliked. Abd al-Rahman ibn Shibli said: *'The Prophet ﷺ prohibited pecking like the crow, sitting like the beast and a man reserving a place for himself to pray in the Masjid like the camel has its place to sit.' [Ahmed]*

3.2.9 Where one fears others passing in front of them while in prayer, it is disliked not to place a barrier (*sutra*) in front of oneself. The Messenger ﷺ said: '*If one of you prays then let them pray towards a barrier, thereby preventing another from passing in front of them.*' [Muslim, 1130]

4.Reconnecting with the spirit: Al-Ghazali on the inner state of the one who prays

4.1 The call to prayer:

"When you hear the call to prayer prepare yourself inwardly to respond promptly. Those that are quick to answer this call are the ones that will be summoned gently on the Day of Resurrection. So review your heart now! If you find it full of joy and happiness, eager to respond immediately, then you can expect the summons to bring you good news and salvation on the Day of Judgement. That is why the Prophet ﷺ used to say "Comfort us O Bilal", for Bilal was the Muezzin, and prayer was the joy and comfort of the Prophet ﷺ .

4.2 Covering the private parts

You cover the private parts [...] but what of the shameful areas of your inner being? Those unworthy secrets of your soul that are examined only by your Lord, Great and Glorious be He?

4.3 Facing the qibla

Do you suppose that you are not also required to turn your heart away from everything else and directing it towards God, Great and Glorious be He? [...] The Prophet ﷺ said "When a man stands up to pray directing his desire, face and heart towards God, Great and Glorious be He, he will come out of the prayer as on the day his mother gave him birth".

4.4 Intention

When performing the intention, resolve to be responsive to God by performing the prayer in obedience to His command, doing it properly and avoiding things that invalidate and sully it. Doing all this sincerely for the sake of God in hope of His reward and fear of His punishment, seeking His grace and favour by His grace.

4.5 Takbir

As for the takbir, your heart must not call lie to the words on your tongue. If you feel in your heart that there is something greater than God, glorified is He, though your words are true, God will attest that you are a liar.

4.6 Standing upright

As for standing upright, it means making oneself erect in body and spirit in front of God. Your head - the loftiest member of your body - ought to be bowed down as a reminder of the need to keep the heart meek and humble, free of haughtiness of pride.

4.7 Reciting the Qur'an

Where reciting the Qur'an is concerned, we can distinguish three types of people;

Those that move their tongues unconsciously; those that pay conscious attention to the movement of the tongue, understanding the meaning while listening as if to a person outside themselves. This is the degree of those on the right path; those that start from an awareness of the meaning and then use the tongue to give expression to this inner consciousness. The tongue may act as an interpreter for inner feelings, or as its teacher. In the case of those nearest to God, the tongue is an interpreter.

4.8 Bowing down

In bowing, you renew your submissiveness and humility, striving to refine your inner feeling through a fresh awareness of your own impotence and insignificance before the might and grandeur of your Lord. To confirm this you seek the aid of your tongue, glorifying your Lord and testifying repeatedly to His supreme majesty both inwardly and outwardly. [Say] "God hears those who give thanks to Him", [and] acknowledging the need to express gratitude you immediately add "Grateful praise to You, our Lord !"

4.9 Prostration

Then you go down into prostration. This is the highest level of submission, for you are bringing the most precious part of your body, namely your face, down to meet the most lowly of all things, the dust of the earth [...]. You are restoring the branch to its root, for of dust you were created and to dust you shall return. At the same time you should renew your inner awareness of God's majesty saying "Glory to my Lord, most High". When your inner feeling has clearly been refined, be confident in hoping for God's mercy, for His mercy quickly flows towards meekness and lowliness, not towards arrogance and vanity.

4.10 Sitting and testifying

When you sit up and make the testimony, sit decorously, declare that all prayers and good works performed are for the sake of God and that everything belongs to Him. Such is the meaning of al-tahiyyat[54]. Be inwardly aware of the Prophet ﷺ and of his noble person as you say "Peace be upon you Prophet as well as God's mercy and blessings", be sure that your salutation will reach him and that he will return an even more perfect greeting to you.

4.11 The final supplication

At the end of your ritual prayer, you should offer a traditional supplication, imploring and entreating with meekness and humility, confidently hoping to be heard. Let your supplication include your parents as well as other believers.

4.12 Salutation

Finally, and with the intention of concluding your prayer, address your salutation to the angels and to the others present, feel a sense of gratitude to God, Glorified is He, having enabled you to complete this act of worship. Imagine that you are saying farewell to this act of yours and you may not live to see another like it. [Summarised from Al-Ghazali, Inner Dimensions, pg44-48]

---

[54] Another name for the *tashahud* supplication, taken from its opening words.

Living the Law 1

Understanding Islamic legal theory in the modern age

Module Slw 1.02.D

Lesson One - Shari'ah law

> **Aim:** By the end of this lesson the student should be able to appreciate the complexity involved in living in accordance with the Shari'ah in the modern world as well as understand the underlying theory used in modern issues discussed by scholars.
>
> **Objectives:** By the end of this lesson the student should be able to display the ability to:
> 1. **Provide** practical scenarios that demonstrate that Muslims are facing challenges within the modern world that require the attention of Islamic scholars.
> 2. Clearly **differentiate** between what is meant by *Shari'ah* and *Fiqh*.
> 3. **Outline** the process through which contemporary Muslim scholars have sought to face up to the challenges posed by modern life, mentioning what is meant by *'fatwa councils'*.
> 4. **Explain** what is meant by *al-Nazilah* (a new legal occurrence) and how this relates to the changing dynamics of human life.
> 5. **State** what is meant by Islamic jurisprudence (*Usul-ul Fiqh*) and what the aims of this science are.
> 6. **List** the main sources of Islamic law as given by scholars.

1. The Shari'ah and the challenges of modern life

Most muslims living in Western countries are having to face dilemmas in their day to day life that they are hard pressed to find solutions to. This is more so the case for people that profess to being faithful to a religious tradition which has its own internal set of ethical standards by which it judges what is good and what is not. Whether it is a medical practitioner deciding in a life or death case, or individuals grappling with the ethics of modern economics with all the associated practices of interest based finance or simply finding something *halal* and *tayyib* (wholesome) to eat, real dilemmas exist.

What a deep and principled study of Islamic law shows us is that even if the scenarios faced be many, the underlying rules and sources used to provide solutions to these issues are the same. The role of finding solutions to these challenges is the role of the *Faqih (scholar of Islamic law)*.

1.1 Some scenarios

1.1.1 Zaynab was adamantly against organ transplantation, having been brought up thinking that it is unacceptable. She later on developed renal failure and was in need of a kidney transplant. A match was found and she was informed as to the existence of a life saving option. *Should she abandon her previously held belief regarding the impermissibility of such procedures? Or is this a case where saving a life takes precedence over a legal technicality?*

1.1.2 A small mosque and community centre is located in a mixed income neighborhood and operates a school with an enrolment of over a hundred students. They are financially struggling to meet the rent payments of the property, but have recently been offered a large sum of money which the person donating states is zakat. Khalid, who runs the centre, asks if zakat funds can be used for such a purpose given the overwhelming need of this community?

1.1.3 Ahmed is a citizen of a country were the majority of the population are non-muslim. Feeling a strong urge to play an active role in protecting the security of the country of his birth, he enrols in the armed forces and receives extensive training. *He feels a sense of fulfillment in his career choice until he is told of an imminent placement to a war-zone in a Muslim country...*

1.1.4 Fatimah is going out with her family for a meal. Before going they end up disagreeing on where to go. Her cousin says that the place they intend to go to is not halal as the meat they serve has been pre-stunned prior to slaughter. Fatimah agrees with her and tells her family that what is important is that the animal be treated with compassion and that because of this she has started only eating organic meat. She is stopped in her tracks by her dad who tells her that all certified organic meat has to stunned.

2. What is *Shari'ah* and what is Fiqh?

> *"... Unto each We appointed a law (shira'tan) and way of life (minhaj)" [5:48]*

Literally, the Arabic language uses the word **Shari'ah** for *"a pathway in a desert which leads to the watering place or oasis" [ibn Mandhur, Lisan al-Arab]*. In Islamic law, the word has been used to denote commands, and prohibitions together with the principles and guidance with which God has obliged mankind. In short, a revealed way of life. It encompasses all the textual sources and proofs of Islam discussed below. It is revealed from God and is divine in origin. In his capacity of conveying and explaining the revelation under protection of divine infallibility, the Prophet ﷺ is known as 'The custodian of the Shar'iah' (Sahib al-Shar'iah).

Fiqh on the other hand, is the understanding and development of the Shari'ah in particular contexts and situations as understood by jurists and legal scholars. *Fiqh* is defined as:

> *'That knowledge containing the practical rules of the Shari'ah which are derived from detailed evidences and proofs.' [al-Subki, Jam' al-Jawami']*

Importantly, scholars state that *Fiqh* is the human understanding of the textual sources and hence the *Shari'ah*. Fiqh is not the *Shari'ah* itself and so differences can occur in this human understanding. This distinction between both terms becomes clear when one looks at the word given to what was produced by the various schools of law which developed in the early history of Islam. One refers to the *fiqh* of Imam Malik and the *fiqh* of Imam Al-Shafi'i and not the *Shari'ah* of Imam Malik and Imam Al-Shafi'i.

3. What are the approaches to deal with modern dilemmas?

One contemporary Muslim author has offered an interesting series of options for Muslims in the West in facing modern issues of Islamic law. Each provides a different way of facing up to the challenges that they encounter in holding true to their faith.

3.1 The ostrich approach: This would be summarised as staying clear of grey areas or refusing to accept that the problem exists in the first place.

3.2 Build a Muslim society: *"If the Italians can have Little Italy we can have a Little Muslim City. This is the next best thing to emigrating and living in a traditional Muslim country. We will have shops selling halal meat; give interest free loans to each other; and live around the Mosque. This approach does not prevent all the thorny issues that face us in the modern world from approaching, but it successfully deals with a number of real problems, while it attenuates the rest"*

3.3 Develop a methodology to integrate ourselves with the society at large without losing our religious identity and integrity: Historically speaking this was the blueprint that was adopted by famous scholars such as Imam Hanifah and al-Shafi'i when they lived and operated in the great metropolis cultures of Egypt and Mesopotamia.

This last option is perhaps the most challenging but in the long term the most successful in preserving a viable Muslim presence in any country. This can be done in one of two ways; (a) lobbying wider society to cater for Muslim sensibilities and needs; (b) by a principled examination of problem areas and ascertaining what options Islamic law offers Muslims in such situations. *[See Abdul Rauf, Islam, A Sacred Law, pg24-26]*

4. Modern Challenges - Classical solutions

The Modern age has given rise to challenges for the whole of humanity and not just Muslims. Advances in technology and changes in social mores have thrown up legal questions that require addressing. This is particularly so for Muslims who hold themselves to the dictates of the Divine law, the *Shari'ah*. It is well known that not all social and legal issues were addressed by the Prophet ﷺ. Early scholars strove to deduce what God's law was on issues where there had been no prior legislation.

As Islam spread in different cultures and lands, new issues continually appeared and had to be addressed by scholars of the time. This led to the concept of *ijtihad* taking a central place in Islamic legal discourse. *Ijtihad* literally meaning to strive with one's upmost ability. As a methodology, it is was the prerogative of the most highly qualified legal minds in the 'Ummah. By researching into patterns and precedent in the sacred sources, Muslim scholars successfully met the challenges of their age.

The legal challenges Muslim face today are perhaps more acute that those in the past, being the result of a spectacular rate of social and technological advance that has raised issues in areas such as finance, morality, medicine, penal law, the environment and culture that Muslims are required to address from an ethical perspective.

4.1 How to face these challenges

The process by which scholars provide their findings on issues brought to them for consideration is by the issuing of a ***fatwa*** (a non-binding Islamic legal pronouncement).

Fatwas in the modern age used in one of two ways:

4.1.1 An individual scholar researchers an issue and presents his or her research and *fatwa* for the attention of other scholars. This can be seen being used in various forms by leading scholars of the day who are recognised by their peers as having the requisite knowledge to undertake the task of *fatwa*.

4.1.2 The setting up of so called *'fatwa councils'* or 'collective *ijtihad*' bodies that look at pressing contemporary issues and offer collective advice based on Islamic law.

4.2 Fatwa councils

In the modern era, a number of collectives have been set up with the expressed aim of providing 'collective fatwa'. Amongst these are:

4.2.1 *The Jeddah Fiqh Council,* consisting of scholars from member states of the *Organization of Islamic Conference (O.I.C)*. These countries send their most distinguished scholars to look over issues of contemporary Islamic law and offer solutions. This is the largest and most distinguished such council.
4.2.2 *The Fiqh Council of Mecca* which is made up of scholars affiliated to the Muslim World League.
4.2.3 *al-Azhar fiqh council* in Egypt.
4.2.4 *European Fiqh Council* with scholars from Muslim countries and those now settled in Europe;
4.2.5 *The Fiqh Council of India.*

There are also a number of standing committees in various other countries researching into contemporary issues of this type. The advantage of such councils is that they allow scholars to debate an issue and reach a degree of unanimity, publishing their findings and material in a systematic format for the information of others. They also allow for specialists in particular fields of research, such as economics and medicine, to provide expert advice which may be unfamiliar to Islamic legal scholars.

4.3 *New Legal Occurrences (Al-Nazilah)*

> *Qasim ibn Abdullah said: "You ask about things we never asked about, and quarrel about things we never quarrelled about. You even ask about things which I'm not familiar with; but if we did know, it would not be permitted for us to remain silent concerning them.' [Al-Darimi, v1,49]*

New scenarios that have no precedents in law are referred to as **al-Nazilah**. This is a word used for a *fatwa* request on a new issue requiring legal expertise. The word also conveys the meaning of an occurrence which requires an urgent response. It is well known that early scholars where particularly cautious in issuing *fatwas* on issues unless they had actually occurred. They would say: *'Has it actually happened' (hal nazalat)?*

It is inevitable that such issues need to be addressed, even though sometimes it is clearly the case that it would have been better had the issue not arisen in the first place. Ignoring the issue is however, not an option.

In this context 'Umar ibn Abdal Aziz, commenting on the vast array of new issues that had arisen in the Muslim community in his time that had not existed before said: *"New issues start to appear in a manner directly corresponding to what people create through their transgressions."*

Similarly Ibn Rushd *['The Grandfather']* says: *'God has specific rules, the preconditions for which did not exist in the first community. If the preconditions later appear then the resultant rulings naturally ensue from them.' [Ibn Bayyah, Sana'at al-Fatwa, pg 184]*

5. The Principles of Islamic Law (*Usul al-Fiqh*)

The central place given in Islam to the science of the principles of Islamic law (*usul al-fiqh*) cannot be overstated. As a discipline, it has attracted the finest minds Islam has produced such as Imam al-Haramayn al-Juwayni, Al-Ghazzali and Ibn Rushd. It not only covers **what** sources, such as the Qur'an, sunnah and analogy, are to be utilised by scholars in providing answers to dilemmas facing Muslims, but also **how** these sources are used.

These principles are alluded to in an oft-discussed hadith related from Mu'adh Ibn Jabal about the occasion he was sent by the Prophet ﷺ to Yemen to teach and judge between people.

> *'When the Messenger of God ﷺ intended to send Mu'adh ibn Jabal to Yemen, he ﷺ asked; 'How will you judge a case?' He answered; 'I will judge in accordance with what is in the Book of God.' The Prophet ﷺ asked; 'And if you do not find it in the Book of God?' 'Then by the Sunnah of the Messenger of God'. 'And if it is not in the Sunnah of the Messenger of God?' He*

answered: 'I will exercise my opinion and not lag behind [in so doing]'. The Prophet ﷺ *tapped his chest and exclaimed: 'Praise be to God who harmonised the messenger of the Messenger of God to what pleases the Messenger of God.'* [Abu Dawud: 3592]

5.1 The aim of *Usul al-Fiqh*

One can state that the primary aim of *usul al-fiqh* is to arrive at the detailed rules of *fiqh* through an informed understanding of the source of Islamic law. It can be said to uncover new *fiqh* rulings from first principles.

What are these sources? The above mentioned *hadith* encapsulates the main sources of Islamic law namely the Qur'anic text; the Prophetic example; and lastly the process of *ijtihad* which is to solve legal problems and dilemmas as they occur. This is done by inferring the rules of *fiqh* from these two textual sources (the Qur'an and the Sunnah) through a number of scholarly techniques. The words of the companion Mu'adh: *'I will exercise my opinion and not fall short [in so doing]',* point to all the techniques used by qualified scholars in order to arrive at an informed answer where a solution is not clearly stated in the Qur'an or Sunnah.

5.2 The sources of Islamic law

The Prophet ﷺ is reported to have said   *"I have left amongst you two things which, if you hold fast to them, you will never stray: the Book of God, and my Sunnah."* [Malik & al-Hakim]

Scholars agree that there are two main sources of Islamic law from which all the others derive their own authority, namely the Qur'an and the Sunnah. All other proofs of law are taken and understood from these two sources. After these two come those of Consensus of opinion (*'Ijma*) and Analogy. These four sources are broadly agreed upon by legal scholars.

There are many other sources that can be the basis of an Islamic legal ruling. They are, however, subject to various levels of discussion and disagreement. Of the more widely used are: Juristic preference (*Istihsan*); Public interest (*Masalih al-Mursalah*); Social custom (*'Urf*); Preventing the means to harm (*Sadd adh-Dhara'i*) and Presumption of Continuity (*Istishab*).

Lesson Two - Sources of Shari'ah law (1)

> **Aim:** By the end of this lesson the student should be able to appreciate the two main sources of law for deriving Islamic rulings: The Qur'an and the Sunnah. Together with this students will be able to understand those aspects of these two sources which are particularly relevant in the understanding and application of Islamic law today.
>
> **Objectives**:
> By the end of this lesson the student should be able display the ability to:
> 1. **Mention** the importance of the Qur'an as the primary source of Islamic law, together with three main types of rulings contained within the Qur'an.
> 2. **Detail**, with examples, the different types of rulings contained within the sunnah.
> 3. **Identify** the issue surrounding our understanding of the intent of the sunnah in as much as it relates to the role of the Prophet (may God bless and grant him peace) as Messenger, Political Leader, Judge and Mufti.
> 4. **Summarise** how the understanding of the intent of the sunnah affects the application of Islamic law, providing a relevant example that shows how different understandings of this result in different rulings.

1. The Qur'an:

This is the primary and undisputed source of Islamic law. Any disagreements that exist relating to rulings existing in the Qur'an are to do with interpretation alone [see Qur'an Module lesson 3]. The central importance of remaining true to its guidance as a source of ethics and law is reiterated in the Qur'an time and again.

> **And whoever judges not by what God has sent down (revealed), these are the disbelievers [...] And whoever judges not by what God has sent down, these are the wrongdoers [...] And whoever judges not by what God has sent down these are the depraved."** [5:44-45-47]

The reliance of scholars on the Qur'anic text in deriving both legal and ethical rulings cannot be overstated. Indeed, in the presence of a clear Qur'anic injunction no one would bypass the Qur'an and instead employ human reason to arrive at a ruling. *'It has never been reported that any of the Companions went to the Prophet ﷺ seeking knowledge in anything for which the answer could be found in the Qur'an.'* [Abu 'Ubaydah, Majaz al-Qur'an]

1.1 Types of Qur'anic rulings

The Qur'an seeks to inform us of what we should believe, how it should change us personally as well as the way in which this then affects the way we deal with others. Hence, there are three main types of rulings that are derived from the Qur'an:

1.1.1 Rulings related to Theology such as the belief in God, His Prophets and issues related to the Hereafter (Eschatology).

1.1.2 Rulings related to purifying the soul, perfecting its character and the like that are laid down to be transformative and habit changing.

1.1.3 Rulings related to the obligations and demands on mature, legally responsible individuals through ostensibly practical rulings. These are the subject matter of *Fiqh*.

This last type of ruling is itself made up of two main categories. Those which relate to matters of worship *(Ibadat)* such as purity, praying and the pilgrimage to Mecca, and others which are concerned with human interaction *(Mu'amalat)*, such as trade, marriage and international relations etc. *[See A. Jum'ah, al-Madkhal, pg 308]*

2.The Sunnah.

> **"But nay, by thy Lord, they will not believe (in truth) until they make you a judge of what is in dispute between them and find within themselves no dislike of that which you decide, and submit with full submission."** [4:65]

Sunnah literally means the exemplary conduct of an individual. In the context of Islamic law it refers to the model behaviour of the Prophet Muhammad ﷺ be it through words, actions, or tacit agreement. The recording of the sunnah is primarily through the Hadith literature. The Sunnah serves as an explanation and supplement to general Qur'anic injunctions. The judgement of the Prophet ﷺ is linked inextricably with submission and *Islam* itself. These issues will be fully dealt with in the module dealing with the recording of the sunnah. Here we will look at a few issues that relate to the Sunnah in the context of Islamic Law.

2.1 Types of rulings in the Sunnah - The four Es. (*emphasis; explanation; exception; extra*)

As the sunnah is the second source of Islamic law after the Qur'an and is subordinated to it, the various types of sunnah rulings can be discussed in relation to what guidance, if any, the Qur'an gives on a particular topic. One may look at this through four main categories.

2.1.1 *Emphasis.* A sunnah that emphasises rulings already contained in the Qur'an.

For example the hadith *'It is not permitted for a person to take the wealth of another without his consent"* reiterates the verse **"O you who have attained to faith! Do not devour one another's possessions wrongfully - except by way of trade based on mutual agreement - and do not destroy one another: for, behold, God is indeed a dispenser of grace unto you! [4:29]**

2.1.2 *Explanation.* A sunnah that explains a general Qur'an injunction.

"And We have sent down to you the Message that you may explain clearly to men what is sent for them." [16:44]

The sunnah provides this explanation and this is the most extensive function of the Sunnah in Islamic law. The nature and amount of zakat to be paid and the way to pray are examples of this.

2.1.3 *Exception.* A sunnah that gives exceptions to rulings in the Qur'an.

'For He commands them what is just and forbids them what is evil; He allows them as lawful what is good and pure and prohibits them from what is bad and impure and he releases them from their heavy burdens and from the shackles that were upon them..." [7:157]

The sunnah gives details of any exceptions to a ruling or clarification as to the precise details of the ruling. An example of this is the verse dealing with prohibited food stuffs where dead animal meat (carrion) is forbidden. *Does this prohibition include what is found dead in the sea?*

"Forbidden to you is carrion, and blood, and the flesh of swine, and that over which any name other than God's has been invoked, and the animal that has been strangled, or beaten to death, or killed by a fall, or gored to death, or savaged by a beast of prey, save that which you [yourselves] may have slaughtered while it was still alive; and [forbidden to you is] all that has been slaughtered on idolatrous altars..." [5:3]

The answer to this was given by the Prophet ﷺ when he was asked about performing ablution *(wudu')* with sea water and whether it was permitted to use it for such a purpose. *"We travel by sea and take a limited amount of water with us. If we use it for wudu' we will have nothing with which to quench our thirst. Can we perform wudu' with sea water?" He said: 'Its water is pure and its carrion is halal.' [al-Tirmidhi, 69]*

2.1.3.1 *Prophetic Educational technique.* It is interesting to note that the Prophet ﷺ did not restrict his answer to the question asked, namely was it permitted to do *wudu'* with sea water. He also provided an answer to what he knew would also have been an issue for those travelling by sea for extended periods. What is the status of fish and seafood that had come to the surface of the sea dead. Was it *haram* as may have been understood from the verse, or is this an exception and the ruling for such food is that it is permitted?

"His ﷺ saying "...and its carrion are halal" is a response not required by the initial query. It is from the finer points of giving fatwa that the questioner be given some extra information so that a fuller benefit be attained, providing important knowledge of something other than that which is directly inquired about.' [Ibn al-Arabi, 'Aridat al-Ahwadhi, V1[14], 89]

2.1.4 *Extra.* Extra rulings that are not in the Qur'an at all.

> *Al-Miqdam ibn Ma'di Karib said that the Prophet* ﷺ *said: 'Verily I have been given the Qur'an and something like it. Soon a man will say, leaning on his couch with his stomach full: 'Follow this Qur'an, whatever you find in it to be [declared] permissible then declare it permissible, and whatever you find in it to be [declared] prohibited then declare it prohibited.' Verily whatever God's Messenger* ﷺ *has declared prohibited is just as what God, Exalted is He, has declared prohibited.' [Abu Dawud, 4604]*

> *'Abu Thalaba relates that the Prophet* ﷺ *forbade the eating of any wild animals with a canine tooth and of any bird with talons.' [al-Bukhari, 5780]*

This is where a ruling is derived independently from the sunnah where the Qur'an is silent on an issue. Examples of this are the the provision of a share of inheritance for the grandmother and the prohibition on consuming predatory animals with canine teeth. *[See A. Jum'ah, al-Madkhal, pg 309]*

3. Understanding the intent of the Sunnah

> *'One of the most pertinent qualities of one seeking to fathom the Maqasid al-Shariah (The higher intent of the law) is to be able to distinguish between the varying intents of the words and actions of the Prophet* ﷺ *. The Prophet* ﷺ *had many roles that act as references in understanding the statements and acts that ensued from him. Therefore scholars seeking to fathom the area of Maqasid al-Shariah need to be able to clearly distinguish these statements and acts in relation to the office from which they ensued.' [Ibn 'Ashur, Maqasid, pg 28]*

It is important in the context of the Sunnah to understand that all Prophetic statements were issued in varying roles that the Prophet ﷺ held in the community, be it in his role ﷺ as a Messenger, leader, judge, or mufti. Understanding this issue aids in appreciating the applicability and scope of certain traditions related from him ﷺ .

Based on this, what is done by the Prophet ﷺ in his capacity as a **Messenger** is binding upon everyone as much as they are able to. As for his acting in the capacity of **leadership** it is not permitted for anybody to enact any such rulings except with prior permission of those with political authority or having been vested with such authority. Those acts carried out as a **judge** are limited in their application to proper judicial procedure being in place, such as both parties being present and the judge giving judgement based on both sides presenting their evidence. It not permitted for others to apply judgements given by the Prophet ﷺ in this capacity except after having been delegated these powers. Lastly, a statement given in the capacity of a **mufti** has universal application on religious and contractual issues such that they can be applied without the restriction placed on the implementation of the rulings of a judge.[55]

4. How do we know in what capacity the Prophet ﷺ spoke in different traditions?

There are general indicators through which we can ascertain the answer to this question.
- The commissioning of military campaigns, organising the affairs of the treasury as well as other fiscal matters together with the appointment of judges are all deemed to be functions of political authority.
- Dealing with people's personal claims and legal disputes against one another are deemed to be issues dealt with in the capacity of being a judge.
- When answering questions about worship or purely religious issues, one can conclude that in such a case the saying or action emanate from the role of *fatwa* and Prophethood.

There are however sometimes hadith texts in which scholars have differed as to the specific role from which the Prophet ﷺ spoke. Based on this they differ on the wider ramifications of the text.

    4.1 Example: The Prophet ﷺ said to Hind bint Utbah; *"Take what suffices you and your child in fairness.'* This was a response to her complaining to the Prophet ﷺ about her husband not providing adequate maintenance for her and her child. Scholars differ with regard to whether this answer was a *fatwa* (in which case it would be applicable to other people in a similar situation without them having to seek recourse to somebody for religious counsel) or whether this was a ruling issued by the Prophet ﷺ in his role as a judge, in which case this would mean that no-one can act upon this hadith until they also first seek recourse to a judge who would hear the side of both the plaintiff and the defendant before issuing such a ruling. *[al-Qarafi' al-Faruq, v1, Pg 206-208].*

---

[55] Certain scholars from the Hanbali and Shafi'i schools went as far as to state that it was disapproved for judges to give *fatwa* in anything other than religious law related to worship since their role as a *qadi* would make their *fatwa* binding on those that appeared before them in a court of law thereby compromising the judicial system itself. *[Ibn Qayyim, 'Ilam al-Muwaqi'in, v4, pg 180]*

Lesson Three - Sources of Shari'ah law (2)

> **Aim:** By the end of this lesson students should have a good conceptual understanding of Consensus, Analogy, juristic preference and Public Interest as sources of Islamic law as well as their usage and importance.
>
> **Objectives:** By the end of this lesson students should be able to display the ability to:
> 1. **Explain** what consensus is and whose agreement is required for consensus to be reached.
> 2. **List** some of the historical benefits of *'Ijma* for the Muslim community.
> 3. **Explain** what is meant by analogy, providing relevant proofs for it being an accepted source of Islamic Law.
> 4. **Provide** an example of the use of analogy outlining clearly the four pillars of analogy.
> 5. **Explain** what is meant by the principle of equity or juristic preference (*istihsan*) in Islamic law, providing an example of its use.
> 6. **Summarise** the issue of public interests in Islamic law, discussing what type of public interests is taken into consideration and what type is not.

1. Consensus of opinion (*'Ijma*)

> *'O you who believe, obey God and obey the Messenger and those in authority amongst you.'* [4:59]

The consensus and unanimous agreement of scholars on an issue in a particular time is considered the third source in Islamic jurisprudence.

This principle of law guarantees the coherence of new legal content that emerges as a result of exercising independent legal reasoning (*ijtihad*) through the process of peer review and commendation. As such it may be seen as a check on the unprincipled use of personal reasoning in the area of Islamic law.

1.1 What constitutes a consensus and who does it include?

The practical issue of who is included in those that have to agree for a consensus to be reached is a point that scholars have debated intensely in the past. The wide array of views on this topic point to the problematic nature of practically using this as a positive source of law in the present day. Some restrict *'ijma* to refer only to the first four orthodox Caliphs or the People of Madinah, while others extend it to the time of the Companions of the Prophet ﷺ . The Shia accept only the consensus of those they refer to as their infallible Imams.

The majority of scholars hold that consensus must be established through the unanimous agreement of all qualified jurisconsults on an issue of law. The fact that all scholars of one age have to agree has meant that although there are many issues upon which there is a consensus, only a small number of issues in Islamic law have been established through consensus alone.

1.2 Benefits of Consensus law

There are a number of positive contributions of *'Ijma* in preserving a unified understanding of faith and practice in the Muslim community and this can be summarised as follows:

    1.2.1 The correct collection, recitation and interpretation of the Qur'an;

    1.2.2 *'Ijma* has led to collective recognition of canonical collections of hadith on the part of the Muslim community and through this an authoritative and balanced understanding of the Sunnah;

    1.2.3 The development of the science of jurisprudence *(usul al-Fiqh)* and the rules for the legitimate use of independent legal reasoning;

    1.2.4 Having reduced the differences of opinion amongst Muslims over given issues, *'Ijma* has ensured the emergence of what can be termed *'Mainstream/Majority Islamic thinking'* and as such has been central in defining who the *Ahl-Sunnah wal-Jama'ah* (those following the norm of the Prophet ﷺand the collective consensus) are.

It is a testimony to the Islamic faith that authority does not lie in a central authority or 'church' but rather in a self-regulating community of learning and scholarship which ensures that balanced and authoritative religious positions are taught and promoted in the wider Muslim community. It thereby safeguards the tradition from heterodox and extreme views. [See Rauf, pg62-67]

2. Analogy: (*Qiyas*)

> *A woman came to the Prophet ﷺ and asked 'My mother has vowed that she would perform the Pilgrimage but passed away before fulfilling this vow. Should I perform the pilgrimage on her behalf. The Prophet ﷺ answered, 'Yes, do you not see that if your mother had passed away with an outstanding debt, would you not have settled it? Repay God's debt for God is more entitled to repayment.'*

Qiyas is the use of an established legal ruling to obtain one for a new case by way of drawing an analogy between the two cases. This is done where a close resemblance exists between an issue for which we know the answer and a new question. Using this principle of law we can reasonably conclude that the ruling will be the same for each.

2.1 The four pillars of analogy

> *'Umar said to Abu Musa al-Ash'ari: 'Acquaint yourself with the parallels and precedents of legal cases and then weigh up the cases (qis al-umur) deciding what judgement would be more pleasing to God and nearest to the truth.' (Al-Mubarrad, al-Kamil, vol. I, p,14.)*

Wine is explicitly prohibited by Qur'anic decree. If we want to know what the ruling would be for whisky then we may use the process of Analogy to do this. The underlying cause for the prohibition of wine is the intoxicating effect. Thus, by analogy, all intoxicating drinks are prohibited. The logic of analogy proceeds as follows (these are also the four pillars of analogy):

2.1.1 The original subject, **asl**, for which there is a decision (in this case wine)

2.1.2 The new subject which is the object of the analogy, **far'** (in this case whiskey)

2.1.3 The cause or link **'illah** (which is shared between the original and new subject and which is the logic for the analogy. Here, it is the intoxicating effect)

2.1.4 The Shari'ah ruling, **hukm** (Here it is prohibition)

It can be assumed that the ruling for the new case is the same as that for the original case based upon the shared causal link which exists in both cases. It is also known that this ruling arrived at by analogy is also established through numerous hadith as well, such as *'Whatever intoxicates in large amounts is also haram in small amounts.' [Abu Daud]*

3. Equity or Juristic Preference (*Istihsan*)

> *'Istihsan is nine tenths of acquired knowledge.' [Malik, in al-Shatibi, Muwafaqat, v4[4],208]*

Is it required or even wise to follow the letter of the law if doing so will go against the wider spirit of the *Shari'ah*?

Juristic Preference is a wide-ranging proof in Islamic jurisprudence where a ruling that has an apparently strong reasoning and proofs supporting it is set aside in relation to another ruling out of consideration for a strong local custom, public good or necessity. Lexically *istihsan* means to hold something to be preferable or good. At the source of Juristic Preference is the setting aside a strict analogy (*qiyas*) or a literal reading of the law in order to alleviate difficulty from people and facilitate ease. It has been described as a type of subtle analogy which requires a great degree of training to master.

3.1 Examples of *Istihsan*

3.1.2 During his period of rule 'Umar ibn al-Khattabsuspended the Qur'anic penalty for non-mitigated theft at a time of famine based upon *Istihsan*. Here the penal code was temporarily suspended in an exceptional situation based on a consideration for the public good.

3.1.3 Another example, again from the time of 'Umar was when he banished Rabiah ibn Umayyah from Madinah as a punishment for fornication. He subsequently joined the Byzantines, at the time at war with Muslims. 'Umar, when he came to know of this, remarked: *'I will never expel anyone for exile again.'*

3.2 Evidences for *Istihsan* being a source of Shari'ah Law

While there is no conclusive evidence for *Istihsan* in either the Qur'an or the Sunnah, a number of supporting proofs have been given such as the verse: '***And follow the fairest (ahsana) of what has been sent***

down to you from your Lord..." **[39:55]** as well as prophetic traditions such as *'There is neither harm nor the reciprocation of harm.' [Ibn Majah, 2340]*

4. Rulings based on Public Interest (*Maslaha al-Mursalah*)

Is it allowed for a Muslim government to impose a speed limit on drivers? How would it seek to justify it? Neither the Qur'an nor the Sunnah provide any direct guidance on this issue so what do we do in such cases?

The concept of *Maslahah al-Mursalah* is particularly important in such cases. It involves arriving at a ruling where none exists based on a reflection on the deeper wisdom of the Shari'ah.

4.1 What does *Maslaha al-Mursalah* mean?

Maslahah literally means benefit or interest. Al-Ghazali holds it to centre on the procurement of benefit and repulsing of harm. When qualified with the word *mursalah* it refers to unrestricted public interest, where the interest and wisdom has not been expressly determined in the two main sources of Islamic Jurisprudence. [al-Mustasfa, 2[4]-139].

As will be seen in Lesson Five, Islamic law seeks to preserve five essential elements of human life. They are, in the order of the priority given to them by Imam al-Ghazali: Religion; Life; Intellect; Lineage and Property. [al- Mustasfa, 1[4]-258]

The correct use of *maslahah al-mursalah* would require taking into account these five essentials of human life in the light of a consideration for the public interest before arriving at a ruling.

Maslahah has been further divided into the following three categories depending on the level of support it has from the primary sources of Islamic Jurisprudence:

4.1.1 Acknowledged [*al-Maslahah al-Mutabarah*] which has already been expressly upheld in the Shari'ah. For example: Establishing the right to ownership by penalising theft.

4.1.2 Suspended [*Maslahah al-Mursalah*] which is neither expressly upheld nor nullified by the Shari'ah. For example: The provision enshrined in statutory law in many Muslim countries for documentary evidence to prove marriage or ownership of property.

4.1.3 Discarded [*Maslahah al-Mulgha*] which has been rejected either explicitly or implicitly by the Shari'ah. For example: Not performing *wudu'* because the water is cold. *[See Zaydan, al-Wajiz, 236-238]*

4.2 Evidences for Public Interest being a source of Shari'ah Law

The Prophet ﷺ said: 'Muslims are held in accordance with their conditions, except for a condition that permits something forbidden or forbids something that is allowed.' [Al-Hakim].

What can be seen from the discussion above is that unnecessary rigidity is not recommended in the application of *shari'ah* rulings and that Muslims should avail themselves of the flexibility and concessions of Shari'ah law if evidence exists pointing to the sacred law allowing such an approach to an issue.

Lesson Four - Sources of Shari'ah law (3)

Aim: By the end of this lesson the student should understand the remaining secondary supporting sources of Islamic law as well as their usage and importance.

Objectives: By the end of this lesson the student should be able to display the ability to
1. **State** the meaning of local custom and its use and importance in Islamic law.
2. **Mention** evidence supporting its use from the Qur'an and Sunnah.
3. **Discuss** whether all types of local custom are upheld, providing relevant examples.
4. **Mention** two examples of the use of this source.
5. **Explain,** with examples, the three categories related to blocking of the means.
6. **Discuss** what is meant by the presumption of continuity in Islamic law and how this can help in providing Islamic rulings to questions where there is no other evidence in existence.

1. Local custom ('*Urf*)

> '*Urf* (Custom) is that which has found acceptance in people's natural disposition by general agreement and which those of a sound persuasion have come to accept.' [al-Ghazali, al-Mustasfa]

The term '*Urf*, from a root meaning 'to know', refers to the local customs and practices of a given society. The *Shari'ah* recognises the local customs that prevailed in the Prophetic era and were not abrogated by the Qur'an or the Sunnah. The Islamic legal tradition has held that what people hold to be good is also considered so by God, if there is no indication in law to the contrary. Taking into account local custom and norms is a basic principle of Islamic law and as such '*Urf* can be seen as equivalent to the western concept of Common (as opposed to Statutory) law.

The main areas where local custom and usage is applied is in the area of Islamic family and Commercial law. This is particularly so when dealing with the language and wording used in these areas. So scholars state for example that '*Judgement is assigned to what is customary in respect to the normal usage [of language] rather than an abnormal usage. This is what is often current in oaths, contracts and divorce by indirect words (kinayah).'* [Al-Muwafaqat, pt. 2, p. 198]

1.1 Evidences for '*Urf* being a source of Shari'ah Law

1.1.1 *"Keep to forgiveness, enjoin 'urf' and turn away from the ignorant"* [7:199].

Imam al Qarafi, the celebrated Maliki Jurist, has held that this verse provides a strong textual proof for the validity of local Custom [al-Qarafi, Al-Faruq, v2:85].

1.1.2 *"Take what is sufficient for you and your child from the property of Abu Sufyan in a customary manner (bil-Ma'ruf)."* In this hadith custom is clearly made the basis of a legal decision.

1.2 The Changing nature of customs

> 'Customs can change from what is considered good to the reverse, such as in the case of uncovering the head (for men). That varies in different regions. In the Eastern (Muslim) lands it is considered offensive and ugly, but not so in Western (Muslim) lands. So the legal judgement for it varies according to that. Thus it detracts from good character (maru'ah) with the people of the East but not with the people of the West.' [Al-Shatibi, al-Muwafaqat, V2 [4], p. 198]

1.3 Local custom and the issuing of Fatwa

> 'Local custom in the sight of the Shari'ah is given credence,
> and for this reason the ruling may be informed by it.'   [Ibn Abidin, Rasa'il, 1-44]

> 'Persons handing down legal judgements while adhering blindly to the texts in their books without regard for the cultural realities of their people are in gross error. They act in contradiction to established legal consensus and are guilty of iniquity and disobedience before God, having no excuse despite their ignorance; for they have taken upon themselves the art of issuing legal rulings without being worthy of that practice [...]. Their blind adherence to what is written down in the legal compendia is misguidance in the religion of Islam and utter

ignorance of the ultimate objectives behind the rulings of the earlier scholars and great personages of the past whom they claim to be imitating.' [Al-Qarafi, quoted by Umar Abdullah, The Cultural Imperative, pg 7]

1.4 Why is 'Urf considered a valid basis for a Shari'ah ruling?

1.4.1 In many cases 'Urf coincides with the wider **public interest** and public interest is indisputably a fundamental principle of the Shari'ah and so 'Urf overlaps with other sources of Islamic jurisprudence.

1.4.2 Custom necessarily entails people's **ease and familiarity** with a matter, and so any judgement based on it will receive general acceptance, whereas divergence from it will cause distress and hardship, which is disliked because God does not seek to impose undue hardship on people.

'Classical Islamic law did not speak of culture per-se, since it is a modern behavioural concept. Instead, the law focused on what we may call culture's most tangible and important components: Custom (al-'urf) and Usage (al-ada), which all legal schools recognised as essential to the proper application of the law, although differing on definitions and their measure of authority. In Islamic jurisprudence, 'al-'Urf and al-Ada' denote those aspects of local culture which are generally recognised as good, beneficial, or merely harmless. In no school did respect for culture amount to blanket acceptance.' [Umar Abdullah, ibd, pg 5-6]

1.5 Are all types of Custom admissible?

1.5.1 Accepted Custom. This is a custom indicated by a religious text, the vast majority of which relate to family law. *'And upon the father of the child is the duty of providing food and clothing for nursing mothers in a manner that is commonly accepted (bil-ma'ruf) [2:233]*

1.5.2 Prohibited custom. This is a custom which is denounced by a clear text of the Lawgiver. This type of custom is, by consensus, not respected or adopted. *'And when the female infant buried alive is asked 'for which sin where you killed?' [81:8-9].* Similarly the custom of disinheriting female heirs from inheritance, as was the pre-Islamic custom, was condemned in Islam.

1.5.3 Disputed Custom. This is a custom for which there is no established prohibition nor are there any indications of it being acceptable. The Malikis and Hanafis generally consider this be a principle of law.

2. Blocking the Means to harm (*Sadd adh-Dhara'i*')

A concise definition of this proof is *'Forbidding or blocking lawful actions because they could be used as a means to the unlawful.'* [al-Shawkani, al-Irshad, pg 246]

It aims at preventing a harm or evil where it is likely to occur before it materialises and implies that what leads to the forbidden is also forbidden. Al-Shatibi states: *'The Shari'ah is based on circumspection, adopting discretion and being on guard against what might lead to harm.'* [al-Muwafaqat, v2[4], pg. 253]

2.1 Examples and proofs for *Sadd adh-Dhara'i*' as a source of Shari'ah Law

2.1.1 *'Do not curse those they call upon besides God that they then curse God out of animosity, without knowledge.' [6:108]*

2.1.2 *'O you who believe, do not say, 'Ra'ina,' but say, 'Undhurna,' and listen well.' [2:104]*

2.1.3 The Prophet ﷺ forbade hoarding. Ma'mar Ibn Abdillah relates that the Prophet ﷺ said : *'No one hoards except someone who acts unlawfully.'* [Muslim, Ahmed, v6 [6], pg400]

Even though there is no inherent prohibition against storing foodstuffs, it may in some situations lead to harm, as it deprives some people of what they are in need of. There is no prohibition of hoarding what does not harm people, like jewellery and items which are not part of necessities or needs [See Lesson 6].

2.1.4 Another example, from the era of the Companions of the Prophet ﷺ , is where they allowed a woman who had been irrevocably divorced in her husband's final illness to inherit from him. This was because there was a well founded suspicion that the husband intended to deprive her of inheritance through the pronouncement of divorce. In certain circumstances, divorce is a means through which one can lose the right to inheritance. [Ibn al-Qayyim I'lam, v 3, pg 122]

2.2 Three categories of Blocking the Means

2.2.1 What definitely leads to harm, like excavating next to a neighbours wall, such that the wall would collapse as a result. The unlawfulness of such actions is unanimously agreed upon.

2.2.2 What most often leads to harm, like selling weapons at a time of civil war or selling grapes to a person who makes a living making wine. Maliki and Hanbali scholars agreed on '*blocking the means*' in such cases. The other schools held that the harm had to be certain to justify such a ruling. The effect of a difference on one point of principle is shown by the fact that Imam al-Qarafi pointed out that a thousand questions of law on which the Shafi'i and Maliki schools differed were based on this one principle. [*al-Qarafi, al-Faruq, 2, 32*]

2.2.3 What rarely leads to harm, such as forbidding a tenant from growing grapes on one's rented land or looking at a prospective partner for marriage. Harm only occurs in rare cases and so the law favours the predominant benefit in such cases and does not take the rare occurrence of harm into consideration. [*al-Qarafi, al-Faruq, 2, 32-3; al-Burhani, Sadd adh-Dhara'i', pg 181-2; Zaydan, al-Wajiz, pg 245-246; Al-Shatibi, al-Muwafaqat,v 2, pg 390*]

2.3 Facilitating the Means

Blocking the Means to Harm also works in reverse as well. In general, what leads to a benefit is as desirable as seeking the benefit itself. If it is obligatory, then the path or act that leads to it is also obligatory. If the benefit is permitted, the means to it is also permitted.

> *'Know that just as it is an obligation to 'block the means', it is also an obligation to facilitate them, or disliked, recommended or allowed. So just as the means to the unlawful is forbidden, the means to an obligation is also an obligation, like undertaking the journey to Hajj or going to the Jumah.' [al-Qarafi, al-Furuq, v2, pg 32]*

It should be noted that this source of law is subject to change depending on the changing social, political and economic conditions in a particular place because what leads to harm in one situation may not in another.

3. The Presumption of continuity - (*Istishab*)

This is a basic logic axiom where one infers that things are as they were in the past unless proven otherwise. One can reasonably assume that because keys were left on the kitchen table they will still be there later. We do so because we have no reason to think otherwise.
Istishab literally means to keep close or have proximity to something. In legal theory, it means the presumption of the existence or non-existence of a set of affairs. As the concept of *Istishab* is based on a mere probability, it is only considered a proof when not in conflict with another proof which is stronger.

3.1 Three main types of *istishab*

3.1.1 Presumption of original absence (*Istishab al-adam al-asli*). A fact or rule which had not existed in the past is assumed to be non-existent until proved otherwise. For example, if one is known to not owe an individual X amount of money, this will also be presumed the case at the present time unless a proof to the contrary is provided.

3.1.2 Presumption of original presence (*Istishab al-wujud al-asli*). The presence of that which is indicated by law or reason is taken for granted and assumed. For example, a husband is liable to pay dowry by virtue of the existence of a valid marriage.

3.1.3 Presumption of the continuity of general rules of law (*Istishab al-hukm*). A known ruling or judgement is assumed to continue until proven not to. An example of the use of this type of *istishab* is the argument made by those that say intentionally missed prayers need not be made up later. [56] This type of *istishab* is sometimes referred to as *al-bara'ah al-asliyyah (The original freedom from an obligation)* [*Zaydan, al-Wajiz, pg268-9*].

---

[56] *See Prayer module 1, lesson 2.*

Lesson 5 - Maqasid: The Higher purpose of the law

Aim: By the end of this lesson the student will have a firm grasp of issues related to the higher purpose and wisdom of the *shari'ah* as well as the essential objectives the sacred law sets out to protect.

Objectives: By the end of this lesson the student should be able to display the ability to
1. **Define** what is meant by the word *maqasid* as elaborated by the scholars.
2. **Discuss** what the ultimate purpose the divine law is said to be.
3. **Outline** with examples the three levels of benefit mentioned by scholars and their relative importance.
4. **Explain** and list with examples, the five essential aims of the *Shari'ah*.
5. **Summarise** the main methods used by scholars to show that the law has a higher objective.
6. **Compare** the areas of worship and worldly dealings in as much as they relate to the area of *maqasid*.
7. **Explain,** providing relevant examples, what is meant by the two terms *maqasid* (*aims*) and *wasail* (*means*) and what significance they have in the understanding of Islamic law.

1. *Maqasid* - Searching for the wisdom of Shari'ah law

> "The objective behind Shari'ah is **to liberate individuals from their desires** in order for them to become true servants of God and that is the ultimate benefit [...]. Violating the Shari'ah under the pretext of following Maqasid al-Shari'ah is like the one who cares about the spirit without the body and since the body without the spirit is useless therefore the spirit without the body is useless too.' [Al-Shatibi]

1.1 What does the word *Maqasid*[57] mean?

Maqasid, the plural of *maqsad*, means the purpose, intent or goal and corresponds to the Greek word *telos* which is used for the ultimate aim of an act for which it exists. One could say therefore that purpose (or *maqsad*) of a pen is to be used to write and that of a bicycle to be used to get from one place to another. What is the ultimate goal of the Shari'ah? To speak about the higher intent of the *Shari'ah* is to look at the underlying wisdom as to why we are commanded and prohibited from certain acts and what these can tell us about why the Divine Law *(Shari'ah)* was revealed.

> "The Shari'ah law is established upon wisdom and the achievement of the welfare of mankind both in this life and the next. It is all about justice, mercy, wisdom, and attaining the good. Therefore, any ruling that replaces justice with injustice, mercy with tyranny, the common good with mischief, or wisdom with irrationality is a judgement that has nothing to do with this code of law, even if it be claimed to be so based upon some or other interpretation." [Ibn Qayyim I'llam v3 pg 3]

2. Why did God reveal Divine Law (*Shari'ah*)?

> "All the obligations of the Shari'ah are predicated on **securing benefits for the people**, in this world and the next, for God Most High is in no need of the obedience of His servants. He is above all creation and cannot be harmed by the disobedience of transgressors." [Ibn Abd as-Salam, al-Qawa'id]

---

[57] *Maqasid* are sought after for their own inherent value and therefore embody the higher aims of the Sacred law. Other legal devices, referred to as *Wasa'il* (means), are the way by which the *maqasid* of Islamic law are realised. Hence any action will have two elements related to its actualisation: Objectives (*maqasid*) which are concerned with the core legal benefits as well as the prevention of harmful matters; Means (*wasa'il*), which are the paths leading to both benefits and harms.

"Since objectives (maqasid) can only be reached by the means and paths which lead to them, those paths and causes which lead to them must be taken into consideration. The means to unlawful things and acts of rebellion are disliked and prohibited inasmuch as they lead to their consequences, and the means to acts of obedience and acts of nearness are recommended and permitted in as much as they lead to their objectives. The means to the objective is subordinate to the objective, and both of them are intended." [Ibn al-Qayyim, I'lam, v 3, pg 119]

Shari'ah law recognises a reciprocal link between the ultimate purpose of an action and the means by which this is attained. If something is beneficial and will be of help to the community such that it is deemed as a communal obligation, the path by which this is achieved and actualised will also be deemed an obligation. Education is a communal obligation that requires the requisite structures and institutions that can facilitate this. This would mean that any means to achieving this is similarly an obligation on the community as long at it entails no forbidden act.

Al-Qarafi says: "The means to the best of goals is the best of means, and the means to the worst of goals is the worst of means. That which is in the middle is in the middle." [Tanqih, p. 200]

There are no clear texts indicating what the higher purpose of sacred law is. Scholars have spent their lives looking into patterns that exist in the *Shari'ah* to try and decipher why God sent down laws for mankind to live by. Though they did not reach a clear consensus on this question, the results of their inquiry point to the internal coherence and consistency of the Sacred law.

> '*Some Muslim scholars of jurisprudence, especially Ibn Taymiyyah, said that Allah revealed such a legislative system or Shari'ah in order to achieve* **Justice.** *Other jurists said it is for the purpose of achieving* **happiness** *[sa'adah] And still some others, especially al-Ghazzali, said it is only for the achievement and the realization of the very* **benefits of man on earth.**' *[al-Allaf, Maqasid Theory, pg 4-5]*

3. How do we know that the Sacred Law has a Higher Objective?

> '*This Community, in fact all religious communities agree, that the religious law was instituted for the protection of five absolute necessities: religion, life, progeny, property and reason. This Community (i.e., the Muslim Community) has unassailable (daruri) knowledge of this. But this has not been established on the basis of any specific proof-text, nor confirmed by any principle that we could isolate and invoke. Rather, its appropriateness to the religious law is simply known* **on the basis of an aggregate of proofs too numerous to count**" *[al-Shatibi as quoted by Jughaym, Turuq al-Kashf, 284]*

There are a variety of methods by which we come to know that certain values are held to be the essentials of the Shari'ah. These include:

3.1 Deducing the *maqasid* based directly on commands and prohibitions. These are taken from the Qur'anic text as well as the Prophetic traditions. Therefore, in the case of the prohibition of wine, we can say that one of the aims of the Shari'ah is a prohibition on the **consumption and procurement of wine**.

3.2 The underlying reason (*illah*) for a ruling. In the case of wine, we can deduce that the aim in prohibiting wine is outlawing the use of any **intoxicant** and that this is one of the aims of the *Shari'ah*.

3.3 The process of induction (*istiqra'*). Here the laws as a whole point to the underlying rationale of the *Shari'ah*. An example of this is the commonly accepted principle that the law came to assure the attainment of benefits for mankind and prevention of harm. As this is nowhere stated in any religious text, one could query as to from where such a conclusion has been arrived at? The answer is quite obvious, in that this is the conclusion reached after a wide survey of the religious texts we have available, all of which point to the law seeking to achieve both worldly and otherworldly benefits for mankind. In the case of the prohibition of wine, this can be related to the widespread social, economic and spiritual ills that put in jeopardy the achievement of what is beneficial for mankind in this world and the hereafter.

3.4 An understanding that the Shari'ah aims at the realization of benefit (*masalih*) and the suppression of harm (*mafasid*). This applies generally to all Shari'ah rulings and is also based on a process of induction, where we have come to understand this on the basis of the religious sources that form the basis of our Law.

4. The three level of legal benefits.

Muslim scholarship has set a hierarchy of interests that the *Shari'ah* seeks to promote and preserve, with each being of a varied degree of importance and each level protecting that next to it. The theory propounded by Abraham Maslow in his theses on the '*Hierarchy of Needs*' does something similar in the field of sociology, where he looks at the basic needs of the individual, ranging from safety to self actualisation. *[Maslow, Motivation and Personality, New York, Harper and Row, 1970]*

> **"Forbidden to you are the flesh of carrion, blood [...] but if anyone is compelled by force of hunger, not intending any wrongdoing, God is ever-Forgiving, Most Merciful" [5:3]**

> **"God does not want to place you in difficulty, but He wants to purify you, and to complete His favour to you, that you may be grateful." [5:6]**

> **"... eat and drink and do not go to excess, for God likes not those that strive to excess" [7:31]**

As we have seen above, one of the most influential Muslim scholars who discussed the wisdom of the *shari'ah, al-Izz Ibn Abd as-Salam,* stated that it was ultimately revealed for the benefit of mankind. This begs the question of whether all benefits are of a similar standing and is there a hierarchy of benefits?

Not all benefits we know of are at the same level of importance. Some benefits have to do with our very survival, while others are related to things which we could all sacrifice if the need arose. This has been taken into account by Muslim jurists in their graded classification of the benefits that man enjoys. Hence they talk about three types of benefits: essential, desirable and complimentary.

> *"The **essential benefits (daruri)** include such areas as food, drinks, clothing, spouses [...] and the like. The minimum of such entities is considered to belong to the category of essentials. The same things, provided in abundance or of the highest quality, such as fine foods and clothing, spacious rooms [...], they belong to the category of **complementary benefits**. Whatever falls between the two belongs to the area of **required benefits.'** [Ibn Abd as-Sallam, al-Qawa'id,v2 pg71]*

4.1 The Five Essential benefits (*al-Kulliyat al-Khams*)

The essentials benefits that the Shari'ah seeks to protect and promote are, in order of priority given by Imam al-Ghazali: Religion; Life; Intellect; Procreation and Property. *[al- Mustasfa, 1-258].*

4.1.1 Rulings related to the Five Essential benefits. These five essentials are of such importance that they permit one to act in a manner that is otherwise unlawful to secure their continued existence. Therefore the specific *fiqh* definition of the essentials (*daruriyyat*) are those things for the protection of which something otherwise *haram* may be done. This is because failure to protect and promote these essentials would result in a systemic failure in the ability of any society to function and survive to further human existence on earth in any meaningful way. *[Bin Bayyah, Sana'at al-Fatwa, pg 190]*

4.1.2 Rulings that seek to preserve and promote the five essential benefits. The concept of *Jihad,* which in this context can be seen as akin to what is referred to in western theory as Just War, has been validated in order to protect human life and safeguard one's right to practice one's religion without fear or hindrance; The law of retaliation (*qisas*) has been proscribed to protect life. The same can be said relating to the laws of adultery, the drinking of intoxicants and theft. Each of these are classed as offences as they destroy the viability of the family unit, disrupt the workings of the intellect and threaten social stability by undermining the ability of people to the right have private property respectively. The *Shari'ah* has instituted canons and laws that protect and promote these five essential values.

4.2 The required benefits (*al-Hajjiyyat*)

Lying directly below these essential benefits in terms of importance are other concerns of the sacred law which help promote and protect these five essential benefits by removing hardship.

Hence related to the essential benefits but of a secondary degree of importance are what are referred to as the '*Hajjiyyat' (lit. items of need)'*. These are to those things related to human needs deemed to be of importance because they remove severity and hardship in day to day life. These also supplement and protect the five essential benefits and so in many cases of law, the Shari'ah provides *rukhas* (concessions) to ensure that these are fulfilled. Examples include the shortening and joining of prayers while travelling, the use of *tayamum* instead of *wudu'* for ritual purity and many of the communal obligations such as attending the funeral prayer. Even though such *rukhas* alleviate hardship, one could, with a degree of difficulty, carry out these act without such concessions. Hence they are not essential, but are still related to the essential benefits.

4.2.1 Required benefits being given the privilege of the Essential benefits.

> '*Correctly delineating the dynamics between required and essential benefits has become a key to unlock complex legal issues in the Modern age related to worldly dealing (mua'malat).' [Bin Bayyah, Sana'at al-Fatwa, pg 189]*

One issue of importance mentioned by scholars is that this second type of benefit, the '*Hajjiyyat',* may in certain situations and under strict conditions, be elevated to the level of the first group in terms of importance such that normally forbidden acts become permitted. This is specifically the case if it is an issue that affects the public at large, in which case the second type of benefit is given the same privileges and rulings as the five essentials. As al-Ghazzali states: '*A general required benefit (al-hajah) affecting all people is given the specific privilege of the essential benefits (darurat) for the individual.*[58]' *[al-Ghazzali, Shifa al-Ghalil, pg 246]*

One should keep in mind that this point of Islamic law is one of the most complex issues of *Usul al-Fiqh* in terms of its practical application and can be misunderstood. Amongst the many conditions of normally forbidden acts becoming permitted based on this rule is that the initial prohibition not be a prohibition sought to safeguard a higher purpose *(muharamat al-maqasid)* as opposed to a prohibition relating to the means or secondary issues *(muharamat al-wasa'il)*. *[Bin Bayyah, Sana'at al-Fatwa, pg 244]*

4.3 The complementary benefits (al-Tahsiniyyat)

The lowest levels of benefits identified by scholars as having been recognised in the *shari'ah* are those thing that perfect and embellish the first two types of benefits mentioned above. These are called the *complementary benefits (tahsiniyyat)*.

For example, the law not only promotes and encourages the performance of the prayer or the seeking of knowledge, but at the same time seeks to do so in a manner that makes this fully effective and perfect. To have suitable methods of delivering knowledge, suitable and clean attire for the purposes of 'ibadah, trusted and professionally run marriage bureaus to facilitate marriage are just some of many examples of this. *[See al-Shatibi, Muwafaqat, 1, 332]*

5. Maqasid in acts of worship (ibadat) and worldly dealing (mua'malat)

Although the law generally exhibits a rationale in the rulings it contains, this does not mean that one can rationalise all action that one is asked to follow. While scholars have enquired into the higher intent of the law in worldly dealings *(mua'malat)*, they have been less forthcoming in terms of the higher intent of acts of worship *(ibadat)*, generally holding that the higher purpose in worship is refining the soul and personality of the individual *(tahdhib al-fard)*. *[Ibn Abd as-Salam, al-Qawa'id]*

A case in point is the jogging around *(raml)* the Ka'bah during the first three rounds of the *tawaf*. This was originally done by the Messenger ﷺ with his companions during the lesser Pilgrimage ('*Umrah*) to show the Quraysh that the Muslims that had emigrated to Madinah had not been weakened by the conditions there and were strong and full of vigour. When 'Umar was asked as to why people still jog around the Ka'bah with their shoulders uncovered even though Islam had now prevailed in Makkah, he replied: '*We do not cease doing anything we used to do during the Prophet's time.*' *[al-Bukhari, Kitab al-Hajj]*

Echoing the words of 'Umar, the Spanish legal theorist al-Shatibi makes a clear differentiation between inquiring over the logic and wisdom in acts of worship on the one hand and more mundane worldly rulings on the other:

> '*Literal compliance (ittiba'a) is the default methodology in the area of acts of Worship, while taking into consideration the higher purposes of the law is the default methodology in the realm of worldly dealings (mua'malat).*' *[al-Shatabi, al-Muwafaqat, 2:6]*

---

[58] الحاجة العامة في حق كافة الخلق تنزل منزلة الضرورة الخاصة في الشخص الواحد.

Lesson 6 - Principles and Legal maxims

> **Aim:** The student will be given an insight into the basic legal principles and maxims that summarises the detailed *fiqh* rulings together with their significance in the practical understanding of Islamic law.
>
> **Objectives: :** By the end of this lesson the student should be able to display the ability to
> 1. **Mention** the historical instance when the science of legal maxims is said to have come into existence.
> 2. **Explain** what is meant by the term as well as the origin of such principles.
> 3. **List** the Five Pivotal legal maxims.
> 4. **Provide** examples of each of the five explaining their usage in Islamic law .
> 5. **Recognise** the related principles for each of the five pivotal maxims together with examples of their use.
> 6. **Summarise** the points in which these principles differ from the science of *Usul al-Fiqh*.
> 7. **Discuss** the practical use of these maxims in the daily practice of Islam.

1. The legal principles and maxims

1.1 The History of a Science

It is related that Imam Tahir al-Dabbas had, after life long research and study, summarised all of the rules of *fiqh* into seventeen all-encompassing principles or maxims (*qawa'id*). It was his habit to revise them out loud in his mosque after the 'Isha prayer once the congregation had left, having the door locked behind them. A scholar from Herat, Abu Sa'd al-Harawi, got news of his extraordinary accomplishments and so travelled to see if he could find out what the results of his study were. It is said that Abu Sa'd entered the mosque and hid after the 'Isha prayer in a rolled-up carpet so as to secretly listen in to the maxims being repeated. Al-Dabbas, who was blind, started to revise them as was his habit. After having revised only a few of them, Abu Sa'd inadvertently coughed and was found out. He was then removed from the mosque after failing to listen in to the rest of the maxims. It is said that the five foundational legal maxims mentioned below are amongst what he actually managed to listen in to. *[al-Suyuti, al-Ashbah, pg7, Ibn Nujaym, pg15-16]*

2. What are Maxims (*Qawaid*) of Fiqh?

A maxim (or principle) is defined as *'a general rule which applies to a large number of its related particulars and which aids in the understanding of those rulings'* *[As-Subqi, al-Ashbah]*. They can therefore be looked at as the common links that connect otherwise different *fiqh* rulings.

They are short and abstract and in their own way summarise a particular objective or even sometimes a higher purpose of the shari'ah.

The origin of these maxims is sometimes directly from the Qur'an or hadith literature, as for example the maxim: *'Acts are judged by the intention behind them.'* (Al-'umuru bi-maqasidiha), which is a paraphrasing of the famous Hadith *"Actions are but by intentions" [al-Bukhari]*.

Similarly, Ibn Taymiyah, commenting on the hadith: *'Whatever intoxicates in large amounts is also haram in small amounts', [Abu Daud]* states*: 'The Messenger ﷺ , through the gift of succinct speech (jawam'i al-kalim) with which he had been endowed, summarised in this short hadith all things that cloud the intellect and intoxicate, not differentiating between one type and another, showing it as being of no relevance whether the intoxicant be in an edible or liquid form.' [Ibn Taymiyah, Majmu al-Fatawa, 27/ 341-342]*

This is a legal maxim as this one hadith not only provides a basis for the prohibition of small and large amounts of alcohol, but also gives an encompassing proof for the consumption of all substances that intoxicate regardless of their physical form.

2.1 The usefulness of Maxims: Three questions one answer

The usefulness of these general principles (or maxims) to generalise what at first appearances seem to be totally different questions with no relation to each other, is demonstrated in the following account recorded of the great scholar Imam Ash-Shafi'i. Notice how he managed to link these issues through one legal principle that sheds light on the *fiqh* ruling for each.

> "He was asked about a lady in a foreign land wishing to get married but who had no legal guardian to act on her behalf in contracting the marriage. He said: 'When a matter becomes constricted, facilitation is made.'

He was also asked about a type of widely used cookware which was of questionable purity. He said: 'When a matter becomes constricted, facilitation is made.'

Finally, he was asked about the impurity that invariably attaches itself to the feet of flies when they land on impurities, should one take any notice of this? 'When a matter becomes constricted, facilitation is made' he replied.' [al-Zarkashi, al-Manthur fil-Qawaid,1\120]

3. The Five Pivotal legal maxims (*al-qawaid al-kulliyah al-khams*)

Although there are many principles that relate to *fiqh* rulings, scholars have singled out five essential principles upon which a large portion of *fiqh* is based. It has been said that there is no ruling except that it falls within at least one of these five principles of *fiqh*. The author of the poem *Maraqi as-Su'ud* on Islamic Jurisprudence collected them together in the following three lines of meter:

*"All of fiqh is a built upon '**The removal of harm**'*
*and the principle that '**Hardship begets ease**'*
*'**Not allowing certainty to be displaced by doubt**'*
*'**Local custom is given the power of the law**' with those attentive adding*
*'**Actions are to be judged by their intentions**'*
though not without, in cases, a degree of far-fetched interpretation.
[Abdallah ibn al-Hajj al-Alawi, Maraqi as-Su'ud, pg 579]

3.1 Harm must be alleviated. (*Al-dararu yuzal*)

"Do not hold your wives in bondage, seeking to harm them; that would be transgression" [2:231]

This not only forbids one from inflicting harm but also from committing harm in response to an alleged aggression. It applies as much to society and the environment as it does to individuals. *'This is a maxim that has its origins in the attainment of the Higher Aims (maqasid) of the law and strengthening them by [either] repulsing harmful matters or alleviating them.' [Ibn Najjar al-Hanbali, Sharh al-Kawakib al-Munir,4/443-4]*

Example

It is forbidden to hoard foodstuffs at a time of shortage based on the maxim: *'Harm must be alleviated.'*

"The Prophet ﷺ said 'He who hoards has indeed committed a wrong' [Sahih Muslim]. It was put to Sa'id ibn Musayib: 'But you hoard!' He responded, saying: 'Ma'mar - who related this Hadith to me - used to hoard as well'. Imam al-Ma'azari said commenting on this: 'The rule underlying this is to look at any ensuing harm from the act, and so whatever leads to harm needs to be alleviated.' [al-Ma'azari, Al-Mu'lim, 2:212]

3.1.1 Related Maxims

'Necessity is measured in accordance with its true proportions' (Al-daruratu tuqdaru bi-qadriha)

'Prevention of evil takes priority over the attraction of benefit' (Dar' al-mafasid muqadam ala' jalb al- masalih).

3.2 Hardship begets facility. (*Al-mashaqqatu tujlab al-taysir*).

"And God does not burden a soul out-with its capacity" [2:286]

This maxim differs from the previous one in that it is understood that rather than simply removing a negative situation, what is entailed here is the replacement of a negative with an alternative that sits better with the overall purpose and intent of the law. The other obvious departure from the previous maxim is that the negative connotations associated with difficulty (*mushaqah*) are usually far less than those associated with harm (*darar*) as is clear in the use of the maxim below.

Example

'[the permissibility of] tayammum where the use of water would lead to difficulty [...] sitting during the course of the prayer where standing would entail hardship [...] shortening the

prayer during a journey [...] Also amongst the absolute facilitations (takhfifat al-mutlaqah) are the communal obligations.' [Ibn Najar al-Hanbali, Sharh al-Kawakib al-Munir, 4/446-7]

3.2.1 Related Maxims

'Necessity makes the unlawful lawful' (Al-daruratu tubiyh al-mahdhurah).

3.3 Certainty is not overruled by doubt. (Al-yaqinu la yazulu bil shakk).

'and do not follow that of which you have no true knowledge.' [17:36]

This means that knowledge of an event or set of affairs remains valid even if one later has doubts about this. It is a manifestation of God's mercy to mankind that they are not burdened with having to take into account lingering doubts and suspicions that fly in the face of sure knowledge. Certainty here includes strong conjecture as well. Related to this maxim is the rule that people are innocent until proven otherwise.

Example

Kulthum, intending to fast, has a doubt over whether she continued eating until after daybreak (*fajr*) had arrived. In accordance with this principle, she has certainty over it being night while eating. This is not affected by the doubt which appeared later over whether dawn broke or not while she was eating. Therefore her fast can be said to remain valid as per the maxim.

3.3.2 Related Maxims

'The norm is that of a lack of liability' (Al-aslu baraa'ah al-dhimmah).

'The norm with regard to things is that of permissibility' (Al-aslu fil-ashyaa' al-Ibahah).

3.4 Custom has the weight of the law. (Al-'addatu muhakkamatun)

The Messenger ﷺ said to Hind, the wife of Abi Sufyan 'Take what suffices you and your child in accordance with what is customary.' [al-Bukhari].

Custom necessarily entails people's familiarity with a matter, and so any judgement based on it will receive general acceptance whereas divergence from it will be liable to cause distress, which is disliked since God has not imposed any hardship on people in His religion.

Example

X sells Y a piece of real estate. In the sale of property and real estate, what is included in the sale is determined by custom. If no commonly accepted custom exists then no ruling can be based on the principle of local custom.

3.4.1 Related Maxims

'What is determined by custom is tantamount to a contractual stipulation.' (Al-ma'rufu 'urfan kal-mashrutu shartan).

3.5 Acts are judged by their purpose. (Al-umuru bi-maqasidiha)

'God does not take you to task on account of inadvertent statements in your oaths, but will take you to task for the intentions that your hearts have made.' [2:225]

Intentions are the pivotal element in any action and the *Shari'ah* gives importance to the intentions behind actions as it helps to differentiate between different types of actions. For example one's intention can alter an otherwise mundane act (*a'dah*) such as eating into an act of worship (*'ibadah*) simply by coupling it with the intention to derive strength from the food to perform righteous actions.

Intention also marks apart similar acts of worship from one another. For example even though the outward form of both the Dhuhr and 'Asr prayers is the same, they are marked apart by the intention that accompanies both. They also sometimes have a role in areas other than those of worship as shown in the example below. *[Ibn 'Abd as-Salam, al-Qawaid al-Kubra,1/176]*

While this maxim obviously plays a central role in acts of worship and devotion and their acceptance by God, this is not always the case with contracts and actions. Since ascertaining an individual's intention in worldly matters is almost impossible without asking, the *Shari'ah* places outward proofs as practical indicators of an individual's intention and rules accordingly. Hence the maxim *"Outward proofs replace intentions in cases where the intention are obscure."* So if a person causes the death of another, judgement will be passed based on the outward actions of the person, such as for example striking a person a number of times with a sharp weapon. Intention will hold no weight in such situations. *[al-Ahkam al-Adliyyah, Article 68]*

Example

Ahmed finds something valuable in the street and picks it up. His intention when taking the item is of importance. If he takes it with the intention of keeping it safe for its owner, it is considered as a legal trust *(amaana)*. This means that if it is destroyed while in his possession, he will not be responsible for it.
If however, if he took it with the intention of usurping *(ghasb)* it, he will be held accountable for it for the duration of the time it is in his possession. This means that if destroyed within this time, he will be responsible for its replacement regardless of whether it was through neglect or not. *[al-Zarqa, Sharh al-Qawaid al-Fiqhiyyah, pg 49]*.

3.5.1 Related Maxims

> *'It is the intent and meaning behind contracts that is given credence, not the mere outward form and wording.'* *[al-Ahkam al-Adliyyah, Article 3]*

4. *Summary:* Qawaid al-fiqh as Rules of thumb

The Legal Maxims *(qawa'id al-fiqhiyyah)* are practical and useful tools in a day-to day setting and can be described as legal rules of thumb or even the law equivalent of 'first aid", useful when one is required to make an on the spot decision on a question where one does not have time to verify an issue through the relevant scholarly channels. They are therefore practical rules that relate directly to day to day *fiqh* issues. [59]

---

[59] *Appendix: How do the Maxims (Qawaid) of Fiqh differ from the science of Usul al Fiqh?*
'Usul al-Fiqh relates to general Proofs, the Maxims relate to general Rulings. [Ibn Taymiyyah, M. al-Fatawa, 29 \167]
One could summarise the differences by looking at the following three questions

[1] Which of the two produces detailed Fiqh laws as a primary function?
Qawaid al-fiqh are generalisations based of the rulings produced by *Usul al-Fiqh* and as such do not bring about *fiqh* rulings. For example, the maxim *"Necessity makes the unlawful lawful"* links together a number of rulings that already exist in books of *fiqh*, such as the *fiqh* ruling of the permissibility of consuming *haram* foodstuffs in order to remain alive, as well as the permission to lie in order to save the life of another.
Usul al fiqh (methodology in Islamic jurisprudence) allows one to derive and produce detailed rulings by the use of source evidence such as a Qur'anic text or Prophetic norm discussed previously. For example the permissibility of consuming otherwise *haram* foodstuffs is derived directly from the verse *"Forbidden to you are the flesh of carrion, blood...but if anyone is compelled by force of hunger, not intending any wrongdoing, God is ever-Forgiving, Most Merciful" [5:3]* through the use of the methodology of Islamic Jurisprudence (*Usul al fiqh*).

[2] Which of the two has exceptions?
Qawaid al-fiqh or legal maxims apply to the majority of cases but not all. There are bound to be exceptions to the general rule.
Usul al-fiqh has rules that have no exceptions as they are general, all-encompassing rules that are used to derive law.

[3] When do they come into being with relation to Fiqh?
Qawaid al-fiqh come into existence after the detailed rules of law are established, grouping a large number of rulings under a general maxim that links them all together
Usul al fiqh on the other hand exist before detailed rules are established as it is through them that one arrives at the detailed rules of fiqh in the first place.

Appendix on the legal terms and definitions

TERM	FARD (ESSENTIAL)	HARAM (UNLAWFUL)
DEFINITION	A ruling established by way of unambiguous Quranic or *Mutawatir* hadith text showing it to be essential	The opposite of *Fard*. Established by way of unambiguous Quranic or *Mutawatir* hadith text showing it to be prohibited
EXAMPLE	Fasting in Ramadan	Drinking alcohol
RULING	A. To deny it is *Kufr* (disbelief) B. Not performing it without a valid excuse leads to moral corruption (*Fisq*) deserving of divine punishment C. Performing it deserves reward	A. Considering it permissible is *Kufr* B. Performing the action leads to moral corruption (*Fisq*) deserving of divine punishment C. Refraining from performing it is essential and entails reward

TERM	WAJIB (OBLIGATORY)	MAKRUH TAHRIMI (GRAVELY DISLIKED)
DEFINITION	Established in non-definitive way (such as a solitary hadith or else an ambiguous Quranic or Mutawatir hadith text) showing it to be obligatory	The opposite of Wajib. Established in non-definitive way (such as a solitary hadith or an ambiguous Quranic or Mutawatir hadith text) showing it to be prohibited
EXAMPLE	Reciting surah Fatiha in the prayer	Praying when one needs to relieve oneself
RULING	A. To deny it is not Kufr B. Not performing it without a valid excuse is sinful and deserving of divine punishment, though less than that given to leaving a Fard act. C. It is obligatory to do it and it entails reward	A. To consider it permissible is not *kufr* B. Performing it is a minor sin which, if done consistently/habitually, leads to moral corruption (*Fisq*) deserving of divine punishment, although the punishment is less than that for doing a *Haram* act. C. Refraining from doing it is required and entails reward

TERM	SUNNAH MUAKADAH (EMPHASISED)	ISA'AH (OFFENSIVE)
DEFINITION	An action done by the Prophet ﷺ consistently and only very rarely left out; or done consistently by him ﷺ but there is an indication that it is not wajib or fard.	It is the exact opposite of sunnah muakadah. It is caused by omitting a sunnah muakadah.
EXAMPLE	Congregational prayer	Omitting the 4 rakah's of sunnah before the dhuhr prayer
RULING	A. Leaving it without a valid excuse occasionally is blameworthy but does not entail a sin B. Leaving it consistently/habitually entails a small element of sin, though less than that of makruh tahrimi C. performing it entails reward	A. It is lower in rank than makruh tahrimi and higher than makruh tanzihi B. Refraining from it is required and doing so entails reward.

TERM	SUNNAH GHAYR MUAKADAH (NON- EMPHASISED)	MAKRUH TANZIHI (DISLIKED)
DEFINITION	An action done by the Prophet ﷺ often and also left sometimes without an excuse	The opposite of sunnah ghayr muakadah. Evidence indicates that is it is undesirable and should be avoided.
EXAMPLE	The 4 rakahs before the Asr prayer and Isha prayer	Splashing water onto the face during wudu
RULING	A. Performing it entails reward B. Omitting it, intentionally or consistently, is not sinful	A. Refraining from performing it entails reward B. Performing it is disliked but not sinful

TERM	MUSTAHAB - MANDUB - ADAB - NAFL (RECOMMENDED)	KHILAF AL-AWLA (NOT RECOMMENDED)
DEFINITION	An action which evidence indicates is preferred or recommended	The opposite of Mustahab. An action which evidence indicates is not recommended to do.
EXAMPLE	Voluntary prayers and fasts	Eating on the day of Eid-al-adha before the Eid prayer
RULING	A. performing it entails reward B. Omitting is not disliked	A. It is better to leave it B. There is no particular dislike in doing it

TERM	MUBAAH (PERMISSIBLE)	N/A
DEFINITION	An action for which there is no recommendation for performing it or omitting it	N/A
EXAMPLE	Eating tasty food	N/A
RULING	A. There is no reward for performing it nor is it discouraged to omit it. B. To do it with a righteous intention will entail reward e.g.. Sleeping with the intention of strengthening one self for worship.	N/A

iSyllabus.org

Printed in Great Britain
by Amazon

43920130R00101